THE
BATTLE
OF JUTLAND

THE
BATTLE
OF JUTLAND

by

Jonathan Sutherland
and
Diane Canwell

Pen & Sword
MARITIME

First published in Great Britain in 2007
and reprinted in this formrat in 2014 by
PEN & SWORD MARITIME
An imprint of
Pen & Sword Books Ltd
47 Church Street
Barnsley
South Yorkshire
S70 2AS

ISBN 978 1 78346 266 7

Typeset in Sabon by
Phoenix Typesetting, Auldgirth, Dumfriesshire

Printed and bound in England
By CPI Group (UK) Ltd, Croydon, CR0 4YY

Pen & Sword Books Ltd incorporates the Imprints of Pen & Sword Aviation,
Pen & Sword Family History, Pen & Sword Maritime, Pen & Sword Military,
Pen & Sword Discovery, Pen & Sword Politics, Pen & Sword Archaeology,
Pen & Sword Atlas, Wharncliffe Local History, Wharncliffe True Crime,
Wharncliffe Transport, Pen & Sword Select, Pen & Sword Military Classics,
Leo Cooper, The Praetorian Press, Claymore Press, Remember When,
Seaforth Publishing and Frontline Publishing

For a complete list of Pen & Sword titles please contact
PEN & SWORD BOOKS LIMITED
47 Church Street, Barnsley, South Yorkshire, S70 2AS, England
E-mail: enquiries@pen-and-sword.co.uk
Website: www.pen-and-sword.co.uk

Contents

Preface

We were both born and brought up in East Anglia, close to what is the most eastern point of Great Britain. Geographically then we live closest to the battlefield of Jutland. Yet to our eternal shame we knew very little about it. We knew still less of another major battle, which took place in 1672, no less important at the time, when an Anglo-French fleet fought a Dutch fleet in Sole Bay, most closely associated with Southwold.

There are great parallels between these two battles: one was that they both decided the control of the North Sea during a time of war, another being the losses to the allied side compared to those of the enemy. The allies, or British, at Jutland lost more vessels yet claimed victory. Regardless of the losses, both the Battle of Sole Bay and the Battle of Jutland made the North Sea a virtual no-go zone for the vanquished fleet. Back in the seventeenth century an inclusive battle was fought, with both sides claiming victory. It was a similar story nearly 150 years later at Jutland, when an inconclusive enagagement saw both sides claim the victory laurels.

Our nearest large town is Great Yarmouth, a port town closely associated with that other great British mariner, Horatio Nelson. Yet the imprints of the Battle of Jutland, its commanders and vessels, have left their marks on Great Yarmouth. So indeed had the shells of the German High Seas Fleet in the early years of the First World War. Great Yarmouth celebrated the British victory by the naming of roads: the Iron Duke public house stands at the end of Jellicoe Road; there is Beatty Road and Sturdee Avenue, immortal memorials to the men and vessels that had fought in the greatest naval sea battle of modern times.

A British vessel lost just prior to the Battle of Jutland was HMS *Aboukir*, on board which was a member of the Woods family from Gorleston, near Great Yarmouth; he would be one of the 527 men lost when the vesel sank in just twenty minutes. Woods is a direct ancestor of Diane Canwell, née Hewitt. Wood's son would serve with distinction in the Second World War, winning himself an MBE for his brave conduct and devotion to duty. German bombs dropped by an aircraft straddled his ship, but he remained on deck until all of his men were saved. Captain Charles Wilfred Woods had only recently recovered from having his legs fractured by a mine and had spent twenty-six weeks in Grimsby Hospital.

Jutland, the battle, the vessels and the men are inextricably linked by family history. Gorleston and Great Yarmouth are seafaring towns, literally on the front line of warfare in the North Sea.

Introduction

Jutland had all of the ingredients of being a great British naval victory to rank alongside Trafalgar. In reality, this enormous sea battle, which sprawled across the North Sea, was somewhat less clear cut.

Jutland was to be the only major, full-scale clash between the British and the Germans in the First World War.

Reinhard Scheer had recently been appointed to command the German High Seas Fleet and had decided to return to the policy of making attacks on the British coast. In the incorrect knowledge that his attacks were safe from the British fleet based in Scotland, Scheer thought that the only serious threat to his vessels were the ships of Admiral Beatty's battlecruisers based in the Firth of Forth. What Scheer did not know was that the British had cracked his codes. Scheer's naval signals had been intercepted and decoded and within minutes of his fleet leaving for the raid, the Royal Navy's Grand Fleet, under Admiral Sir John Jellicoe, was underway.

The Germans had planned to use Vice Admiral Franz von Hipper's battlecruisers ahead of the main fleet, the intention being to lure Beatty out and destroy him with the German High Seas Fleet. Little did the Germans know that Jellicoe was already on his way to link up with Beatty.

Sure enough, von Hipper's force made contact with Beatty's ships on the afternoon of 31 May 1916. The German ships gave way and fled south towards Scheer's main force. Beatty then encountered the High Seas Fleet and he, too, turned away, luring the Germans on to Jellicoe.

The Germans were in for a terrible shock. From 1830 to 2030 the British main fleet and the Germans engaged one another. The British heavy guns forced Scheer to reconsider and he made what could have been a disastrous decision: instead of turning away from the British fleet, Scheer ordered a turn to the east. His intention was to escape into the Baltic.

Jellicoe's scouts failed to pick up the true course being taken by the Germans and British Naval Intelligence failed to intercept crucial positioning reports. Aware that his fleet could not operate well at night, Jellicoe screened his fleet with smaller vessels and hoped for a conclusive engagement at first light. As it was, the Germans managed to slip away. The German fleet had been mauled and would never again dare to risk a full-scale engagement with the British. It was a flawed victory, one that could have been so much more conclusive for the British. Had British armour- piercing shells not exploded on impact with the German ships, the German losses would have been enormous.

Why had Jellicoe allowed the Germans to escape the trap? Had he been too cautious? Why risk defeat when you already have control of the seas? Was it Scheer's brilliance that saved the German fleet or, perhaps, Beatty's lack of control over his own vessels?

In this all-new look at the Battle of Jutland we examine the tactics used in the naval war, the opposing fleets and the admirals. Central to the book is the detailed analysis of the battle itself, split into the key phases. We also feature the notable accounts of the battle by contemporary writers, some of whom actually took part in the battle itself, plus a chapter that deals with the official reports of the battle, from Jellicoe, Beatty and Scheer. Finally, we turn our attention to the lessons learned from the battle and examine the 'Jellicoe controversy'.

Although Jutland is a much-misunderstood battle, its significance is enormous, both in framing the outcome of the naval war in the First World War, and also determining German tactics and willing-ness to face the Royal Navy head on in the Second World War.

Chapter One

Britain's Naval Supremacy

The victory at Trafalgar in 1805 had removed the threat of invasion for more than a century. It also established the Pax Britannica, which would hold sway until 1914. To a large extent the spectre of Nelson hung over the Royal Navy and permeated into the sub-conscious of the general public. To win a sea battle meant that the opposing fleet should be utterly destroyed, as it had been at Trafalgar and earlier, when British tactics and the weather devastated the Spanish Armada.

The First World War generation of naval commanders had their opportunity to inflict a grievous defeat on the enemy at Jutland in 1916, but the outcome of the battle was in no way as clear-cut as it had been against the French or the Spaniards. It is probably fairer to view the outcome of Jutland as a tactical victory for the Germans, but a strategic victory for the British. After Jutland the German High Seas Fleet was not to put to sea again until it headed for Scapa Flow in 1918 to ignominious surrender. The much-vaunted German vessels that had dared to deny the British their naval supremacy would soon lie deep in the waters of Scapa Flow, having emitted barely a whimper.

After the battle, no one was really convinced by the British claims that they had won a great victory at Jutland that could rank along-side Nelson's victory at Trafalgar. Jellicoe would be moved upstairs and his job would be taken by Beatty.

The road to Jutland was a long one that can be traced back to the latter half of the nineteenth century and an incident that could have

1

claimed the life of a man who was lying in his cabin, suffering from severe dysentery. That man was John Rushworth Jellicoe.

The Royal Navy's Mediterranean Fleet was approaching Tripoli on 22 June 1893. The commanding officer, Vice Admiral Sir George Tryon, had been directing manoeuvres off the coast of Lebanon and decided there would be one more exercise before the vessels slipped into port. The fleet was steaming in two lines, roughly 1,200 yards apart; the first line consisted of 5 battleships and a cruiser and the second line 3 battleships and 2 cruisers. Tryon was on board HMS *Victoria,* in the first line and his second in command, Rear Admiral Sir Albert Markham, was in the second line, on board HMS *Camperdown.*

Tryon decided to execute a dangerous manoeuvre where the ships in each line would turn towards the other line to form two new lines. The ships needed a 2,000-yard turning circle. Tryon signalled for the manoeuvre to begin. Markham ordered *Camperdown* to swing hard to starboard, whilst simultaneously, *Victoria* swung to port. As it quickly became obvious that the two vessels were on a colli-sion course, orders were given to close the watertight doors and at the last minute both ships were thrown into reverse. *Camperdown* had an underwater ram and smashed into the hull of *Victoria,* causing grievous damage – the hole was some 9ft deep and it stretched to some 12ft below the waterline. As *Camperdown* continued to move an even larger hole was torn in the side of *Victoria* and in under ten minutes over 2,000 tons of water had poured into her. With *Victoria* listing heavily, a belated order was given to abandon ship. A cadet helped Jellicoe on deck; he was one of the lucky ones. Tryon and 358 officers and men went down with the ship, some of whom were killed by *Victoria*'s propellers.

The crews of both ships faced court martial. They were acquitted of the charges, but what it proved was that despite the danger of the manoeuvre, no one on board had questioned Tryon's decision to conduct it in the first place.

No country had dared to challenge Britain since 1805. Meanwhile, the Royal Navy had been transformed from an effec-tive fighting force to a service obsessed with spit and polish. Even as late as four years after this collision, British ships had their hulls painted in red and black; the superstructures were white and the masts and funnels buff coloured – all this at a time when other nations were painting their fighting ships grey so that they would be less conspicuous.

There were bizarre rules: knives and forks were considered unmanly, so seamen had to eat with their fingers, although they were allowed spoons for soup. The pay was poor, the discipline harsh and the men lived in appallingly cramped conditions.

The Royal Navy spent much of its time steaming from port to port in a rather aimless fashion. Gunnery practice took place four times a year, but there were no clear instructions, only that the ship should head out to sea, expend a quarter of its ammunition and return to port – this often meant that the ship's officers would order the ammunition to be jettisoned over the side, rather than fire the guns and dirty the paintwork.

At the time of Queen Victoria's Diamond Jubilee in 1897, the Royal Navy consisted of 92,000 men and 330 vessels, around thirty of which were battleships. At the same time the Germans had 68 ships, the Russians 85 and the French 95. The Japanese and the Americans had fewer than seventy each. It had been decided, back in 1889, under the terms of the Navy Bill, that Britain's fleet should be the equivalent in strength to at least the two other largest naval powers; normally this was based on the total of the French and Russian fleets. When the First World War broke out, of course, both of these countries were allies of the British.

The Royal Navy was supremely confident in itself and exuded this confidence to the general public. The danger lay elsewhere, with Germany, whose navy at this stage was primarily designed to protect its coastline. But the Germans were aggressively expanding and consolidating.

Back in 1867, Prussia had annexed several smaller German kingdoms, duchies and free cities and had decisively defeated the French in the Franco-Prussian War of 1870–1871. As a result of this the King of Prussia became the Emperor of the first German Reich. Kaiser Wilhelm I and his chancellor, Prince Otto von Bismarck, had no great desire to come to blows with Britain – this would have been inevitable had they decided to expand their naval strength. However, when Kaiser Wilhelm I died in 1888, his grandson succeeded him as the Kaiser.

Wilhelm II was a far more aggressive and ruthless ruler. He was also described as being impulsive, lacking in judgement and somewhat erratic; his grandmother was Queen Victoria. He had long cherished the notion of emulating the impressive Royal Navy and determined to begin a vast shipbuilding programme. In 1897 Wilhelm II appointed Rear Admiral Alfred von Tirpitz as Secretary of State of the Imperial Navy Office. Tirpitz knew that it would be difficult to convince the government to plough huge funds into a shipbuilding programme, but he carefully began to gain support and was ably assisted by German industrialists.

Germany, in any case, was enjoying a period of industrial expansion and its population was growing equally as rapidly. It had begun to build a colonial empire and had adopted a far more aggressive form of foreign policy. In order to achieve its longer-term aims, Germany could not risk being held back by a strong Royal Navy, which they could not challenge. The Germans were pragmatic about naval expansion and their chances against the Royal Navy; they knew that their aims would be fulfilled if the British believed that the German fleet was big enough and powerful enough to inflict serious casualties on the Royal Navy. It was believed that the British would not risk losing their trump card and would, therefore, avoid any direct confrontation with the German navy if that situation arose.

Naval laws were passed in Germany in 1898 and 1900 that allowed funds to be set aside for shipbuilding projects. In 1895 the Germans had just five battleships, but by 1902 they would have nineteen, supported by a dozen armoured cruisers. It was also proposed that from 1900 onwards, three new battleships would be built each year.

An important civil project, the Kiel Canal, had been completed in 1895, which meant that the fleet could now deploy swiftly between the North Sea and the Baltic Sea.

On a smaller scale than the 1897 Diamond Jubilee Spithead Review, the Germans mounted their own in Kiel, in 1904. As the British First Lord of the Admiralty, the Earl of Selborne, and King Edward VII watched twenty-three German battleships sail past, both men were clearly apprehensive.

Had the First World War not broken out in 1914, the Germans had planned to have forty-one battleships and twenty armoured cruisers ready by 1917. Indeed, by 1920, the Germans had hoped to have at least the same amount of vessels as the Royal Navy.

4

The British, however, had not been idle and in 1889 the Naval Defence Act had set up a programme to build more warships. By 1898 it had been planned to have twenty-nine first-class battleships, with a dozen more under construction. The British were worried by the intentions of the Germans as it was obvious to them that the German battleships were not being built purely to defend and support German overseas colonies. There had to be another, more sinister, reason for the German navy's massive expansion programme. Rather than the German fleet being used to protect German commerce and possessions abroad, it was obviously being designed for an entirely different purpose, and that had to be to challenge the Royal Navy.

Even by 1904, when the Germans carried out their naval review in Kiel, Britain still had a 300 per cent advantage in battleships. In fact, over the period 1903 to 1906, the Germans produced eleven battleships while the British produced eighteen. The British had always operated on this Two Power Standard, inasmuch as they compared their fleet's strength to two other major powers to give them at least a 10 per cent margin of safety.

The Germans had been stockpiling naval guns and had also been increasing their steel production, but no matter how much effort Germany put into the shipbuilding project, it seemed that they were unable to catch up with the British. Whilst both countries spent excessive amounts of money on warships, other vital expenditure had to be set aside.

The Germans also had another major advantage: although they would have to despatch some of their vessels to protect their colonies, the vast majority of them could be deployed in the North Sea. On the other hand, the British had a vast empire to protect and police and therefore a considerable part of the Royal Navy would not be available for a conflict in the North Sea itself. Some British vessels could not even be expected to respond in a reasonable amount of time as they were deployed as far afield as Australia, the Indian Ocean or the South Atlantic.

The British, therefore, set out on a series of diplomatic and political deals, with the primary aim of freeing up more Royal Navy vessels so that they could be used for home defence. In 1902 the British signed a treaty with Japan, by which the Japanese would take primary responsibility for matching the Russians in the Far East. A deal was done with France in 1904, in which the French fleet would take primary responsibility for dealing with the Austrian fleet in the Mediterranean. In 1907 the Russians were brought into the equation by which they could add their naval strength to counter Germany.

These agreements were all serious threats to Germany. The original Triple Alliance of Germany, Austria-Hungary and Italy could not match the strength of Britain, France and Russia and it was even worse when Italy withdrew from the Triple Alliance in 1913. With these alliances adding significantly to Britain's power and the Royal Navy's ability to redeploy, the Germans were left with a very stark set of options.

The German navy was, in effect, trapped in the Baltic. In order to access the Atlantic and from there any other ocean, it would have to fight its way through the Royal Navy in time of war. There was also the serious threat that with this effective blockade German merchant vessels would be easy prey for the Royal Navy and that, in a relatively short period of time, Germany would be starved of resources. In fact, the Germans themselves believed that an effective blockade by the Royal Navy would bring Germany to its knees within a year.

The Royal Navy was extremely powerful on paper, but in reality some of the vessels deployed around the world were at best obsolete. They might have been superior numerically, but with the German fleet being almost entirely newly designed, up-to-date vessels, some of the older Royal Navy ships would be easy prey. In haste, Britain would have to pay for a root and branch refit of the Royal Navy. Luckily, the ideal man came to the fore at the right time.

When Admiral Sir John Arbuthnot Fisher was Commander-in-Chief of the Mediterranean Fleet, he had been desperate to ensure that he improved the efficiency of his fleet. The ships were made to carry out realistic gunnery practice, firing at moving targets, and he was constantly looking at strategy and tactics. As Winston Churchill said of Fisher: 'His energy and drive were already legendary in the service.'

Fisher first became Second Sea Lord, then First Sea Lord, effectively in control of the Royal Navy, saying of those who would stand in his way: 'Those who get in my way had better look out. I'll ruin anyone who tries to stop me.'

Fisher knew, as did his long-standing ally, Winston Churchill, that the Royal Navy would be comprehensively defeated in the event of a war if sweeping reforms did not take place – he even half-jokingly suggested that the Royal Navy sail for Kiel and destroy the German fleet as a pre-emptive strike. He took office as First Sea Lord on 21 October 1904, the 99th anniversary of Trafalgar.

Fisher's reforms were soon transforming a lazy and complacent Royal Navy into an effective fighting machine once again. He began by modernizing the training at Dartmouth and Osborne Naval Colleges – henceforth, the cadets would be taught all areas of seamanship, engineering, navigation and more special areas. The lot of the common sailor was improved: better food was introduced, as was better pay; severe punishments were abolished. Most importantly, Fisher tackled the problem of obsolete vessels. He identified 154 that were surplus to requirements and these were decommissioned. Some were sold on to smaller nations, whilst others were sent to the breaker's yard. This released experienced crews who were redeployed, and it also reduced the maintenance costs, allowing more money to be spent on newly commissioned vessels.

Fisher determined that henceforth a full 75 per cent of the Royal Navy's strength would be assigned to the Home Fleet. To begin with the Home Fleet was renamed the Channel Fleet, but this was later changed again to the Grand Fleet; its sole responsibility was to guard the North Sea. What had been the Channel Fleet became the Atlantic Fleet. This was to be based at Gibraltar so that it could easily be deployed into either the Mediterranean or the English Channel.

Fisher also created a new Reserve Fleet which retained key crew members, allowing the vessels, which would be partially moth-balled, to be redeployed as quickly as possible. The old Reserve Fleet had been virtually scrapped and these new reserve vessels could now be sent as reinforcements wherever they were needed.

One of Fisher's other major initiatives was to develop the torpedo boat and submarine, both of which had hitherto been considered to be ungentlemanly vessels, particularly in the case of the submarine.

Fisher's most important development, however, was to begin the standardization of the armament carried by the Royal Navy's battle-ships. Most of the existing battleships had 11 or 12in guns that were designed to penetrate an enemy vessel's hull, together with a large number of other guns of smaller calibres, designed to knock out enemy gun turrets. As a result of this, the Royal Navy was having huge problems ensuring that they had adequate stocks of ammunition for the different calibres of guns. The Royal Navy also relied on pummelling enemy ships with a hail of fire from these various weapons, but it was almost impossible for an individual gun to judge whether it was on target, falling short or firing long. Something had to be done to make this far more scientific. Fisher therefore decided that battleships needed to be able to do the job that they were designed to do – neutralize enemy battleships. In order to do this they needed to fire a salvo of heavy armour-piercing shells of a similar calibre.

Fisher was determined to produce battleships armed only with big guns, following the example of the Americans who were working on the *Michigan* and the *South Carolina* (completed in 1910) and a pair of Japanese ships, the *Settsu* and the *Kawachi* (work on these two began in 1909).

The final piece in the jigsaw was speed and Fisher determined to use new steam turbines. They had not been used in warships before and the only real experience of them was the sea trials that were underway with transatlantic liners. The new engines would give the warships a speed of 21 knots, at least 3 knots more than existing battleships. As steam turbines were more efficient, they needed less space on board, allowing sections of the ship to be compartmentalized; the decks would be armoured, as would the sides of the ships and the turrets.

The first ship of this type was HMS *Dreadnought* which was launched at Portsmouth on 10 February 1906. She had twelve 12in guns, four more than existing battleships, and she could deliver a broadside of eight guns. This meant that the broadside was at least twice the weight of shells than any other battleship that had been built to date. When in pursuit, she could fire three guns ahead instead of the normal one. There were other, smaller, guns – 12-pounders – to deal with smaller vessels, such as torpedo boats.

Dreadnought had a displacement of 20,000 tons and had armour of between 4 and 12 inches thick. She was developed and tested in record time and it only took four months from the time she was laid down for her to be launched; within twelve months she had completed her sea trials.

Many people believed that Fisher had made a big mistake and that he was risking all on the development of *Dreadnought*, but in truth it had chilled the Germans to the bone and they immediately halted construction of their new class of battleships. The Germans were desperate to copy the *Dreadnought*. By the time the first German Dreadnoughts, which were in fact modified versions, came into service in May 1910, Britain already had ten in service.

Fisher was also pushing through the development of another type of vessel: a heavy-gunned, armoured cruiser, with significant speed. These were to be used to find the enemy fleet, provide a protective screen and hold until the main fleet arrived. More often than not, cruisers proved too weak for this task and therefore armoured cruisers, with eight 12in guns were developed. The first ship, HMS *Invincible*, was completed in 1907; she weighed 17,000 tons, but could achieve a speed of 27 knots. The thickest part of her armoured belt was just 4 to 6 inches thick, but the deck, which would prove to be the undoing of this vessel, was barely an inch.

The British and the Germans entered into a Dreadnought-building race from 1906. In 1909 the Admiralty asked for the number of Dreadnoughts being built each year to be increased from four to six. The Liberal government decided to stick with the four, but to introduce a contingency plan for four more. As it was, the government finally decided to approve the eight. By the time 1912 dawned, Germany had managed to build eleven Dreadnought battleships and battlecruisers; Britain had built seventeen. By 1914 Germany had been able to increase their total to twenty-one, but Britain had sped ahead and had thirty-six.

Both the British and the Germans had problems with these new, enormous vessels. Britain had to create new naval bases at Rosyth and Cromarty, but even by 1914 they were not completed. The North Sea Fleet base at Scapa Flow was just an anchorage, without any defences. The more established naval bases at Portsmouth and Devonport were too far away from the Grand Fleet's main area of operations, the North Sea, and even Chatham was too far south. The Germans, on the other hand, had begun an expensive and time-consuming deepening and widening of the Kiel Canal, which took eight years to complete. Until then, the Germans were unable to transfer vessels with ease from and into the Baltic.

It was Fisher who had taken Jellicoe under his wing, recognizing his potential to become an important senior naval officer. Fisher had first spotted him back in 1898 and he would engineer successive appointments so that Jellicoe would become the Director of Naval Ordnance as soon as he himself became First Sea Lord.

By the time the Royal Navy carried out its Spithead Review in 1911, to mark the coronation of King George V, it was an entirely different navy to the one that had been on display in 1897. Fisher had created a modern battle fleet that bore no resemblance to the Victorian navy of a few years before.

Unfortunately, the previous year Fisher had felt obliged to resign, having fallen victim to some well-placed enemies. He had had a very public dispute with the Commander-in-Chief of the Channel Fleet, Admiral Lord Charles Beresford and had manoeuvred Beresford out of his command. The Admiralty set up a committee to investigate the dispute between the two men and when they reported back they did not fully support Fisher, who decided to resign, although he would be back and his enemies would pay in 1914.

As 1914 dawned, it began to look inevitable that Britain and Germany would soon be at war. Fisher had predicted that war with Germany would come in the autumn of 1914; in fact it came a little earlier than that, in August.

Throughout his short period out of office, Fisher kept close contact with his political ally, Winston Churchill. Churchill had become First Lord of the Admiralty in October 1911, had thrown himself into his role with enormous vigour and had involved himself in virtually everything, much to the resentment of senior officers in the Royal Navy. Churchill manoeuvred Wilson out of his job as First Sea Lord and, after trying Admiral Sir Francis Bridgman, he appointed Admiral Prince Louis of Battenburg. Churchill continued the revolutionary work that had been started by Fisher, approving the development of the super-Dreadnoughts and ordering the laying down of the *Queen Elizabeth* class; these would be armed with 13.5in guns and would be oil fired and capable of at least 24 knots. The first one was to be laid down in 1912 and five of them would be launched between 1913 and 1915.

Both Churchill and Fisher were in agreement about Jellicoe. The current commander, Admiral Sir George Callaghan, was not due to be replaced until late 1914, so Churchill had Jellicoe appointed as Callaghan's second in command. With Battenburg's agreement,

Churchill proposed to replace Callaghan, whose health was poor, with Jellicoe should hostilities break out. Churchill also chose Vice Admiral Sir David Beatty to command the battlecruiser squadrons.

Beatty already had a good reputation. He had received the Distinguished Service Cross at Omdurman in the war against Sudan in the 1890s, had fought during the Boxer Rebellion and had commanded several cruisers and a battleship. Significantly, he had even beaten Nelson to the rank of Rear Admiral, attaining this rank at the age of just thirty-nine years.

Beatty had been offered the position of second in command of the Atlantic Fleet, but he wanted an independent command and the Board of Admiralty had therefore put him on half pay from 1910. He asked to see Churchill and the two men immediately hit it off. As Churchill said of his meeting and his view of Beatty:

> He viewed naval strategy and tactics in a different light from the average naval officer. He did not think of matériel as an end in itself but only as a means. He thought of war problems in their unity by land, sea and air. His mind had been rendered quick and supple by the situations of polo and the hunting field and enriched by varied experiences against the enemy. I had no doubts whatever, when the command of the Battle Cruiser Squadron fell vacant in the spring of 1913, in appointing him over the heads of all to this incomparable command.

In fact Beatty was not to be given just one battlecruiser squadron, but three squadrons, known as the Battle Cruiser Force. In effect, he had become the second most important officer in the Grand Fleet.

Neither Beatty's nor Jellicoe's appointments had met with universal acclaim or approval. They were very different men, but they got on well together. Churchill had now engineered a strong command team with him at the top: Battenburg, and then Jellicoe and Beatty. It was a coherent combination that shared a similar view and purpose.

The Germans, on the other hand, had all sorts of problems. The Kaiser was somewhat erratic, while Tirpitz was almost in open conflict with the naval cabinet and senior naval staff. Most importantly, however, Tirpitz did not have the ability to make operational decisions. This was the role of Admiral von Pohl and the Commander-in-Chief of the German High Seas Fleet, Admiral von Ingenohl. When Tirpitz proposed that he would become head of operations, no one, including the Kaiser, seemed to support this. Von Pohl and von Ingenohl were not exactly decisive leaders either, and in any case the Kaiser himself too easily influenced them.

Whereas the Germans had always assumed that at the outbreak of war the British would move in close to the German ports to effect a tight blockade, the British had determined not to do this, but would instead blockade the German ports from a distance. It was a practical decision as most of the British vessels could only stay at sea for around a week, while some of the smaller vessels, including the destroyers, could only remain in position for a few days before having to refuel. The British were also aware of the dangers posed by minefields and submarines if they moved in close to the German ports, having heeded the lesson that Admiral Togo, the Japanese commander, had learned so bloodily in 1904. Togo had moved his battleships close to the Russian base of Port Arthur and had lost upwards of 30 per cent of his battleship force to mines.

It should be borne in mind that the vessels facing one another in 1914 had absolutely no protection against mines. They had even less chance against submarines, although mercifully the submarines were relatively slow and the torpedoes had a very limited range. The only hope that a surface vessel would have in dealing with a submarine was to close with it as quickly as possible and try to ram it.

The British knew very well that the estuaries leading to the main German bases were fortified. Several plans had been considered, including landing troops on the Pomeranian coast to seize or threaten the German bases. Nonetheless, a blockade had to be attempted, otherwise the German fleet would be at liberty to range far and wide, and do untold damage.

Effectively, the British plan was very simple: to present the German High Seas Fleet with an unmissable opportunity. If it could lure the German vessels out into the North Sea then the German High Seas Fleet could be cornered and eliminated by the more powerful Grand Fleet of the Royal Navy. The Germans, however, were not about to fall for such a simple trick, knowing how difficult it would be to enter the North Sea and break out to the North Atlantic. If they went north the Grand Fleet would get them, as they

12

were based in Scotland. If they went south, through the English Channel, they could force the weaker Channel Fleet aside, but inevitably the Grand Fleet would then block the English Channel and there would be nowhere to run.

So, despite the vast sums of money spent on the German High Seas Fleet, its role would remain limited. When the opportunity arose, it would venture out and attack British towns on the east coast, at the same time luring weaker British forces towards it so that it could destroy parts of the Royal Navy in detail. In the meantime it would hope to reduce the number of Royal Navy vessels by such actions, whilst more German vessels were launched. Once the German fleet had reached equal numbers with the British Grand Fleet it would then attempt a major sea battle.

Neither the Royal Navy nor the German navy was prepared to take any serious risks, even though it meant that two huge, highly expensive and heavily manned forces would sit and stare at one another until one of them made a move. Only then would there be a chance of action.

It was incredibly difficult to organize coordinated movements between such large numbers of vessels. Wireless telegraphy was used, but for security and technical reasons it was never quite trusted. As a result, the majority of communication between vessels was done either by flags or signal lamps.

With both the British and the Germans working on ways in which to deal with the newer, long-range guns, it would be of vital importance to be able to judge the movements of an enemy ship. Complex mathematical calculations would need to take into account the enemy ship's speed, range and bearing. If the ships were firing at targets as much as 8 miles away, the shells would be in the air for more than twenty seconds, which meant that judging all of the factors necessary to hit the enemy ship at the point at which the guns were about to fire could well change over those few seconds. The British employed technicians to work on aids that could improve the overall gun control.

Lieutenant Dumaresq created a device to calculate changes in bearing and range – effectively a slide rule. The values worked out were applied to a range clock that made calculations in order to plot the enemy's expected course. The range clock itself, or at least the most effective one, was known as the Argo clock, invented by

Arthur Pollen. Captain Frederic Dreyer devised another mechanical device, known as the Dreyer Fire Control Table Mark I, which was a manually operated device and was often too slow to cope with rapid changes. In the end, many of the ships used the Dreyer system, although few had the Argo clock.

The Germans, meanwhile, were working on a similar device to the Dumaresq slide rule. The problem was that the gun layers needed months of training, although the Germans had a much better range finder than the one used by the Royal Navy. Each ship had up to seven stereoscopic range finders, each of which gave quite accurate values, but again the operator needed to be extremely well trained and an awful lot of pressure was placed on them.

By mid-July 1914 the Royal Navy was testing naval mobilization, but was due at Spithead for the annual review on 20 July, after which it would proceed to the Channel for exercises. The Germans were undergoing exercises in the Skagerrak, following which they would move into Norwegian waters. The political situation was beginning to deteriorate and events were in progress that were about to trigger off the First World War.

The situation had deteriorated to such an extent by 25 July that the Kaiser ordered the German High Seas Fleet to move to the Baltic to attack Russia. Von Ingenohl managed to convince the Kaiser that part of the fleet should be sent into the North Sea, just in case.

The following day, when Churchill was on his way to Cromer, in Norfolk, to visit his sick wife, Battenburg decided to send Callaghan an order: 'No ships of First Fleet or Flotillas are to leave Portland until further orders.'

Later in the day Battenburg wired Callaghan once again: 'First Fleet is to leave Portland tomorrow, Wednesday, for Scapa Flow. Destination is to be kept secret.'

When Austria declared war on Serbia on 28 July, the world was on the brink of war. The Royal Navy was warned to take all measures and precautions, and all leave was cancelled. On 31 July the Russians began mobilizing and on 1 August the Germans told the Russians to demobilize within twelve hours. The Russians ignored the warning and Germany declared war on Russia the same day.

When both the British Grand Fleet and the German High Seas

Fleet received general mobilization orders on 1 August, it was still not clear what Britain and France would do. After enquiring about the intentions of the French, the Germans decided to declare war on France on 3 August.

The previous day, Churchill had replaced Callaghan with Jellicoe, who wired Churchill, warning him that changing command at such a late date was bound to have an impact on the morale of the fleet, at the same time admitting that he needed to know more about the fleet before he could lead it. Churchill replied: 'I can give you 48 hours after joining Fleet. You must be ready then.'

Jellicoe was still unsure. Callaghan had simply been told: 'You are to strike your flag forthwith, reporting yourself to the Admiralty thereafter at your earliest convenience.'

Many felt that Callaghan's dismissal was unfair, but in a very short time Jellicoe won the respect of the fleet. As Jellicoe was assuming command of the Grand Fleet, the British government had sent an ultimatum demanding that the Germans respect Belgian neutrality, and giving them until 2300 hrs on 4 August to confirm that Belgium's neutrality would be honoured. When the Germans did not reply the Admiralty signalled all ships and installations: 'Commence hostilities against Germany.'

Sitting in the Jade Estuary was the High Seas Fleet of fourteen Dreadnought battleships and five battlecruisers. Against this was ranged the Grand Fleet's twenty-one Dreadnought battleships at Scapa Flow and eight battlecruisers at Rosyth. The British had certainly won the arms race. There were other British vessels underway in the dockyards: three super-Dreadnoughts, destined for the Ottoman Turks and the Chileans, had been commandeered. Churchill would not countenance the prospect of British-built vessels falling into enemy hands.

Although, in terms of the larger ships, the British had a distinct advantage, they lacked a clear superiority in terms of light cruisers – by August 1914 the Germans had mustered twenty to Britain's twenty-three. In terms of smaller vessels, the Germans were better off, mustering ninety torpedo boats compared to the British destroyer screen of some forty vessels. But it was in submarines that the Germans had a distinct advantage, with some nineteen U-boats attached to the German High Seas Fleet, whereas there were none in the Grand Fleet.

The Germans were to strike the first blow. On the night of 4 August 1914 a converted steamer managed to work its way past Royal Navy patrols and lay mines between the Thames Estuary and the Dutch coast. Royal Navy destroyers operating out of Harwich the following morning intercepted the German vessel, the *Königin Luise*, and she was sunk. But the German mines were to do their work and the light cruiser HMS *Amphion* was sunk by one with heavy loss of life.

On the same day there was action in the Mediterranean. Admiral Wilhelm Souchon commanded the German battlecruiser *Goeben* and the light cruiser *Breslau*. Opposing him was Admiral Sir Berkeley Milne, on board an old battlecruiser, HMS *Inflexible*, accompanied by four armoured cruisers. The British spotted the German ships off the coast of French Algeria as they bombarded the ports. There was nothing the British could do as the ultimatum to Germany had not yet expired and by the time Milne received the go-ahead to engage the German ships they had vanished during the night.

Milne's second in command, Rear Admiral Ernest Troubridge, and his light cruisers had picked up the trail of the German ships to the south of Corfu on the evening of 6 August. Troubridge had contradictory orders: on the one hand Milne had told him to prevent the Germans joining up with the Austrian fleet in the Adriatic; on the other hand, the Admiralty had said he was not to engage a superior force. Troubridge only had the four cruisers and decided that trying to tackle a battlecruiser would constitute a superior force. As it was, the German ships headed towards the Dardanelles on 10 August and although the *Goeben* hit three Turkish mines, they both reached Constantinople the following day, which helped to bring the Ottoman Turks into the war. The two German ships were then placed into the hands of the Turkish navy.

Troubridge faced a court martial, charged with cowardice: 'Through negligence or through another default, forbear to pursue the chase of His Imperial Majesty's Ship *Goeben* being an enemy then flying.'

Troubridge was found not guilty, but his career was over. Milne did not escape criticism. Fisher said: 'Personally I should have shot Sir Berkeley Milne.'

So far not a shot had been fired between the two fleets, but the

British were itching to get to grips with the Germans, so they decided to lay a trap. The Germans sent out patrols each day to prevent British operations in the Heligoland Bight, so it was proposed that a pair of light cruisers and thirty-five destroyers should intercept the German patrols at around dawn. The hope was that the Germans would send in larger vessels to support their patrol ships, the British ships would withdraw and, to the north of Heligoland, eight submarines would be waiting for them. The plan was approved on 24 August and the raid was scheduled for 28 August.

The Grand Fleet also wanted to be part of the plan. Jellicoe was particularly keen and finally decided to let Beatty go, taking five vessels, supported by a light-cruiser squadron, although he neglected to let anyone know that Beatty was on his way until 27 August. In any case the information never reached those planning to bait and spring the trap.

On the morning of 28 August, a pair of German warships were spotted chasing a British submarine; the British gave chase. Tyrwhitt, in command of the Harwich force, pursued them and came within range of the German vessels, the *Stettin* and the *Frauenlob*, both of which were light cruisers. They engaged HMS *Arethusa* and HMS *Fearless* and in the running battle HMS *Arethusa* was damaged, as were both of the German vessels. As Tyrwhitt's destroyer flotillas hunted for other German ships, he discovered that no fewer than six German light cruisers were heading in his direction. The first to appear at 1100 was the *Strassburg* which opened fire on the already crippled *Arethusa*. At 1110 the flagship of Rear Admiral Maass, the *Köln*, came into view and three of Tyrwhitt's destroyers were badly damaged.

With Beatty's force still 40 miles to the north-west, he ordered the First Light Cruiser Squadron, under Goodenough, to move in Tyrwhitt's support. Meanwhile Beatty's battlecruisers came under fire from British submarines which reported Goodenough's cruisers as being German ships.

The Germans were now reinforced by the *Stralsund, Danzig* and *Ariadne,* all cruisers; the *Stettin* had been repaired and was now back in action.

Beatty realized the danger that Tyrwhitt was in and moved to within 30 miles of the heavily defended coast. Five British battle-cruisers, led by Beatty himself in HMS *Lion*, headed towards the battle at a speed of 28 knots. Goodenough, meanwhile, was chasing another German cruiser, the *Mainz*, which found itself surrounded when six destroyers appeared. She had been hit several times already but despite continued fire the Germans refused to surrender. Eventually HMS *Lydiard* hit the *Mainz* with a torpedo and some 300 members of her crew were taken on board HMS *Lurcher* as prisoners.

Beatty's battlecruisers were about to make the Germans pay dearly for having been so easily ensnared in the trap. The first target was the *Köln*. HMS *Lion* quickly overtook her and fired point-blank salvos into her until eventually Admiral Maas drowned on board his flagship with 380 of his men.

The *Strassburg* was badly hit, but the next victim would be the *Ariadne* which was quickly reduced to a mass of flames, although she stayed afloat for another three hours. The Germans had been scattered and Tyrwhitt's force had been saved from being overwhelmed.

A mist appeared and the British ships were in dangerous enemy waters, eight hours from safety. HMS *Arethusa* was towed home to Chatham for repairs; Beatty had won the Battle of Heligoland Bight. The Germans had lost 1,200 killed, wounded or taken prisoner, including an admiral and a destroyer commodore, one of the prisoners being none other than Tirpitz's own son, Wolf. They had also lost three light cruisers, a destroyer and had had three more light cruisers badly damaged. The British casualties amounted to thirty killed and forty-five wounded, nearly all of whom were confined to the badly damaged *Arethusa*. In all, three British destroyers and one cruiser were damaged – a decisive victory.

Lessons were learned from the battle, the most important one by the Germans: British shells had broken up on impact with their ships, rather than penetrating the superstructure.

The First Battle of Scapa Flow took place on 1 September 1914. Anything less like a battle could barely be imagined. A British cruiser spotted a periscope inside the fleet's anchorage at around dusk; a cruiser found and rammed a German U-boat; the discovery unnerved Jellicoe and he took twelve battleships out to sea and remained there until dawn. It has never been completely proven whether there ever was a periscope, as no wreckage or bodies were ever found. Many people believe that the periscope was probably a seal, but the incident had spooked the British.

The British had ample reason to fear submarines, proven beyond any doubt on the night of 21/22 September 1914. Three old cruisers, HMS *Hogue*, HMS *Aboukir* and HMS *Cressy* were patrolling off the Dutch coast. At 0630 on 22 September a torpedo hit the *Aboukir*, unfortunately destroying all her lifeboats. HMS *Hogue* came in to rescue the crew from the water, despatching her own lifeboats to pick up the survivors. The *Aboukir* sank at approximately 1655. At around the same time HMS *Hogue* was hit twice within five minutes and she too had to be abandoned; this time HMS *Cressy* came in to pick up survivors. A pair of torpedoes were fired at her and one of them hit; she almost immediately rolled over, sinking fifteen minutes later. In all nearly 1,400 men were drowned. The perpetrator of this attack was Otto Weddingen in the U-9, who was awarded the Iron Cross First Class, but later drowned while in command of the U-12 when his submarine was rammed by HMS *Dreadnought* in March 1915.

The false alarm at Scapa Flow and the disastrous loss of three obsolete ships off the Dutch coast made the British even more paranoid about the threat from submarines. Jellicoe was particularly affected by all of this and until submarine defences had been constructed at Scapa Flow, he moved the Grand Fleet to Loch Ewe on 7 October. He was stunned again when a submarine was seen in the loch and moved his fleet to the north-west coast of Ireland. During this time the whole of the British east coast was open to attack and the Germans could have mounted the raids that they had intended with impunity.

The Germans despatched the liner *Berlin* to sow mines to the north of Ireland and she began laying the minefield on 22 October 1914. Five days later Jellicoe sent out his Second Battle Squadron to engage in gunnery practice, but disaster struck when HMS *Audacious* hit one of the mines. The captain, Dampier, tried to make for shore although she was already sinking. The liner *Olympic* arrived and started picking up the crew members. Attempts to tow *Audacious* to safety failed and just twelve hours later she blew up and sank. This incident further worried Jellicoe who felt certain that the Germans would try to lure him into a trap if he was to engage their High Seas Fleet in the southern North Sea:

If the enemy turned away from us, I should assume the intention was to lead us over mines and submarines, and decline to be drawn. This might result in failure to bring an enemy into action as soon as is expected and hoped, but with new and untried methods of warfare, new tactics must be devised. These, if not understood, might bring odium upon me, but it is quite possible that half our battle fleet might be disabled by underwater attack before the guns open fire at all. The safeguard will consist in moving to a flank before the action commences. This will take us off the ground on which the enemy desires to fight, and may result in a refusal to follow me; but if the battle fleets remain in sight of one another, I should feel that after an interval of high speed manoeuvring, I could safely close.

Far away in the Indian Ocean the German raider, *Emden*, was attacking British convoys and merchant ships. Meanwhile, in the Pacific, Rear Admiral Sir Christopher Cradock was desperately trying to find Vice Admiral Graf von Spee's East Asiatic Squadron. They were finally to close off the Chilean coast on 1 November when the German armoured cruisers outgunned HMS *Good Hope,* Cradock's flagship, and another armoured cruiser, HMS *Monmouth*. The pair of ships went down with all hands, including Cradock and 1,600 officers and men.

While the Germans strongly believed that the myth of British naval invincibility had been shattered for ever, Battenburg took most of the criticism and resigned, allowing Churchill to reinstate Fisher as First Sea Lord. Fisher's first act was to send Vice Admiral Sir Doveton Sturdee, with a pair of battlecruisers, to deal with von Spee's vessels.

Meanwhile, there was another German attack on the British coast on 3 November, this time at Gorleston and Great Yarmouth, when five German battlecruisers and four smaller cruisers began firing on the two towns at dawn. The majority of the shells landed harmlessly on the beaches, and after an hour the Germans gave up and headed home. Despite British attempts to intercept them, the German ships got away.

The bad news which had rocked the Royal Navy and the Admiralty was largely offset by a tremendous breakthrough in

December 1914, when quite by chance the British were handed the German naval code system on a plate. At the end of August 1914 a German cruiser, the *Magdeburg,* ran aground in the Gulf of Finland after a pair of Russian cruisers had battered her into submission. The Russians clambered aboard the wrecked German vessel and discovered what Churchill described as 'sea-stained priceless documents'. These arrived in London at the end of October 1914 and it was discovered that they were an intact copy of the German naval codebook.

A second discovery took place when a German secret operational grid of the North Sea was scooped up in the nets of a British trawler. The grid was used by the Germans to identify a vessel's position in the North Sea and would prove to be invaluable.

The Admiralty set up Room 40, under Sir Alfred Ewing, whose staff would listen in to German W/T messages and pass the information through the Operations Division to Jellicoe.

As part of the overall covert operations against the Germans, Captain William Hall, Head of Naval Intelligence, ordered the establishment of a number of direction-finding stations along the East Coast that could take bearings on ships sending signals. By taking multiple bearings the exact location of the vessel could be established.

The Germans soon got wise to the breaking of their codes and changed their ciphers and codebooks, but no sooner had they done so than Ewing's men deciphered these too. In any case a new signal book had already been found in a crippled U-boat and another in a Zeppelin.

Way to the south, in the Falkland Islands, Sturdee reached Port Stanley on 9 December 1914, by which time five other cruisers had joined him. As he planned to hunt systematically for von Spee, and with the British vessels re-coaling, von Spee rounded Cape Horn, having decided to attack Port Stanley and sink any ships he might find there. To his horror, as he approached Port Stanley, von Spee did not see a motley collection of merchant vessels but battle-cruisers. Instead of taking advantage and destroying the helpless British ships, von Spee turned and fled. By the time Sturdee's ships left the harbour the Germans had a 20-mile lead on them. The Germans knew that the faster British ships would soon catch them and hoped for fog.

Sturdee gave chase, first sinking the *Scharnhorst,* von Spee's flagship. The next German vessel to be caught was the *Gneisenau,* which was so badly damaged that it was scuttled by its crew. Last to be caught were the *Leipzig* and the *Nurnberg* and they, too, were sunk; the only German cruiser to escape was the *Dresden* which ran for the Pacific Ocean but was cornered a few months later when she had run out of coal. Unable to escape, her captain chose to scuttle her.

The Battle of the Falklands, as the engagement became known, was an overwhelming British victory. Four major German vessels had been destroyed and von Spee was dead, along with his two sons, Otto and Heinrich, and 2,000 German sailors.

Room 40 discovered that Franz von Hipper's German squadron was going to move on the morning of 14 December and that it was due to return to base on the evening of the following day. As far as British Naval Intelligence was concerned it seemed that Hipper and his five large warships, accompanied by destroyers and light cruisers, were aiming to hit the East Coast, just as on 3 November. The British saw this as an ideal opportunity to cut off the German ships and destroy them before they could return to base.

Jellicoe despatched Beatty with four battlecruisers and Vice Admiral Sir George Warrender, with six super-Dreadnoughts, to trap Hipper. As an insurance measure, Rear Admiral Sir William Pakenham, Goodenough's First Light Cruiser Squadron, Tyrwhitt's Harwich Force and Sir Roger Keyes' submarines would be sent in support. Tyrwhitt and Keyes would wait near the Dutch coast and pick off any German stragglers or damaged vessels that had escaped the main fleet action.

Beatty and Warrender were to rendezvous close to the Dogger Bank on the morning of 16 December, in order to put them in an ideal position to intercept Hipper. The Germans, however, had plans of their own.

Friedrich von Ingenohl, the Commander-in-Chief of the German High Seas Fleet, was planning a trap of his own. Knowing that three British battlecruisers were absent from Beatty's force, he intended to put to sea and ambush the Royal Navy in the belief that they would send out only part of their battle fleet to deal with Hipper's battlecruisers. He would wait for Hipper to withdraw and lure whatever vessels the Royal Navy had put to sea into the hands of the German High Seas Fleet, where they would be smashed. In a single stroke von Ingenohl hoped to destroy enough of the Grand Fleet to equalize the balance of power at sea.

In the event, it all turned out to be somewhat confused. Warrender arrived at the rendezvous well before the appointed time of 0730. To the south of the Dogger Bank he saw German torpedo boats and ordered his destroyer screen to engage them. Soon after, German light cruisers appeared and these, too, were engaged. Warrender had stumbled into a screen hiding the German High Seas Fleet. By this stage it was still more than two hours before daybreak.

Von Ingenohl was terrified that as he had run into destroyers, the British Grand Fleet was in the immediate vicinity. Although Beatty was made aware of Warrender's engagement and sped to the position, both he and Warrender were completely unaware of the fact that they were not chasing Hipper's force but were in fact pursuing the entire German High Seas Fleet. If Ingenohl had had the guts to stop and turn, he would have realized that his twenty-two battleships would have been more than a match for the half dozen super-Dreadnoughts and four battlecruisers. As it was, before Hipper could react, Warrender and Beatty received news at 0800 that the *Derfflinger* and the *Von der Tann* were shelling Scarborough. They broke off their pursuit and headed to engage the raiders.

The German vessels shelled Scarborough for thirty minutes and Whitby for ten minutes, but all they managed to achieve was to inflict forty-seven civilian casualties before fleeing to the north to rejoin Hipper who had been directing the shelling of Hartlepool since 0815. Hipper was on board his flagship, *Seydlitz*, which was accompanied by the *Moltke* and the *Blucher*. Hartlepool was badly damaged with eighty-six civilians killed and over 400 injured.

Hipper broke off the bombardment at 0900 and turned to meet up with the *Derfflinger* and the *Von der Tann*. He now had three options, all of which would take him through the German minefields near the Tyne and the Humber. Meanwhile Warrender was moving to cover the southern route, Jellicoe had sent Vice Admiral Sir Edward Bradford to cover the north and Beatty's battlecruisers were covering the central gap. As it was, Hipper chose the route guarded by Beatty, not realizing he was in any danger – after all,

23

von Ingenohl had not told him that the British had broken off from the engagement near the Dogger Bank four hours before.

It seemed now that Hipper was trapped, but at 1130, with Beatty and Hipper only 50 miles apart, the weather came to his rescue. Goodenough's flagship, HMS *Southampton,* spotted the Germans first and opened fire. *Southampton* was quickly joined by HMS *Birmingham* and they reported that the Germans were heading south. HMS *Nottingham* and HMS *Lowestoft* were moving to support Goodenough.

Hipper was now aware that an enemy force was somewhere in front of him. He turned south-easterly to avoid Beatty's battle-cruisers and immediately ran into part of Warrender's squadron. In thickening fog, Hipper now turned north-east and disappeared. Keyes was told to try to intercept the Germans as they reached Heligoland Bight. As it was only one of the submarines managed to get a shot off but missed the German battleship *Posen* at nearly point-blank range.

Although the engagement had been entirely inconclusive, it had caused enormous public consternation. Many civilians had been killed, civilians who had thought that the Royal Navy was there to protect them. The Germans were accused of operating contrary to the terms of the Hague Convention as they were targeting virtually undefended towns and butchering civilians, quite apart from causing the Royal Navy intense embarrassment. Churchill, Fisher, Jellicoe and Beatty were determined to catch and destroy the Germans the next time.

The Germans were planning a reconnaissance of the Dogger Bank area, believing that there were spies operating in the area, informing the British of German ship movements. They had not appreciated the fact that their naval codes had been compromised. At 1000 on 22 January 1915 von Ingenohl sent Hipper a coded wireless signal: 'To Seydlitz for Senior Officer Scouting Vessels. First and Second Scouting Groups, Senior Officer of torpedo boats and two flotillas chosen by Senior Officer of Scouting Vessels to reconnoitre the Dogger Bank. Proceed to sea this evening after dark, and return after dark on the following evening.'

When the signal was intercepted by the British and deciphered, Sir Arthur Wilson, the Admiral of the Fleet, along with the Chief of

Staff, Admiral Oliver, ran into Churchill's office in the Admiralty. It was now 1235 and it was too good a chance to miss. Beatty was told to prepare to leave Rosyth immediately.

Hipper's force was made up of four battlecruisers and half a dozen light cruisers. The British were ready to send a number of vessels against them, hoping to trap Hipper in such a way that he would not be able to escape this time. Beatty, leading five battle-cruisers and supported by Goodenough with four light cruisers, would arrive just after dawn on 24 January to the north-east edge of Dogger Bank. Tyrwhitt would rendezvous with them at the head of three light cruisers and thirty-five destroyers. It was hoped that the British would be no more than 10 miles from Hipper's fleet at dawn. Beatty would be between Hipper and his base and Hipper would be trapped. As an insurance measure, Pakenham and his Third Cruiser Squadron, and Bradford's Third Battle Squadron, were told to rendezvous 50 miles to the north of the Dogger Bank to prevent any escape in that direction.

Just in case the German High Seas Fleet ventured out, three of Jellicoe's battle squadrons would be patrolling around 130 miles to the north of the Dogger Bank. Way to the south Keyes would lie in wait to interdict any German vessels. The only flaw in the plan was if Hipper somehow escaped to the south-east, however, when the Admiralty discovered that one of the German ships was the *Blucher*, they realized there was no way Hipper could outrun Beatty's battle-cruisers.

By 2100 on 23 January 1915 the majority of the British forces were close to their assigned rendezvous positions. At 0705 on the 24th, HMS *Aurora* spotted four German torpedo boats and a German light cruiser about 4 miles to the east of her and opened fire. The *Aurora* was trading shots with the *Kolberg*, to the far left of the advance screen protecting Hipper's force, both vessels scoring direct hits on one another. Beatty saw the gun flashes and turned to the south-east, increasing the speed of his battlecruisers to 23 knots. At 0730 HMS *Southampton* spotted a pair of German cruisers, the *Stralsund* and the *Graudenz*, which were to the starboard of Hipper's main force. Goodenough immediately informed Beatty. Meanwhile, *Aurora* saw traces of black smoke in the distance, which she believed to be enemy battlecruisers.

The weather conditions were ideal for a naval engagement, but

Hipper had just received a message from the *Stralsund* telling him that they had seen eight large British warships to the north-west. Hipper was now in a quandary having been led to believe that Beatty only had five battlecruisers. Fearing these vessels were part of Jellicoe's Grand Fleet, Hipper immediately ordered his vessels to swing to the south-east and head for Wilhelmshaven.

Beatty headed south-east and shortly before 0800 he could see clouds of smoke rising from German battlecruisers. He estimated the range to be 25,000 yards and ordered his vessels to increase speed to 25 knots. Goodenough had a better view of the Germans and confirmed that there were four battlecruisers heading east/south-east. Beatty was determined to catch them, first cranking up the speed of the battlecruisers to 26 knots and then 27. Beatty's flagship, HMS *Lion,* was in the lead, followed by HMS *Tiger* and HMS *Princess Royal.* Behind them were the older HMS *New Zealand* and HMS *Indomitable.*

Lagging behind in the German group was the *Blucher,* with the *Moltke* and the *Derfflinger* just ahead, behind Hipper's flagship, the *Seydlitz.*

By 0900 the range had closed to 22,000 yards. Beatty ordered HMS *Lion* to fire a sighting shot at the *Seydlitz* but the shot fell well short. With growing impatience Beatty increased the battle cruiser's speed to 29 knots, but already HMS *New Zealand* was falling behind and HMS *Indomitable* was finding it hard to keep up even with HMS *New Zealand. Lion* continued firing ranging shots, this time focusing on the *Blucher.* Shortly after 0900 the range to the *Blucher* had fallen to 20,000 yards. It was then that Beatty ordered his other vessels to open fire.

HMS *Lion* began firing salvos at the *Derfflinger,* while HMS *Tiger* and HMS *Princess Royal* focused on the *Blucher.* The two other British ships desperately tried to catch up and join in the fight. Beatty ordered up his destroyers so that if Hipper launched his torpedo boats they would be able to screen the larger ships. During the salvos the *Blucher* was hit once and the *Derfflinger* and *Seydlitz* were both hit twice, as was HMS *Lion.*

By 0935 the range had fallen to 17,000 yards, but HMS *Indomitable* was still unable to lend any weight of fire, as HMS *New Zealand* began firing at the *Blucher,* HMS *Princess Royal* at the *Derfflinger,* HMS *Tiger* at the *Moltke* and HMS *Lion* at the Seydlitz.

Unfortunately the crew of HMS *Tiger* mistook HMS *Lion*'s fire and began firing at the *Seydlitz,* leaving the *Moltke* unengaged, so this vessel and the *Seydlitz* concentrated their fire on HMS *Lion.*

At 0945 a shot from HMS *Lion* shattered the afterdeck of the *Seydlitz.* As Admiral Scheer later described it:

> The first shell that hit her had a terrible effect. It pierced right through the upper deck in the ship's stern and threw the barbette armour of the near turret, where it exploded. In the reloading chamber, where the shell penetrated, part of the charge in readiness for loading was set on fire. The flames rose high up into the turret and down into the munition chamber, and thence through a connecting door usually kept shut, through which the men from the munition chamber tried to escape into the fore turret. The flames thus made their way through to the other munition chamber, and thence again up to the second turret, and from this cause the entire gun crews of both turrets perished almost instantly. The flames rose as high as a house above the turrets.

Some 6 tons of propellant were on fire. Amazingly, three men managed to get through the heat and fumes and open the flooding valves to the magazines. The *Seydlitz* was not out of action.

Hipper decided to concentrate on destroying HMS *Lion.* The *Derfflinger,* along with the *Moltke* and the remaining guns on the *Seydlitz,* concentrated on Beatty's flagship.

With the *Blucher* under heavy fire, Hipper desperately needed von Ingenohl to come and save him, but there was no way the German High Seas Fleet could be in a position to assist before 1430. By then it would be too late. The *Derfflinger* was belching smoke and HMS *New Zealand* and HMS *Princess Royal* believed they had crippled her, but they were wrong.

All of a sudden, German torpedo boats began arriving, but by now Tyrwhitt was closing with his destroyers to help drive them off. HMS *Lion* was still under fire from three German ships having been hit at least four times; one shell which hit her at 1001 penetrated her side armour, but mercifully failed to explode. In return HMS *Lion* was firing as fast as possible at the *Seydlitz,* but only achieved one additional hit.

Suddenly a pair of shells from the *Derfflinger* hit the *Lion* at the same time. One of the shells went straight through her armour belt at the waterline; the second hit the side armour underneath the waterline, flooding several compartments. HMS *Lion* began to list. Beatty was still hoping to drive Hipper north so that he would run into Jellicoe's Grand Fleet, which unfortunately was still over 140 miles away.

Beatty signalled for his ships to continue to close and at 1035, heading close to the enemy torpedo-boat screen, he had closed the range to just over 16,000 yards. The *Blucher* had been hit several times and was even further behind the other German battlecruisers. Suddenly HMS *Princess Royal* hit her with a pair of 13.5in shells that went straight through her main deck. One of them set off an ammunition fire and the other knocked out two of her engines; the detonation jammed the steering gear. The *Blucher* moved abruptly to port and as she did so she was hit twice more. Beatty order HMS *Indomitable* to finish off the crippled *Blucher* while his other four ships closed to finish off the rest of Hipper's squadron.

All of a sudden Beatty's flagship, HMS *Lion,* under fire from three German battlecruisers, was hit ten times in just twenty minutes. With his flagship losing speed and listing heavily, Beatty was beginning to lose his ability to determine the course of the battle.

At 1100 HMS *Lion* was hit again. Sea water flooded in and the port engine had to be closed down. She had taken on 3,000 tons of water and was struggling along at 15 knots with an 11-degree list; there was no light or power. With the Germans still withdrawing and pulling away from the crippled *Lion*, HMS *Tiger* passed her and was almost immediately hit four times. There was a spectacular explosion and the Germans thought they had destroyed her, but it was only petrol on the deck, stored there for the ship's motor launches, which had exploded.

There was sudden panic when a lookout on HMS *Lion* claimed that he had spotted the periscope of a submarine, although in fact there were no German submarines within 50 miles of the engagement. The false report panicked Beatty and he ordered a 90-degree turn to port. This would not only take them away from the direction in which Hipper was fleeing, but also bring them perilously close to the German torpedo boats. Beatty quickly realized he had made a mistake and corrected his order to turn 45-degrees and attack the rear of the enemy.

The British move threw Hipper. He had considered turning back to try to save the *Blucher*, but his ships were running out of ammunition. He had hoped to turn in a wide, starboard arc to draw the British towards him before launching an attack on them with his torpedo boats, but now that Beatty's ships were heading to the north-west he abandoned the *Blucher* and headed south-east towards Heligoland.

The *Blucher* was soon surrounded by four British battlecruisers. Although she was hit countless times, perhaps as many as seventy, she refused to surrender and continued to fire back. One of the survivors of the ship later wrote:

> Shells came thick and fast with a terrible droning hum. When the ranges shortened their trajectory flattened and they tore holes in the ship's sides and raked her decks. The terrific air pressure resulting from explosion in a confined space left a deep impression on the minds of the men of the Blucher. The air, it would seem, roars through every opening and tears its way through every weak spot. As one poor wretch was passing through a trapdoor a shell burst near him. He was exactly halfway through. The trapdoor closed with a terrific snap. The men were picked up by that terrible Luftdruck [air pressure] and tossed to a horrible death amidst the machinery.

HMS *Arethusa* came up and fired a pair of torpedoes into the *Blucher*. The British battlecruisers ceased fire and suddenly she rolled over; what remained of the crew tried to jump clear. When the *Blucher* capsized at 1215, HMS *Arethusa* and other destroyers managed to save 234 men out of a total complement of 1,026. Amazingly, a German seaplane came over after the *Blucher* had sunk and the men were being picked up from the water. They dropped hand bombs on the little boats, believing the scene to be a crippled British ship.

In the meantime HMS *Attack,* a destroyer, transferred Beatty to HMS *Princess Royal,* which he temporarily made his flagship at 1227. The Germans were still retreating and by now were at least 30,000 yards away. Beatty calculated that it would take him two hours to catch them up and by then the Germans would be close to Heligoland. Rather reluctantly he called off the pursuit at 1245.

29

HMS *Lion* was under tow by HMS *Indomitable*, with cruisers and destroyers surrounding the two ships so that the Germans would not get a cheap victory out of the engagement by sinking the slowly moving vessels. When the Admiralty discovered, from decoded signals, that the Germans were planning a night attack to finish off HMS *Lion*, Jellicoe decided to send two destroyer flotillas to help screen the pair of battlecruisers. As it was Hipper was low on fuel and the attack was never made. Eventually HMS *Lion* arrived near the Firth of Forth at 0635 the following day.

Thus ended the Battle of the Dogger Bank. Although HMS *Lion* had received something of a battering, it had been a British victory. *Lion* would be in the Tyne dockyards for six weeks, but in truth the casualties had been comparatively light. Only eleven men had been killed on *Lion* and thirty-one wounded. The Germans, by comparison, had lost over 1,000 men.

Beatty was desperately disappointed and wrote: 'The disappointment of that day is more than I can bear to think of. Everybody thinks it was a great success, when in reality it was a terrible failure. I had made up my mind that we were going to get four, the lot, and four we ought to have got.'

What had really been the downfall of the British was their poor gunnery. HMS *Lion*, HMS *Tiger* and HMS *Princess Royal* had fired 869 x 13.5in shells, but between them they had scored just six hits. The Germans, on the other hand, had fired off 976 shells and had scored twenty-two hits on HMS *Lion* and HMS *Tiger*. The worst culprit was HMS *Tiger* which had fired 355 shells and only hit the Germans twice.

Some heads would roll, including that of Admiral Archibald Moore, who was relieved of command of the Second Battle Cruiser Squadron and sent off to relative obscurity to command the Ninth Cruiser Squadron in the Canary Islands.

As far as the Germans were concerned, the loss of the *Blucher* had a devastating effect. Von Ingenohl was roundly criticized for not supporting Hipper, although Hipper himself made a bad decision by deciding to take the *Blucher* with him: she was too old, too slow and was unable to protect herself. The Kaiser was livid that the *Blucher* had been destroyed and dismissed von Ingenohl, replacing him with Admiral Hugo von Pohl.

As for the British, they learned lessons from the damage that had been done to HMS *Lion* – henceforth British battlecruisers would have strengthened side armour. Improvements were also made to prevent magazine explosions, but only on HMS *Lion* and not the other battlecruisers. It would be a deciding factor at the Battle of Jutland.

The Germans, for their part, had nearly lost Hipper's flagship and took steps to prevent fires from travelling from turret to turret. They had also discovered that many of the British armour-piercing shells had failed to penetrate their armour.

Pohl decided to change German naval tactics. Rather than risk German surface vessels on raids across the North Sea he threw his weight behind the use of mines and submarines. In fact, at the beginning of 1915 the German navy was already planning a U-boat offensive, having told the world that henceforth all of the seas around Great Britain were war zone and that they could not guarantee the safety of merchant ships, even if they belonged to neutral governments. Up until that point German U-boats had stopped merchant ships and if they found that war materials were on board they would make the crew abandon ship and sink the vessel with gunfire.

U-boats of this period were very basic and Royal Navy patrols were numerous. U-boats also had to contend with British Q-ships, which purported to be tramp steamers, but were actually crewed by the Royal Navy and sported a concealed 4in gun. If a U-boat surfaced to examine the vessel, the Q-ship could easily sink its German adversary.

Up to now, the British had been winning the blockade war. They were able to reinforce their troops around the world, as well as bring in Commonwealth units to fight in France. The Germans, however, did not have this luxury and therefore hoped that a successful U-boat campaign would redress the balance.

Meanwhile, the British were desperately trying to improve their gunnery, as well as looking at ways in which new shells could be developed that would not suffer the same problems as the ones currently in use. Unfortunately, the new shells would not be ready by the time the Battle of Jutland was fought. Whilst Jellicoe was carrying out intensive training of his Grand Fleet in terms of gunnery and manoeuvring, Beatty was reluctant to accede to Jellicoe's suggestion to send his ships up to Scapa Flow, one or two at a time, fearing that Hipper would make another raid. In any case, some of Beatty's officers believed that practice firing was not necessary as they did so using real targets. This was a somewhat unfair jibe against the Grand Fleet, which had not seen much action.

The British decided, at the behest of Churchill and Fisher, to create a Battle Cruiser Force as a separate fleet. There would be three squadrons, each of seven vessels to begin with, and nine by the Battle of Jutland, plus a pair of light cruisers, based at Rosyth. The force became known as the Battle Cruiser Fleet. Against them the Germans had five battlecruisers; their much-vaunted and powerful *Hindenburg* would not be ready in time for the Battle of Jutland.

There was considerable debate about where Jellicoe's Grand Fleet and Beatty's Battle Cruiser Fleet were to be deployed. Both Churchill and Fisher believed that Jellicoe should move to Rosyth and that Beatty should move to the Humber, so that the latter could be in the thick of the action eight hours quicker than before. It would also knock four hours off steaming time for Jellicoe. As Fisher said to Jellicoe: 'The fundamental fact is that you can never be in time as long as you are at Scapa Flow and therefore there will never be a battle with the German High Seas Fleet unless von Pohl goes north especially to fight you and that he never will.'

There were objections, however, to the suggested redeployments. Beatty believed that the Humber could be too easily mined, or covered by German submarines. He also reckoned that the entrance at Rosyth was too tight for Jellicoe, and it was susceptible to fog. In the end Vice Admiral Sir Thomas Jerram's Second Battle Squadron moved from Scapa Flow to Cromarty and Vice Admiral Sir Edward Bradford's pre-Dreadnought Third Battle Squadron shifted from Rosyth to the Thames. When Beatty asked Jellicoe to let him have Rear Admiral Sir Hugh Evan-Thomas and his five super-Dreadnoughts of the Fifth Battle Squadron, Jellicoe refused, believing that it would tempt Beatty to try and face off the German High Seas Fleet without the support of the British Grand Fleet.

There was talk of landing ground troops along the Baltic coast, and an attempt to capture Heligoland and the Friesian Islands, but these ideas were rejected.

Jellicoe and Beatty put forward a plan to attack the coast of Jutland, coupled with seaplane raids on Zeppelin bases in Schleswig-Holstein. They proposed to attack with light vessels, supported by Beatty's battlecruisers, that in turn would be supported by the Grand Fleet. Jellicoe wrote to Beatty towards the end of March 1915:

I imagine the Germans will try and entrap you by risking their battlecruisers as a decoy. They know the odds are that you will be 100 miles away from me, and can draw you down to the Heligoland Bight without my being in effective support. This is alright if you keep your speed, but if some of your ships have their speed badly reduced in a fight with their battlecruisers, or by submarines, their loss seems inevitable if you are drawn onto the High Seas Fleet with me too far off to extricate them before dark. The Germans know you very well and will try to take advantage of that quality of 'not letting go when you have once got hold', which you possess thank God. But one must concern oneself with the result to the country of a serious decrease in relative strength. If the game looks worth the candle the risks can be taken. If not, one's duty is to be cautious. I believe you will see which is the proper course, and pursue it victoriously.

Elsewhere, the British were looking for a way to defeat the Germans and their allies. The war in Flanders was a stalemate, with thousands of men locked in an impossible struggle in the mud. When Churchill proposed attacking the Ottoman Turks by sending a squadron of battleships through the Dardanelles to threaten Constantinople, many people feared that Churchill's plan would weaken the Royal Navy's ability to control the North Sea.

The Royal Navy duly began bombarding the outer forts at the entrance to the Straits. The initial attacking force consisted of five vessels belonging to the British and four belonging to the French, most of which were considered to be expendable, old pre-Dreadnoughts. Seven other pre-Dreadnoughts, including the battle-cruiser HMS *Inflexible* and the super-Dreadnought, HMS *Queen Elizabeth*, reinforced the squadron. The Turks worked hard to hold off the British and French, and with a combination of gunfire and mines sank three of the battleships and damaged three others, including HMS *Inflexible*.

When the delayed land invasion finally began on 25 April 1915, the Turks were ready. Meanwhile, in another naval attack on the Dardanelles, three more battleships were lost. By the time the Gallipoli Campaign, as it became known, was abandoned in 1916, both the Allies and the Turks had lost a quarter of a million men each.

The ensuing uproar over the Gallipoli Campaign was to cost Churchill and Fisher their jobs. On 14 May 1915, Churchill asked Fisher to release more vessels for Gallipoli, whereupon Fisher promptly resigned. Ultimately Churchill would take the blame, although Kitchener deserves some of the criticism, as he had blocked Churchill's plan to launch an amphibious assault on the forts guarding the Dardanelles. Balfour took Churchill's job and Henry Jackson became the First Sea Lord.

Meanwhile, the German campaign of unrestricted attacks on merchant shipping around the British Isles continued. On 7 May 1915, the U-20 famously sunk the *Lusitania* off Ireland. The passenger ship went down in twenty minutes, causing nearly 1,200 deaths. The United States was outraged by the attack, but even this sinking, which had cost 128 American lives, was not enough to bring them into the war. Another British liner, the *Arabic,* was sunk off the coast of southern Ireland on 19 August, this time by the U-24. Once more the Americans were vociferous in their condemnation of German tactics. Three of those lost in the attack were US citizens and at one stage the United States threatened to break off diplomatic relations with Germany. The Germans reluctantly ordered their U-boat captains not to sink liners without first giving a warning – henceforth passengers and crew were to be given the opportunity to abandon ship. This, however, was not enough for the Americans and with great reluctance the Germans were forced to abandon their policy of unrestricted submarine warfare on 30 August 1915.

With the German submarine threat ended for the time being, the counter blockade of Great Britain weakened. The British, on the other hand, continued to police and intercept vessels that they believed to be bringing war materials to Germany. This led almost immediately to rationing in Germany, as they could not produce enough food and were relying on imports from Sweden. The contraband control base was established at Kirkwall in the Orkney Islands. If contraband was discovered Great Britain would either buy it themselves or confiscate it. This caused problems between Britain and the United States, as American ships were not immune from being intercepted and searched. German blockade-runners continued to operate along the Norwegian coast, which was the only realistic route into Germany for contraband.

There were no major sea engagements in 1915, as both fleets tried to improve their fighting abilities, as well as their manoeuvring skills. With morale particularly low within the German High Seas Fleet at this time, many German officers and men, frustrated by the lack of action, asked for transfers to the submarine branch. But the German High Command was not about to risk their surface vessels on raids of dubious value only to be pounced upon by the British Grand Fleet. In fact, von Pohl only carried out five sorties during the whole year, never venturing more than 150 miles from the mouth of the Jade.

Pressure to take a more aggressive stance did not come from within the navy, but from the Commander-in-Chief of the German army, General Erich von Falkenhayn. He wanted the navy to break the blockade, knowing, as did many others, that if it continued it would have a detrimental effect on Germany's ability to wage any kind of war. And the only real way to do this was to replace von Pohl. However, by December 1915, von Pohl was already gravely ill with a brain tumour, finally resigning on 18 January 1916, to be replaced by Vice Admiral Reinhardt Scheer on 24 January 1916.

Scheer was a far more aggressive commander and wanted the blessing of the Kaiser to risk the whole of the German High Seas Fleet in an attempt to draw out Beatty and Jellicoe, and defeat them in detail. He already had an excellent reputation as a tactician, so knew that it would be suicidal to meet the British Grand Fleet head on. He hoped to find a favourable opportunity to cut off parts of the Grand Fleet and deal with them, thus bringing Germany back to a degree of parity with the British in terms of naval power. He intended to despatch surface vessels to interdict British trade with Scandinavia, and resolved to use submarine and mine warfare whenever possible. He also ordered the Imperial Navy's zeppelin force to launch night-bombing raids against British cities. Finally, he planned further raids on the British coast with his battlecruisers, under Hipper.

Scheer's first major attack took place on 10 February 1916, when a flotilla of British minesweepers, operating close to the Dogger Bank, was attacked by light cruisers and torpedo boats. The British had intercepted signals concerning the raid, but by the time Tyrwhitt's Harwich force had got out to sea the Germans were already heading for home, having succeeded in scattering the British minesweeping force and sunk a sloop, the *Arabis*.

The next major raid took place over the period 24 to 25 April 1916. Due to illness, Rear Admiral Friedrich Boedicker had temporarily replaced Hipper. Unfortunately for the Germans, the *Seydlitz* hit a mine close to the Friesian Islands, as a result of which Boedicker made the *Lützow* his flagship. With the Germans steaming towards Great Yarmouth and Lowestoft, once again the British had intercepted signals regarding the raid. Beatty was too far north to intercept them, and when Tyrwhitt's force of cruisers and destroyers approached the German force near Great Yarmouth, they had already hit Lowestoft. Tyrwhitt's force was no match for the German battlecruisers and unfortunately his flagship, HMS *Conquest,* was badly damaged. But he had managed to draw the Germans away from Great Yarmouth and no great damage had been done.

By the time the Germans turned for home, Beatty was three hours away. The Germans had not managed to inflict any real damage of military importance on the British, but Lowestoft had suffered the most, with around 200 houses being destroyed.

As a result of this raid five Queen Elizabeth Class super-Dreadnoughts were sent to reinforce Beatty's battlecruiser fleet. In the short term this would allow Beatty to send parts of his own fleet to Scapa Flow for gunnery practice.

Jellicoe, meanwhile, launched a series of raids against German mine-laying operations and against German zeppelin bases. On at least two occasions he had hoped to tempt the Germans out and had deployed his entire Grand Fleet to deal with them if they had been so foolish. However, it was to be the Germans who were to sow the seeds for what would become the first battle fought between fleets of Dreadnoughts.

Chapter Two

The Opposing Fleets

Before describing the two fleets in action, it might be useful to look at the comparative qualities of the major ships that were in action at the Battle of Jutland. This chapter examines the types of ships and their qualities by analysing their armament, armour, speed and other distinguishing features. Note that where appropriate we have included sister ships that may not have necessarily been present at the Battle of Jutland for a variety of reasons. In some cases, they had been posted elsewhere, or perhaps they were undergoing repairs arising out of earlier incidents.

Throughout the account of the battle itself in later chapters, there are references to different types of vessel. Sometimes, the type of ship can be somewhat confusing, but we must begin with the battleship. These were usually the biggest vessels and were primarily designed to deal with the larger ships in the enemy's fleet. They were comparatively slow, had an impressive armament and substantial armour to protect them.

Dreadnoughts were, of course, named after HMS *Dreadnought*. They had a uniform design in terms of their armament and the fact that they had the same calibre of guns. They were also armed with smaller calibre weapons to protect themselves against smaller and faster moving vessels such as torpedo boats.

Pre-Dreadnought was a catch-all term used to describe vessels still in service but built before HMS *Dreadnought*. They invariably had four main guns and were, by the time of Jutland, somewhat slow and weak. In most cases, they were being relegated to supporting roles and were not front-line vessels.

Semi-Dreadnoughts were the intermediate stage between the pre-Dreadnought and the real Dreadnought. They were armed with 8- to 10-inch guns.

Cruisers were used as multi-purpose vessels, the smallest type of vessel deemed able to cope on its own. They ranged in size enormously, but were generally used to lead destroyer groups and support battleships.

Battlecruisers were very powerful vessels as large as battleships and with very similar armament. They tended to have less guns, were faster and did not have as much armour as the battleships.

Armoured cruisers were large cruisers with an additional armoured belt and had gradually been developed over the preceding ten or more years. Their role, however, had been taken over by the battlecruiser.

Other cruiser types included the protected cruiser which had a curved armoured deck, the scout cruiser used to lead destroyers by relying on its speed, and the light cruiser. The latter is a confusing descripton as it includes light-armoured, small or medium-sized vessels.

Destroyers were originally named Torpedo Boat Destroyer (TBD) and were fast, relatively large torpedo boats. They tended to be used to screen the larger vessels in the fleet. Torpedo boats were still being used, but were gradually being replaced by the destroyer.

British Ships by Type

King George V Class Dreadnought Battleship
Length 589 feet 6 inches waterline 597 feet 9 inches overall, beam 89 feet 1 inches, draught 28 feet 8 inches, displacement 25,420 tons, load 27,120 tons deep. 4 shaft Parsons turbines, 27,000 shp, 21 knots. 12 to 8in belt, 10 to 3in barbettes, 11in turret faces, 4 to 1in decks. 10 x 13.5in 45cal Mk V (5 x 2), 16 x 4in (16 x 1), 4 x 3 pounder (4 x 1), 3 x 21in TT.

HMS *King George V*
Built Portsmouth Dockyard, laid down January 1911, completed October 1912, cost £1,961,096. Trial speed 22.373 knots. 2nd Battle Squadron Grand Fleet. October 1914–February 1915 refit. Present at the Battle of Jutland 1916. Fired 9 x 13.5in rounds. Received no damage. December 1926 sold for scrap.

HMS *Centurion*
Built Portsmouth Dockyard, laid down January 1911, completed February 1913, cost £1,950,671. Trial speed 22.866 knots. 2nd Battle Squadron Grand Fleet. February 1915 refit. Present at the Battle of Jutland 1916. Fired 19 x 13.5in rounds. Received no damage. August 1916 refit. 1944 sunk as part of Mulberry harbour.

HMS *Audacious*
Built Cammell Laird, laid down March 1911, completed August 1913, cost £1,918,813. 2nd Battle Squadron Grand Fleet. 27 October 1914 struck a mine and sank.

HMS *Ajax*
Built Scott, laid down February 1911, completed May 1913, cost £1,889,387. Trial speed 21.22 knots. 2nd Battle Squadron Grand Fleet. Present at the Battle of Jutland 1916. Fired 6 x 13.5in rounds. Received no damage. December 1926 sold for scrap.

Erin Class Dreadnought Battleship
Length 553 feet waterline 559 feet 9 inches overall, beam 91 feet 7 inches, draught 28 feet 5 inches (load), displacement 22,780 tons, load 25,250 tons deep. 4 shaft Parsons turbines, 26,500 shp, 21 knots. 12 to 4in belt, 10 to 3in barbettes, 11in turret faces, 3 to 1.5in decks. 10 x 13.5in 45cal Mk VI (5 x 2), 16 x 6in (16 x 1), 6 x 6 pounder (6 x 1), 2 x 3in (2 x 1), 4 x 21in TT.

HMS *Erin*
Built Vickers, laid down December 1911, completed August 1914, cost estimated £2,500,000. Originally commissioned by the Ottoman Empire. 22 August 1914 taken over by British. September 1914 4th Battle Squadron Grand Fleet. October 1914 transferred to 2nd Battle Squadron. Present at the Battle of Jutland 1916. December 1922 sold for scrap.

Orion Class Dreadnought Battleship
Length 576 feet waterline 581 feet overall, beam 88 feet 6 inches, draught 27 feet 6 inches normal, displacement 20,797 tons light, 27,120 tons deep. 4 shaft Parsons turbines, 27,000 shp, 21 knots. 12 to 8in belt, 10 to 3in barbettes, 11in turret faces, 4 to 1in decks.

10 x 13.5in 45cal Mk V (5 x 2), 16 x 4in (16 x 1), 4 x 3 pounder (4 x 1), 3 x 21in TT. The first of the Super Dreadnoughts.

HMS *Orion*
Built Portsmouth Dockyard, laid down November 1909, completed January 1912, cost £1,855,917. Trial speed 21.05 knots. 2nd Battle Squadron Grand Fleet. Present at the Battle of Jutland 1916. Fired 51 x 13.5in rounds. Received no damage. December 1922 sold for scrap.

HMS *Conqueror*
Built Beardmore, laid down April 1910, completed November 1912, cost £1,891,164. Trial speed 22.13 knots. 2nd Battle Squadron Grand Fleet. 27 December 1914 rammed HMS *Monarch*. March 1915 rejoined Grand Fleet after repairs at Scapa Flow, Invergordon and Devonport. Present at the Battle of Jutland 1916. Fired 57 x 13.5in rounds. Received no damage. December 1922 sold for scrap.

HMS *Monarch*
Built Armstrong, laid down April 1910, completed February 1912, cost £1,888,736. Trial speed 21.88 knots. 2nd Battle Squadron Grand Fleet. 8 August 1914 unsuccessfully attacked by U-15 off Fair Isle. 27 December 1914 rammed from behind by HMS *Conqueror*. 20 January 1915 rejoined Grand Fleet after repairs at Scapa Flow and Devonport. Present at the Battle of Jutland 1916. Fired 53 x 13.5in rounds. 1925 sunk as target.

HMS *Thunderer*
Built Thames Iron Works, laid down April 1910, completed May 1912, cost £1,892,823. Trial speed 20.79 knots. 2nd Battle Squadron Grand Fleet. December 1914 refit. Present at the Battle of Jutland 1916. Fired 37 x 13.5in rounds. Received no damage. November 1926 sold for scrap.

Iron Duke Class Dreadnought Battleship
Length 614 feet 3 inches waterline 623 feet 9 inches overall, beam 90 feet 1 inches, draught 32 feet 9 inches (deep), displacement 26,100 tons load, 31,400 tons deep. 4 shaft Parsons turbines, 29,000 shp, 21 knots. 12 to 4in belt, 10 to 3in barbettes, 11in turret

faces, 2.5 to 1in decks. 10 x 13.5in 45cal Mk V (5 x 2), 12 x 6in (12 x 1), 4 x 3 pounder (4 x 1), 2 x 3in (2 x 1), 4 x 21in TT.

HMS *Iron Duke*
Built Portsmouth Dockyard, laid down January 1912, completed March 1914, cost £1,945,824. Trial speed 21.6 knots. August 1914–January 1917 Flagship of Grand Fleet under Admiral Sir John Jellicoe and then Sir David Beatty. 12 January 1916 collided with oil tanker *Prudentia* which sank. Present at the Battle of Jutland 1916. Fired 90 x 13.5in rounds and received no damage. Sold for scrap 1946.

HMS *Marlborough*
Built Portsmouth Dockyard, laid down January 1912, completed June 1914, cost £2,043,437. Trial speed 21.8 knots. 1st Battle Squadron Grand Fleet. Squadron flagship until February 1917. Present at the Battle of Jutland 1916. Fired 162 x 13.5in rounds. Hit by torpedo and suffered 2 killed and 2 wounded. 29 July 1916 rejoined Grand Fleet after repairs. Sold for scrap 1932.

HMS *Benbow*
Built Beardmore, laid down November 1912, completed October 1914. Trial speed 21.5 knots. November 1914 joined 4th Battle Squadron Grand Fleet. Squadron flagship until June 1916. Present at the Battle of Jutland 1916. Fired 40 x 13.5in rounds and received no damage. Sold for scrap 1931.

HMS *Emperor of India*
Built Vickers, laid down May 1912, completed October 1914. Trial speed 21 knots. December 1914 joined 1st Battle Squadron Grand Fleet. Under refit at time of Jutland. Sold for scrap 1932.

Royal Sovereign Class Dreadnought Battleship
Length 614 feet 6 inches waterline 620 feet 7 inches overall, beam 88 feet 6 inches, draught 33 feet 7 inches (deep), displacement 29,590 tons load, 32,820 tons deep. 4 shaft Parsons turbines, 40,000 shp, 21 knots. 13-1in belt, 10 to 4in barbettes, 13in turret faces, 4 to 1in decks. 8 x 15in 45cal Mk I (4 x 2), 14 x 6in (14 x 1), 4 x 3 pounder (4 x 1), 2 x 3in (2 x 1), 4 x 21in TT.

HMS *Royal Sovereign*
Built Portsmouth Dockyard, laid down January 1914, completed May 1916, cost £2,570,504. Trial speed 21.7 knots. May 1916 joined 1st Battle Squadron Grand Fleet. Missed Jutland owing to engine problems. 1949 sold for scrap.

HMS *Revenge*
Built Vickers, laid down December 1913, completed March 1916, cost £2,406,368. Trial speed 21.9 knots. February 1916 joined 1st Battle Squadron Grand Fleet. Present at the Battle of Jutland 1916. Fired 102 x 15in shells and received no damage. 1948 sold for scrap.

HMS *Resolution*
Built Palmers, laid down November 1913, completed December 1916, cost £2,449,680. Trial speed unknown. December 1916 joined 1st Battle Squadron Grand Fleet. 1948 sold for scrap.

HMS *Royal Oak*
Built Devonport Dockyard, laid down January 1914, completed May 1916, cost £2,468,269. Trial speed 22 knots. May 1916 joined 4th Battle Squadron Grand Fleet. Present at the Battle of Jutland 1916. Fired 38 x 15in shells and received no damage. 14 October 1939 sunk by German submarine U-47.

HMS *Ramillies*
Built Beardmore, laid down November 1913, completed September 1917, cost £3,295,810. Trial speed 21.5 knots. When launched in September 1916 her keel was damaged which delayed her completion. September 1917 joined 1st Battle Squadron Grand Fleet. 1948 sold for scrap.

Bellerophon Class Dreadnought Battleship
Length 522 feet waterline 526 feet overall, beam 82 feet 6 inches, draught 31 feet 5 inches, displacement 18,596 load, 22,540 tons deep. 4 shaft Parsons turbines, 23,000 shp, 21 knots. 10 to 5in belt, 9 to 5in barbettes, 11in turret faces, 3 to 0.5in decks. 10 x 12in 45cal Mk X (5 x 2), 16 x 4in (16 x 1), 4 x 3 pounder (4 x 1), 3 x 18in TT.

HMS *Bellerophon*

Built Portsmouth Dockyard, laid down December 1906, completed February 1909, cost £1,763,491. Trial speed 21.25 knots. August 1914 1st then 4th Battle Squadron Grand Fleet. 27 August 1914 collided with SS *St Clair* off the Orkney Islands, no significant damage sustained. May 1915 refit at Devonport. Present at the Battle of Jutland 1916. Fired 62 x 12in rounds and received no damage. June–September 1917 served as second flagship 4th Battle Squadron whilst HMS *Colossus* in refit. November 1921 sold for scrap.

HMS *Superb*

Built Elswick, laid down February 1907, completed June 1909, cost £1,744,287. Trial speed 21.56 knots. 1st Battle Squadron Grand Fleet. January–March 1915 refit at Portsmouth. 10 November 1915 transferred to 4th Battle Squadron. May 1916 served as flagship 4th Battle Squadron whilst HMS *Emperor of India* in refit. Present at the Battle of Jutland 1916. Fired 54 x 12in rounds and received no damage. October 1918 detached to Eastern Mediterranean Squadron and became Flagship of Vice Admiral Gough-Calthrope. December 1922 sold for scrap.

HMS *Temeraire*

Built Portsmouth Dockyard, laid down January 1907, completed May 1909, cost £1,641,114. Trial speed 21.55 knots. 4th Battle Squadron Grand Fleet. 18 March 1915 unsuccessfully attempted to ram German submarine U-29 which had attacked HMS *Neptune*. Summer 1915 refit at Devonport. Present at the Battle of Jutland 1916. Fired 54 x 12in rounds and received no damage. October 1918 detached to Eastern Mediterranean Squadron. End 1921 sold for scrap.

Canada Class Dreadnought Battleship

Length 654 feet 10 inch waterline 661 feet overall, beam 92 feet, draught 29 feet 6 inches (normal), displacement 26,968 tons light, 32,188 tons deep. 4 shaft Parsons/Brown Curtis turbines, 37,000 shp, 22 knots. 9 to 4in belt, 10 to 6in barbettes, 10in turret faces, 4 to 1in decks. 10 x 14in 45cal Mk I (5 x 2), 16 x 6in (16 x 1), 4 x 3 pounder (4 x 1), 2 x 3in (2 x 1), 4 x 21in TT.

HMS *Canada*

Built Armstrong, laid down December 1911, completed November 1915, cost estimated £2,500,000. Trial speed 24.3 knots. Originally ordered for Chile, but purchased by Britain in September 1914. October 1915 joined 4th Battle Squadron Grand Fleet. Present at the Battle of Jutland 1916. Fired 42 x 14in rounds and received no damage. 12 June transferred to 1st Battle Squadron. April 1920 repurchased by Chile. 1959 sold for scrap.

St Vincent Class Dreadnought Battleship

Length 531 feet waterline 536 feet overall, 84 feet 1 inch beam, draught 28 feet 11 inches load, displacement 19,700 tons load, 22,800 tons deep. 4 shaft Parsons turbines, 24,500 shp, 21 knots. 10 to 7in belt, 9-5in barbettes, 11in turret faces, 3 to 0.75in decks. 10 x 12in 50cal Mk XI (5 x 2), 20 x 4in (20 x 1), 4 x 3 pounder (4 x 1), 3 x 18in TT.

HMS *St Vincent*

Built Devonport Dockyard, laid down December 1907, completed May 1909, cost £1,721,970. Trial speed 21.66 knots. 1st Battle Squadron Grand Fleet. Present at the Battle of Jutland. Fired 98 x 12in rounds, received no damage. June 1916 transferred to 4th Battle Squadron. December 1921 sold for scrap.

HMS *Collingwood*

Built Vickers, Barrow, laid down February 1908, completed April 1910, cost £1,680,888. Trial speed 20.62 knots. 1st Battle Squadron Grand Fleet. HRH The Duke of York, later King George VI, served on her as a lieutenant. Present at the Battle of Jutland 1916. Fired 84 x 12in rounds, received no damage. Transferred to 4th Battle Squadron. December 1922 sold for scrap.

HMS *Vanguard*

Built Devonport Dockyard, laid down April 1908, completed March 1910, cost £1,606,030. Trial speed 22.3 knots. 1st Battle Squadron Grand Fleet. 1 September 1914 fired on a false alarm submarine at Scapa Flow. April 1916 transferred to 4th Battle Squadron. Present at the Battle of Jutland 1916. Fired 80 x 12in rounds, received no damage. 7 July 1917 accidentally exploded at Scapa Flow with the loss of 804 crew.

Colossus Class Dreadnought Battleship
Length 541 feet 6 inch waterline 545 feet 9 inches overall, 86 feet 8 inch beam, draught 29 feet 5 inch deep, displacement 20,030 tons load, 23,266 tons deep. 4 shaft Parsons turbines, 25,000 shp, 21 knots. 11 to 7in belt, 11 to 4in barbettes, 11in turret faces, 3 to 1.75in decks. 10 x 12in 50cal Mk XI (5 x 2), 16 x 4in (16 x 1), 4 x 3 pounder (4 x 1), 3 x 21in TT.

HMS *Colossus*
Built Scotts, laid down July 1909, completed July 1911, cost £1,672,103. Trial speed 21.58 knots. 1st Battle Squadron Grand Fleet as flagship. Present at the Battle of Jutland 1916. Fired 93 x 12in rounds. Received two hits causing minor damage and nine wounded. June–September 1917 refit. August 1928 sold for scrap.

HMS *Hercules*
Built Palmers, laid down July 1909, completed August 1911, cost £1,661,240. Trial speed 21.57 knots. 1st Battle Squadron Grand Fleet. Present at the Battle of Jutland 1916. Fired 98 x 12in rounds. February 1916 refit at Scapa Flow. June 1916 transferred to 4th Battle Squadron as flagship. 19 August 1916 carried out experiments with towed kite balloon. August 1922 sold for scrap.

Neptune Class Dreadnought Battleship
Length 541 feet 2 inches waterline 546 feet overall, beam 85 feet 1 inches, draught 28 feet 6 inches, displacement 19,680 tons load, 23,123 tons deep. 4 shaft Parsons turbines, 25,000 shp, 21 knots. 10 to 2.5in belt, 9-5in barbettes, 11in turret faces, 3 to 0.75in decks. 10 x 12in 50cal Mk XI (5 x 2), 16 x 4in (16 x 1), 4 x 3 pounder (4 x 1), 3 x 18in TT.

HMS *Neptune*
Built Portsmouth Dockyard, laid down January 1909, completed January 1911, cost £1,668,916. Trial speed 21.29 knots. 1st Battle Squadron Grand Fleet. December 1914–March 1915 under refit. 18 March unsuccessfully attacked by German submarine U-29. 22/23

April 1916 accidentally hit at night by SS *Needvaal* but only sustained minor damage. Present at the Battle of Jutland 1916. Fired 48 x 12in rounds and received no damage. June 1916 transferred to 4th Battle Squadron. September 1922 sold for scrap.

Agincourt Class Dreadnought Battleship

Length 668 feet waterline 671 feet 6inches overall, beam 89 feet, draught 29 feet 10 inches (mean deep), displacement 24,792 tons light, 30,860 tons deep. 4 shaft Parsons turbines, 34,000 shp, 22 knots. HMS *Agincourt* was originally ordered for Brazil, but the Brazilian government ran into financial difficulties and sold the ship to the Ottoman government, whereupon the ship was seized by the Royal Navy.

HMS *Agincourt*

Built by Armstrong, laid down September 1911, commissioned August 1914, cost estimated £2,900,000. Trial speed 22.42 knots. 9-4in belt, 9-2in barbettes, 12in turret faces, 2.5-1in decks. 14 x 12in 45cal MK XIII (7 x 2), 20 x 6in (20 x 1), 10 x 3in (10 x 1), 3 x 21in TT. Joined the 4th Battle Squadron of the Grand Fleet on 25 August 1914. Transferred to the 1st Battle Squadron 1915. Present at the Battle of Jutland 1916. Fired 144 x 12in rounds and received no damage. Transferred to the 2nd Battle Squadron in late 1918. December 1922 sold for scrap.

Invincible Class Battlecruiser

Length 560 feet waterline 567 feet overall, beam 78 feet 9 inches, draught 26 feet 8 inches, displacement 17,420 load, 20,135 tons full load. 4 shaft Parsons turbines, 41,000 shp, 25 knots. 6 to 4in belt, 7in barbettes, 7in turret faces, 2.5 to 1in decks. 8 x 12in 45cal Mk X (4 x 2), 16 x 4in (16 x 1), 5 x 18in TT.

HMS *Invincible*

Built Elswick, laid down April 1906, completed March 1909, cost £1,767,515. Trial speed 26.64 knots. 6 August 1914 completed refit and despatched to Queenstown for trade protection duties. 19 August 1914 ordered to return to become flagship of 2nd Battlecruiser Squadron. 28 August 1914 took part in the Battle of Heligoland Bight. September 1914 transferred to 1st Battlecruiser

Squadron. October 1914 rejoined 2nd Battlecruiser Squadron. 4 November ordered to South American waters to hunt for Admiral Graf von Spee. 11 November 1914 flagship of Vice Admiral Sturdee. 8 December 1914 Battle of the Falkland Islands. January–February 1915 refit at Gibraltar then joined 3rd Battlecruiser Squadron. 31 May 1916 sunk by SMS *Derfflinger* and *Lützow* at the Battle of Jutland having inflicted fatal damage on *Lützow*.

HMS *Inflexible*
Built Clydebank, laid down February 1906 completed October 1908, cost £1,720,739. Trial speed 26.48 knots. 2nd Battlecruiser Squadron as flagship of the British Mediterranean fleet. August 1914 hunting SMS *Goeben* and *Breslau*. 18 August 1914 set off for home waters to join 3rd Battlecruiser Squadron. 11 November sailed to South American waters with HMS *Invincible* to hunt for Admiral Graf von Spee. 8 December 1914 Battle of the Falkland Islands. 24 January 1915 became flagship of British Dardanelles squadron. 19 February took part in bombardment of Dardanelles outer forts. 25 February 1915 again bombarded Dardanelles outer forts. 18 March 1915 bombardment of Dardanelles forts. Was hit nine times and then struck a mine. 10 April reached Malta for repairs. 19 June 1915 joined 3rd Battlecruiser Squadron with the Grand Fleet. Present at the Battle of Jutland 1916. Fired 88 x 12in rounds and was not damaged. 5 June transferred to 2nd Battlecruiser Squadron. 19 August 1916 attacked unsuccessfully by German submarine U-65. 31 January 1918 collided with the submarine K-14. 1921 sold for scrap.

HMS *Indomitable*
Built Fairfield, laid down March 1906, completed June 1908, cost £1,752,337. Trial speed 26.11 knots. 2nd Battlecruiser Squadron in the Mediterranean. Early August 1914 hunting SMS *Goeben* and *Breslau*. 3 November 1914 bombardment of Dardanelles forts. 26 December 1914 joined 1st Battlecruiser Squadron with the Grand Fleet. Early January 1915 refit then joined 2nd Battlecruiser Squadron Grand Fleet. 24 January 1915 took part in the Battle of Dogger Bank. February 1915 repairs after accidental electrical fire. 11 March 1915 unsuccessfully attacked by German submarine.

Present at the Battle of Jutland 1916. No damage and fired 175 x 12in rounds. 5 June 1916 transferred to 2nd Battlecruiser Squadron. August 1916 refit. 1921 sold for scrap.

Minotaur class armoured cruisers

Length 490 feet waterline 519 feet overall, beam 74 feet 6 inches, draught 26 feet, displacement 14,600 tons load. 2 shaft triple expansion engines, 27,000 ihp, 23 knots. 6 to 3in belt, 7 to 3in barbettes, 8in turret faces, 1.5 to 0.5in decks. 4 x 9.2in Mk XI (2 x 2), 10 x 7.5in Mk II (10 x 1), 16 x 12 pounder (16 x 1), 5 x 18in TT.

HMS *Minotaur*

Built Devonport Dockyard, laid down February 1905, completed April 1908, cost £1,410,356. At China Station at start of war. August 1914 captured and sank German merchant ship *Elsbeth*. 6 August 1914 bombarded German wireless station at Yap. November 1914 escorted Australian troop convoys. December 1914 Flagship Cape Station. January 1915 refit then joined 2nd Cruiser Squadron Grand Fleet. Present at the Battle of Jutland 1916. 1920 sold for scrap.

HMS *Defence*

Built Pembroke Dockyard, laid down January 1905, completed February 1909, cost £1,362,970. Trial speed 23 knots. 1st Cruiser Squadron Mediterranean Fleet. August 1914 involved in hunt for SMS *Goeben* and *Breslau*. November 1914 sent to South Atlantic in hunt for Admiral Graf von Spee. January 1915 1st Cruiser Squadron Grand Fleet. 31 May 1916 sunk at the Battle of Jutland.

HMS *Shannon*

Built Chatham Dockyard, laid down January 1905, completed October 1908, cost £1,415,535. Trial speed 22.41 knots. 2nd Cruiser Squadron Grand Fleet. November 1914 refit at Cromarty. Present at the Battle of Jutland 1916. November 1916 Murmansk. 1917–18 Atlantic convoy escort. 1922 sold for scrap.

Warrior Class Armoured Cruisers

Length 480 feet waterline 505 feet 4 inches overall, beam 73 feet 6 inches, draught 25 feet, displacement 13,550 tons load. 2 shaft triple expansion engines, 23,000 ihp, 23 knots. 6 to 3in belt, 6in barbettes, 7.5in turret faces, 1.5 to 0.5in decks. 6 x 9.2in Mk IX (6 x 1), 4 x 7.5in Mk II (4 x 1), 26 x 3 pounder (26 x 1), 3 x 18in TT.

HMS *Warrior*
Built Pembroke Dockyard, laid down November 1903, completed December 1906. Cost about £1.18m. 1st Cruiser Squadron Mediterranean Fleet. August 1914 involved in hunt for SMS *Goeben* and *Breslau*. November 1914 Sierra Leone. December 1914 onwards 2nd Cruiser Squadron Grand Fleet. 1 June 1916 sunk at the Battle of Jutland.

HMS *Cochrane*
Built Fairfield, Govan, laid down March 1904, completed February 1907. Cost about £1.18m. 2nd Cruiser Squadron Grand Fleet. Present at the Battle of Jutland 1916. 1917 West Indies and North America Station. May–September 1918 Archangel. 14 November 1918 ran aground and wrecked in the Mersey estuary.

HMS *Natal*
Built Vickers, Barrow, laid down January 1904, completed March 1907. Cost about £1.18m. Trial speed 22.9 knots. 2nd Cruiser Squadron Grand Fleet. 30 December 1915 destroyed by internal explosion at Cromarty, thought to be faulty cordite.

HMS *Achilles*
Built Armstrong, Elswick, laid down February 1904, completed April 1907. Cost about £1.18m. Trial speed 23.27 knots. 2nd Cruiser Squadron Grand Fleet. November 1914 suffered accidental gun explosion. Under refit at the time of Jutland. 16 March 1917 along with armed boarding steamer *Dundee* sank the German raider SMS *Leopard*. 1917 used for escort duties. 1918 training ship. 1920 sold for scrap.

Duke of Edinburgh class armoured cruisers

Length 480 feet waterline 505 feet 6 inches overall, beam 73 feet 6 inches, draught 26 feet, displacement 13,550 tons load. 2 shaft triple expansion engines, 23,000 ihp, 23 knots. 6 to 3in belt, 6in barbettes, 7.5in turret faces, 1.5 to 0.5in decks. 6 x 9.2in Mk IX (6 x 1), 10 x 6in Mk XI (10 x 1), 22 x 3 pounder (22 x 1), 3 x 18in TT.

HMS *Duke of Edinburgh*

Built Pembroke Dockyard, laid down June 1903, completed January 1906. Cost about £1.15m. Trial speed 22.84 knots. 1st Cruiser Squadron Mediterranean Fleet. August 1914 involved in hunt for SMS *Goeben* and *Breslau*. August 1914 Captured German merchant ship *Altair* in the Red Sea. November 1914 Persian Gulf including bombardment of Ottoman Turk positions. December 1914 onwards 1st Cruiser Squadron Grand Fleet. Present at the Battle of Jutland 1916. June 1916 Joined 2nd Cruiser Squadron Grand Fleet. 1917 escorted Atlantic convoys. August–November 1918 West Indies and North American Station. 1920 sold for scrap.

HMS *Black Prince*

Built Thames Iron Works, laid down February 1903, completed March 1906. Cost about £1.15m. Trial speed 23.66 knots. 1st Cruiser Squadron Mediterranean Fleet. August 1914 involved in hunt for SMS Goeben and Breslau. August 1914 captured a German merchant ship in the Red Sea. November 1914 Gibraltar. December 1914 onwards 1st Cruiser Squadron Grand Fleet. 1 June 1916 sunk at the Battle of Jutland.

Devonshire class armoured cruisers

Length 450 feet waterline 473 feet 6 inches overall, beam 68 feet 6 inches, draught 24 feet, displacement 10,850 tons load. 2 shaft triple expansion engines, 21,000 ihp, 22 knots. 6 to 2in belt, 6in barbettes, 5in turret faces, 2 to 0.5in decks. 4 x 7.5in (4 x 1), 6 x 6in Mk VII (6 x 1), 18 x 3 pounder (18 x 1), 2 x 18in TT.

HMS *Devonshire*

Built Chatham Dockyard, laid down March 1902, completed October 1905. Cost about £0.85m. Trial speed 22.97 knots. 3rd Cruiser Squadron Grand Fleet. 6 August 1914 captured German merchant ship. September 1914 refit at Cromarty. July 1916 7th Cruiser Squadron. December 1916 West Indies and North America Station. 1920 sold for scrap.

HMS *Antrim*
Built London and Glasgow, Glasgow, laid down August 1902, completed June 1905. Cost about £0.85m. Trial speed 23.2 knots. 3rd Cruiser Squadron Grand Fleet. 6 August 1914 captured German merchant ship. 9 October 1914 unsuccessfully attacked by German submarine. June 1916 Archangel. 1916 to December 1917 West Indies and North America Station. August 1918 trials ship. 1922 sold for scrap.

HMS *Argyll*
Built Scott, Greenock, laid down September 1902, completed December 1905. Cost about £0.85m. Trial speed 22.28 knots. 3rd Cruiser Squadron Grand Fleet. 6 August 1914 captured German merchant ship. 28 October 1915 ran aground and wrecked on Bell Rock.

HMS *Carnarvon*
Built Beardmore, Dalmuir, laid down October 1902, completed May 1905. Cost about £0.85m. Trial speed 23.3 knots. 5th Cruiser Squadron as Flagship. 24 August 1914 captured German merchant ship. October 1914 Montevideo in hunt for Admiral Graf von Spee. 12 December 1914 took part in the Battle of the Falklands. February 1915 ran aground off Abrolhos Rocks and repaired at Rio de Janeiro. 1916 West Indies and North America Station. 1921 sold for scrap.

HMS *Hampshire*
Built Armstrong, Elswick, laid down September 1902, completed July 1905. Cost about £0.85m. Trial speed 23.4 knots. China Station. 11 August 1914 captured a German merchant ship. August 1914 took part in hunt for SMS *Emden*. December 1914 Grand Fleet, joining 7th Cruiser Squadron the following month. November 1915 escort of merchant shipping in the White Sea. 1916 2nd Cruiser Squadron Grand Fleet. Present at the Battle of Jutland 1916. 5 June 1916 sunk by a mine with the loss of 650 men including Lord Kitchener.

HMS *Roxburgh*
Built London and Glasgow, Glasgow, laid down June 1902, completed September 1905. Cost about £0.85m. Trial speed 23.63 knots. 3rd Cruiser Squadron Grand Fleet. 6 August 1914 captured German merchant ship. 20 June 1915 damaged by torpedo from German submarine U-39. April 1916 operated in Norwegian waters. 1916 West Indies and North America Station. 24 May 1917 escorted first convoy from Hampton Roads, Virginia. 12 February 1918 rammed and sank German submarine U-89 off Northern Ireland. 1921 sold for scrap.

Calliope Class Light Cruisers
Length 420 feet waterline 446 feet overall, beam 41 feet 6 inches, draught 14 feet 9 inches, displacement 4,228 tons normal, 4,695 tons deep load. 4 shaft Parsons turbines, 37,500 shp, 29.5 knots, Champion 2 shaft, 40,000shp, 29 knots. 4 to 1.5in belt, 1in decks. 2 x 6in 45cal Mk XII (2 x 1), 8 x 4in 45cal Mk IV (8 x 1), 1 x 13 pounder (13 x 1), 2 x 21in TT.

HMS *Calliope*
Built Chatham Dockyard, laid down January 1914, completed June 1916. 4th Light Cruiser Squadron Grand Fleet. 19 March 1916 major boiler room fire. Present at the Battle of Jutland 1916. 1 September 1917 involved in sinking of four German trawlers. 1931 sold for scrap.

HMS *Champion*
Built Hawthorn Leslie, laid down March 1914, completed December 1915. Leader 13th Destroyer Flotilla Grand Fleet. Present at the Battle of Jutland 1916. 1934 sold for scrap.

Cambrian Class Light Cruisers
Length 420 feet waterline 446 feet overall, beam 41 feet 6 inches, draught 14 feet 9 inches, displacement 4,320 tons normal, 4,799 deep load. 4 shaft Parsons/Brown-Curtis turbines, 40,000 shp, 29 knots. 3 to 1.5in belt, 1in decks. 2 x 6in 45cal Mk XIII (2 x 1), 8 x 4in 45cal Mk IV (8 x 1), 1 x 13 pounder, 2 x 21in TT.

HMS *Cambrian*
Built Pembroke Dockyard, laid down December 1914, completed April 1916. 4th Light Cruiser Squadron Grand Fleet. 1934 sold for scrap.

HMS *Canterbury*
Built John Brown, laid down October 1914, completed April 1916. Attached to Grand Fleet. Present at the Battle of Jutland 1916. 1916 5th Light Cruiser Squadron Harwich Force. 5 June 1917 sank German torpedo boat S-20 off Belgian coast. 1918 Aegean. 1934 sold for scrap.

HMS *Castor*
Built Cammell Laird, laid down October 1914, completed November 1915. Leader 11th Destroyer Flotilla Grand Fleet. Present at the Battle of Jutland 1916. 1935 sold for scrap.

HMS *Constance*
Built Cammell Laird, laid down January 1915, completed January 1916. 4th Light Cruiser Squadron Grand Fleet. Present at the Battle of Jutland 1916. 1936 sold for scrap.

Arethusa Class Light Cruisers
Length 410 feet waterline 436 feet overall, beam 39 feet, draught 13 feet 5 inches, displacement 3,750 tons load, 4,400 tons deep load. 4 shaft Parsons/Brown-Curtis turbines, 40,000 shp, 28.5 knots. 3 to 1in belt, 1in decks, 2 x 6in 45cal Mk XII (2 x 1), 6 x 4in 45cal Mk IV (6 x 1), 1 x 3 pounder, 4 x 21in TT. Average cost of £285,000 per vessel.

HMS *Arethusa*
Built Chatham Dockyard, laid down October 1912, completed August 1914. Leader 3rd Destroyer Squadron Harwich Force. 28 August 1914 took part in the Battle of Heligoland Bight. 25 December 1914 took part in the Cuxhaven Raid. 24 January 1915 took part in the Battle of the Dogger Bank. June 1915 5th Light Cruiser Squadron Harwich Force. September 1915 captured four German trawlers. 11 February 1916 sunk by mine off Felixstowe.

HMS *Aurora*
Built Devonport Dockyard, laid down October 1912, completed September 1914. Leader 1st Destroyer Flotilla Grand Fleet. 1915 Leader 10th Destroyer flotilla Harwich Force. June 1915 5th Light Cruiser Squadron Harwich Force. August 1915 took part in sinking of German raider *Meteor*. 1918 7th Light Cruiser Squadron Grand Fleet. 1927 sold for scrap.

HMS *Galatea*
Built Beardmore, laid down January 1913, completed December 1914. Leader 2nd Destroyer Squadron Harwich Force. February 1915 Leader 1st Destroyer Squadron Grand Fleet. 4 May 1916 took part in shooting down of Zeppelin L-7. 1st Light Cruiser Squadron Grand Fleet. Present at the Battle of Jutland 1916. 1921 sold for scrap.

HMS *Inconstant*
Built Beardmore, laid down April 1913, completed January 1915. 1st Light Cruiser Squadron Grand Fleet. Present at the Battle of Jutland. 1922 sold for scrap.

HMS *Penelope*
Built Vickers, laid down February 1913, completed December 1914. Harwich Force. August 1915 5th Light Cruiser Squadron Harwich Force. 25 April 1916 damaged by torpedo from German submarine U-29 off Norfolk coast. March 1918 7th Light Cruiser Squadron Grand Fleet. 1924 sold for scrap.

HMS *Phaeton*
Built Vickers, laid down March 1913, completed February 1915. 4th Light Cruiser Squadron Grand Fleet. February–September 1915 Dardanelles. 1st Light Cruiser Squadron Grand Fleet. 4 May 1916 took part in shooting down of Zeppelin L-7. Present at the Battle of Jutland 1916. March 1918 7th Light Cruiser Squadron Grand Fleet. 1923 sold for scrap.

HMS *Royalist*
Built Beardmore, laid down June 1913, completed March 1915. 4th Light Cruiser Squadron Grand Fleet. Present at the Battle of Jutland

1916. February 1917 1st Light Cruiser Squadron Grand Fleet. 1922 sold for scrap.

HMS *Undaunted*
Built Fairfield, laid down December 1912, completed August 1914. Leader 3rd Destroyer Flotilla Harwich Force. 28 August 1914 took part in the Battle of Heligoland Bight. 17 October 1914 involved in action with German torpedo boats resulting in the sinking of four German ships. 25 December 1914 took part in the Cuxhaven Raid. 24 January 1915 took part in Battle of the Dogger Bank. April 1915 damaged in collision with British destroyer HMS *Landrail*. 24 March 1916 damaged in collision with British cruiser HMS *Cleopatra*. 1917 Leader 10th Destroyer Flotilla Harwich Force. November 1918 4th Light Cruiser Squadron Grand Fleet. 1923 sold for scrap.

Caroline Class Light Cruisers
Length 420 feet waterline 446 feet overall, beam 41 feet 6 inches, draught 14 feet 9 inches, displacement 4,219 tons load, 4,733 tons deep. 4 shaft Parsons turbines, 40,000 shp, 28.5 knots. 2 x 6in 45cal Mk XII (2 x 1), 8 x 4in 45cal Mk IV (8 x 1), 1 x 6 pounder, 4 x 21in TT. 3 to 1in belt, 1in decks.

HMS *Caroline*
Built Cammell Laird, laid down January 1914, completed December 1914. Trial speed 29.07 knots. Leader 4th Destroyer Flotilla Grand Fleet. 1915 1st Light Cruiser Squadron Grand Fleet. 1916 4th Light Cruiser Squadron Grand Fleet. Present at the Battle of Jutland 1916. Currently afloat at Belfast.

HMS *Carysfort*
Built Hawthorn Leslie, laid down February 1914, completed June 1915. Leader 4th Destroyer Flotilla Grand Fleet. 1916 5th Light Cruiser Squadron Harwich Force. 1917 7th Light Cruiser Squadron Grand Fleet. 1931 sold for scrap.

HMS *Cleopatra*
Built Cammell Laird, laid down February 1914, completed June 1915. 5th Light Cruiser Squadron Harwich Force. 23–24 March

1916 rammed and sunk German destroyer G-194 and damaged in collision with HMS *Undaunted*. 4 August 1916 damaged by mine off Belgian coast. 1918 7th Light Cruiser Squadron Grand Fleet. 1931 sold for scrap.

HMS *Comus*
Built Swan Hunter, laid down November 1913, completed January 1915. 4th Light Cruiser Squadron Grand Fleet. 29 February 1916 sank the German raider *Grief*. Present at the Battle of Jutland 1916. 1934 sold for scrap.

HMS *Conquest*
Built Scott, laid down March 1914, completed June 1915. 5th Light Cruiser Squadron Harwich Force. 25 April 1916 damaged by German battlecruisers during German raid on Lowestoft. 5 June 1917 sank German destroyer S-20. July 1918 damaged by mine. 1930 sold for scrap.

HMS *Cordelia*
Built Pembroke Dockyard, laid down July 1913, completed January 1915. 1st Light Cruiser Squadron Grand Fleet. Present at the Battle of Jutland 1916. 1917 4th Light Cruiser Squadron Grand Fleet. 1923 sold for scrap.

Active Class Scout Cruisers
Length 385 feet waterline 406 feet overall, beam 41 feet 6 inches, draught 15 feet 7 inches, displacement 3,440 tons. 4 shaft Parsons turbines, 18,000 shp, 25 knots. 1in decks. 10 x 4in 50cal Mk VIII (10 x 1), 4 x 3 pounder (4 x 1), 2 x 18in TT.

HMS *Active*
Built Pembroke Dockyard, laid down July 1910, completed December 1911. Leader 2nd Destroyer Flotilla with the Harwich Force. 1915 Grand Fleet. Present at the Battle of Jutland 1916. 1916 Leader 4th Destroyer Flotilla at Portsmouth. 1917 Queenstown. 1917 Mediterranean. 1920 sold for Scrap.

HMS *Amphion*
Built Pembroke Dockyard, laid down March 1911, completed March 1913. Leader 3rd Destroyer Flotilla with the Harwich Force. 6th August 1914 sunk by mine.

HMS *Fearless*
Built Pembroke Dockyard, laid down November 1911, completed October 1913. Leader 1st Destroyer Flotilla with the Harwich Force. 1916 Leader 12th Submarine Flotilla Grand Fleet. 31 January 1918 accidentally rammed and sank submarine K-17. 1921 sold for scrap.

Boadicea Class Scout Cruisers
Length 385 feet waterline 405 feet overall, beam 41 feet, draught 14 feet, displacement 3,300 tons. Average cost £330,000. 4 shaft Parsons turbines, 18,000 shp, 25 knots. 1in decks. 6 x 4in 50cal Mk VIII (6 x 1), 4 x 3 pounder QF (4 x 1), 2 x 18in TT.

HMS *Boadicea*
Built Pembroke Dockyard, laid down June 1907, completed June 1909. Attached to Grand Fleet Battle Squadrons. 15 December 1914 bridge lost in storm with several men drowned. Present at the battle of Jutland 1916. December 1917 converted to lay mines. 1926 sold for scrap.

HMS *Bellona*
Built Pembroke Dockyard, laid down June 1908, completed February 1910. Attached to Grand Fleet Battle Squadrons. Present at the Battle of Jutland 1916. June 1917 converted to lay mines. 1921 sold for scrap.

Blonde Class Scout Cruisers
Length 385 feet waterline 405 feet overall, beam 41 feet 6 inches, draught 15 feet 6 inches, displacement 3,350 tons. 4 shaft Parsons turbines, 18,000 shp, 24.5 knots. 1.5in decks. 10 x 4in 50cal Mk VIII (10 x 1), 4 x 3 pounder (4 x 1), 2 x 21in TT.

HMS *Blonde*
Built Pembroke Dockyard, laid down December 1909, completed May 1911. Attached to Grand Fleet Battle Squadrons. September 1917 converted to lay mines but never used as a minelayer. 1920 sold for scrap.

HMS *Blanche*
Built Pembroke Dockyard, laid down April 1909, completed November 1910. Attached to Grand Fleet Battle Squadrons. Present at the Battle of Jutland 1916. March 1917 converted to lay mines. 1921 sold for scrap.

Birkenhead Class Light Cruiser
Length 430 feet waterline 446 feet overall, beam 50 feet, draught 16 feet, displacement 5,185 tons normal 5,795 tons deep load. 4 shaft Parsons turbines, 25,000 shp, 25.5 knots. 2in belt, 1.5 to 0.5in decks. 10 x 5.5in 50cal Mk I (10 x 1), 1 x 3in, 2 x 21in TT.

HMS *Birkenhead* (formerly *Antinavarhos Kontouriotis*)
Built Cammell Laird, laid down April 1914, completed May 1915. 3rd Light Cruiser Squadron Grand Fleet. Present at the Battle of Jutland 1916. 1921 sold for scrap.

HMS Chester (formerly *Lambros Katsonis*)
Built Cammell Laird, laid down October 1914, completed May 1916. 3rd Light Cruiser Squadron Grand Fleet. Present at the Battle of Jutland 1916. 1921 sold for scrap.

Lion Class Battlecruiser
Length 675 feet waterline 700 feet overall, beam 88 feet 7 inches, draught 28 feet, displacement 26,350 normal, 30,084 tons deep. 4 shaft Parsons turbines, 70,000 shp, 27 knots. 9 to 4in belt, 9in barbettes, 9in turret faces, 2.5-1in decks. 8 x 13.5in 45cal Mk V (4 x 2), 16 x 4in (16 x 1), 4 x 3 pounder (4 x 1), 2 x 21in TT.

HMS *Lion*
Built Devonport Dockyard, laid down November 1909, completed May 1912, cost £2,083,999. Trial speed 27.62 knots. 1st Battlecruiser Squadron Grand Fleet as flagship of Vice Admiral

Beatty. 28 August 1914 took part in the Battle of Heligoland Bight. 16 December failed attempt to intercept German battlecruisers bombarding English east coast. 24 January 1915 at the Battle of the Dogger Bank. April 1915 returned from repair after battle. Present at the Battle of Jutland 1916. Hit by 13 x 12in and 1 x 5.9in rounds with 99 killed and 51 injured. Fired 326 x 13.4in rounds. July 1916 returned from repairs. 17 November 1917 part of covering force at the Second Battle of Heligoland Bight. 1924 sold for scrap.

HMS *Princess Royal*
Built Vickers, laid down May 1910, completed October 1912, cost £2,076,222. Trial speed 28.5 knots. 1st Battlecruiser Squadron Grand Fleet. 28 August 1914 Battle of Heligoland Bight. 28 September 1914 detached to escort Canadian troop convoy across Atlantic. 26 October 1914 rejoined Grand Fleet. 21 November 1914 arrived at Halifax to hunt for Admiral Graf von Spee. 19 December left Kingston for home after the destruction of Graf von Spee. 24 January 1915 took part in Battle of the Dogger Bank. Present at the Battle of Jutland 1916. Hit by 8 x 12in and 1 x 11in rounds with 22 killed and 81 injured. Fired 230 x 13.5in rounds. June–July 1916 refit at Portsmouth. 17 November 1917 part of covering force at the Second Battle of Heligoland bight. 1922 sold for scrap.

Queen Mary Class Battlecruiser
Length 698 feet waterline 703 feet 6 inches overall, beam 89 feet, draught 28 feet, displacement 26,780 tons. 4 shaft Parsons turbines, 75,000 shp, 27.5 knots. 9 to 4in belt, 9in barbettes, 9in turret faces, 2.5 to 1in decks. 8 x 13.5in 45cal Mk V (4 x 2), 16 x 4in (16 x 1), 4 x 3 pounder (4 x 1), 2 x 21in TT.

HMS *Queen Mary*
Built Palmers, laid down March 1911, completed March 1912, cost £2,078,491. 1st Battlecruiser Squadron Grand Fleet. Present at the Battle of Heligoland Bight. January–February 1915 refit at Portsmouth. 31 May 1916 sunk at the Battle of Jutland.

Tiger Class Battlecruiser
Length 697 feet 9 inches waterline 704 feet overall, beam 90 feet 6 inches, draught 32 feet load, displacement 28,800 normal, 33,677

tons deep. 4 shaft Brown-Curtis turbines, 85,000 shp, 28 knots. 9 to 3in belt, 9in barbettes, 9in turret faces, 3 to 1in decks. 8 x 13.5in 45cal Mk V (4 x 2), 12 x 6in (12 x 1), 2 x 3in (2 x 1), 4 x 3 pounder (4 x 1), 4 x 21in TT.

HMS *Tiger*
Built John Brown, laid down June 1912, completed October 1914, cost £2,100,000. Trial speed 29 knots. October 1914 joined 1st Battlecruiser Squadron. Present at the Battle of the Dogger Bank. Received 6 hits with 10 killed. Present at the Battle of Jutland 1916. Hit by 15 x 11in rounds with 24 killed and 46 wounded. Fired 303 x 13.5in rounds. Under repair until July 1916. Battlecruiser Fleet flagship whilst *Lion* being repaired. 17 November 1917 present at the Second Battle of Heligoland Bight. 1932 sold for scrap.

Indefatigable Class Battlecruiser
Length 588 feet waterline 590 feet overall, beam 79 feet 10 inches, draught 30 feet, displacement 18,750 load, 22,080 tons deep. 4 shaft Parsons turbines, 44,000 shp, 25 knots. 6 to 4in belt, 7in barbettes, 7in turret faces, 2.5 to 1in decks. 8 x 12in 45cal Mk X (4 x 2), 16 x 4in (16 x 1), 3 x 18in TT.

HMS *Indefatigable*
Built Devonport Dockyard, laid down February 1909, completed April 1911, cost £1,520,591. Trial speed 26.89 knots. 2nd Battlecruiser Squadron as flagship of the British Mediterranean Fleet. August 1914 hunting SMS *Goeben* and *Breslau*. 18 August became flagship of Dardanelles squadron. 3 November 1914 bombarded Dardanelles forts. 24 January 1915 left for refit at Malta. 14 February 1915 left Malta for home waters. 20 February joined 2nd Battlecruiser Squadron of the Grand Fleet. 31 May 1916 sunk by *SMS* Von der Tann at the Battle of Jutland.

HMS *New Zealand*
Built Fairfield, laid down June 1910, completed November 1912, cost £1,783,190. Trial speed 26.38 knots. A gift from New Zealand. 1st Battlecruiser Squadron Grand Fleet. 19 August transferred to 2nd Battlecruiser Squadron. Present at the Battle of Heligoland Bight. 1 September 1914 rejoined 1st Battlecruiser Squadron. 15

January 1915 became flagship of 2nd Battlecruiser Squadron. Present at the Battle of the Dogger Bank. 22 April 1916 collided with HMAS *Australia*. 30 May 1916 returned from repairs. Present at the Battle of Jutland 1916. Fired 420 x 12in rounds (the most of any ship in the battle) and received 1 x 11in hit. November 1916 refit at Rosyth. 17 November 1917 present at Second Battle of Heligoland Bight whilst temporarily attached to 1st Battlecruiser Squadron.

HMAS *Australia* (Royal Australian Navy)

Built John Brown, laid down June 1910, completed June 1913, cost £1,783,190. Trial speed 26.89 knots. Paid for for by the Australian government as part of the Royal Australian Navy. Flagship of Australian Squadron under Rear Admiral Patey. August 1914 hunting Admiral Graf von Spee. 15 September 1914 escorted convoy of Australian and New Zealand Army Corps. 17 September 1914 diverted to cover to German New Guinea. 31 December 1914 left Pacific via Straights of Magellan. 1 January 1915 damaged propeller on rocks. 2–5 January 1915 repairs at Port Stanley. 28 January 1915 arrived at Portsmouth and underwent a short refit. 17 February 1915 joined 2nd Battlecruiser Squadron Grand Fleet becoming flagship. 22 April 1916 collided with HMS *New Zealand*. 1 June 1916 returned from repairs having just missed Battle of Jutland. 12 December 1917 collided with HMS *Repulse*. January 1918 covering Scandinavian convoys. October 1918 as part of September 2nd Battlecruiser Squadron covered US navy minelaying as part of the Northern Barrage. 12 April 1924 scuttled east of Sydney to form artificial reef.

Queen Elizabeth Class Dreadnought Battleship

Length 634 feet 6 inches waterline 639 feet 9 inches overall, beam 90 feet 8 inches, draught 33 feet, displacement 27,470 tons light, 33,260 tons deep. 4 shaft Parsons/Brown-Curtis turbines, 6,000/75,000 (normal/overload) shp, 23/24 knots. 13-6in belt, 10 to 4in barbettes, 13in turret faces, 3 to 2in decks. 8 x 15in 45cal Mk I (4 x 2), 14 x 6in (14 x 1), 4 x 3 pounder (4 x 1), 2 x 3in (2 x 1), 4 x 21in TT.

HMS *Queen Elizabeth*
Built Portsmouth Dockyard, laid down October 1912, completed
January 1915, cost £3,014,103. 19 February 1915 arrived at the
Dardanelles and saw action bombarding forts, during which she
was hit by shore batteries but sustained no serious damage. 27 April
1915 fired on the former SMS *Goeben* overland using a kite balloon
for spotting. 12 May sent home from Dardanelles owing to risk
from submarines. 26 May arrived at Scapa Flow and joined the 5th
Battle Squadron. Not present at Jutland as undergoing refit.
November 1916 to February 1917 refit at Newcastle to enable her
to become Grand Fleet flagship for Admiral Sir David Beatty. 1948
sold for scrap.

HMS *Warspite*
Built Devonport Dockyard, laid down October 1912, completed
April 1915, cost £2,524,148. April 1915 2nd Battle Squadron
Grand Fleet. 16 September grounded in the Forth. 24 November
1915 rejoined Grand Fleet after repairs as part of the 5th Battle
Squadron. 3 December 1915 collision with HMS *Barham*. Present
at the Battle of Jutland 1916. Fired 259 x 15in rounds. Received 2
x 11in and 13 x 12in hits with 14 killed and 32 injured. 23 July 1916
rejoined Grand Fleet after repairs. 24 August 1916 collided with
HMS *Valiant* and under repair until 29 September 1916. 1947 sold
for scrap.

HMS *Barham*
Built John Brown, laid down February 1913, completed October
1915, cost £2,470,113. October 1915 Grand Fleet, joining 5th
Battle Squadron in November. 3 December 1915 collision with
HMS *Warspite*. 1 January 1916 rejoined Grand Fleet after repairs.
Present at the Battle of Jutland 1916 as flagship of 5th Battle
Squadron. Fired 337 x 15in rounds. Received 1 x 11in and 5 x 12in
hits with 26 killed and 46 injured. 4 July 1916 rejoined Grand Fleet
after repairs. 27 May 1941 sunk by German submarine U-331.

HMS *Valiant*
Built Fairfield, laid down January 1913, completed February 1916,
cost £2,537,037. January 1916 Grand Fleet 5th Battle Squadron.
Present at the Battle of Jutland 1916. Fired 288 x 15in rounds.

Received splinter damage with one injured. 24 August 1916 collided with HMS *Warspite* and under repair until 18 September 1916. 1948 sold for scrap.

HMS *Malaya*
Built Portsmouth Dockyard, laid down October 1913, completed February 1916, cost £2,945,709. Paid for as a gift by the Federated Malay States. April 1916 Grand Fleet 5th Battle Squadron. Present at the Battle of Jutland 1916. Fired 215 x 15in rounds. Received 7 x 12in hits with 63 killed and 68 injured. 24 June 1916 rejoined Grand Fleet after repairs. 1948 sold for scrap.

Chatham Second Class Protected Cruisers
Length 430 feet waterline 458 feet overall, beam 49 feet, draught 16 feet, displacement 5,400 tons normal, 6,000 tons deep load. Average cost £334,053. 4 shaft Parsons turbines (Southampton 2 shaft Brown-Curtis turbines), 25,000 shp, 25.5 knots. 2in belt, 1.5 to 0.5in decks. 8 x 6in 45cal Mk XII (8 x 1), 4 x 3 pounder (4 x 1), 2 x 21in TT.

HMS *Chatham*
Built Chatham Dockyard, laid down January 1911, completed December 1912. 2nd Light Cruiser Squadron Mediterranean. 1914 detached to Red Sea. November 1914 operations against the *Königsberg*. May 1915 Dardanelles. 1916 3rd Light Cruiser Squadron Grand Fleet. 26 May 1916 damaged by mine. 1926 sold for scrap.

HMS *Dublin*
Built Beardmore, laid down April 1911, completed March 1913. 2nd Light Cruiser Squadron Mediterranean. February 1915 Dardanelles. 9 June 1915 damaged by torpedo from Austro-Hungarian submarine. 1916 2nd Light Cruiser Squadron Grand Fleet. Present at the Battle of Jutland. 1926 sold for scrap.

HMS *Southampton*
Built John Brown, laid down April 1911, completed November 1912. Flagship 1st Light Cruiser Squadron Grand Fleet. 28 August 1914 present at the battles of Heligoland Bight and the Dogger

Bank. February 1915 Flagship 2nd Light Cruiser Squadron Grand Fleet. Present at the Battle of Jutland 1916. 1917 8th Light Cruiser Squadron Grand Fleet. 1926 sold for scrap.

Birmingham Second Class Protected Cruisers
Length 430 feet pp 457 feet overall, beam 50 feet, draught 16 feet, displacement 5,440 tons normal, 6,040 tons deep. 4 shaft Parsons turbines, 25,000 shp, 25.5kts. 2in belt, 1.5 to 0.5in decks. 9 x 6in 45cal Mk XII (9 x 1), 4 x 3 pounder (4 x 1), 2 x 21in TT.

HMS *Birmingham*
Built Elswick, laid down June 1912, completed February 1914. 1st Light Cruiser Squadron Grand Fleet. August 1914 sank two German merchant ships. 9 August 1914 rammed and sank the German submarine U-15. Present at the battles of Heligoland Bight and the Dogger Bank. February 1915 2nd Light Cruiser Squadron. Present at the Battle of Jutland 1916. 1931 sold for scrap.

HMS *Lowestoft*
Built Chatham Dockyard, laid down July 1912, completed April 1914. 1st Light Cruiser Squadron Grand Fleet. August 1914 sank a German merchant ship. Present at the battles of Heligoland Bight and the Dogger Bank. February 1915 2nd Light Cruiser Squadron. 1916 8th Light Cruiser Squadron Mediterranean. 1931 sold for scrap.

HMS *Nottingham*
Built Pembroke Dockyard, laid down June 1912, completed April 1914. 1st Light Cruiser Squadron Grand Fleet. 28 August 1914 Battle of Heligoland Bight. 24 January 1915 took part in Battle of the Dogger Bank. February 1915 2nd Light Cruiser Squadron. Present at the Battle of Jutland 1916. 16 August 1916 torpedoed and sunk by the German submarine U-52.

Weymouth Class Second Class Protected Cruisers
Length 430 feet waterline 453 feet overall, beam 48 feet 6 inches, draught 15 feet 6 inches, displacement 5,250 tons normal, 5,800 tons full load. Average cost £396,363. 4 shaft Parsons turbines, 22,000 shp, 25 knots. 2 to 0.5in decks. 8 x 6in 50cal Mk XI (8 x 1), 4 x 3 pounder (4 x 1), 2 x 21in TT.

HMS *Weymouth*
Built Elswick, laid down January 1910, completed October 1911. 2nd Light Cruiser Squadron Mediterranean. August 1914 detached to Indian Ocean to look for *Emden*. February 1915 East Africa as part of operations against the *Konigsberg*. December 1915 Adriatic. 1916 6th Light Cruiser Squadron Grand Fleet. 1917 8th Cruiser Squadron Brindisi in the Mediterranean. 2 October 1918 damaged by torpedo from Austrian submarine U-28. 1928 sold for scrap.

HMS *Dartmouth*
Built Vickers, laid down February 1910, completed October 1911. 1914 East Indies. October 1914 Captured German tug *Adjutant*. January 1915 2nd Light Cruiser Squadron Grand Fleet but operated in South Atlantic in search for *Karlsruhe*. February 1915 Dardanelles. May 1915 8th Light Cruiser Squadron Brindisi. 15 May 1917 damaged by torpedo from German submarine U-25. 1930 sold for scrap.

HMS *Falmouth*
Built Beardmore, laid down November 1909, completed September 1911. 5th Cruiser Squadron mid Atlantic. August 1914 sank four German merchant ships. August 1914 1st Light Cruiser Squadron Grand Fleet. Present at the battles of Heligoland Bight, the Dogger Bank and Jutland. 19 August 1916 sunk by German submarines U-66 and U-52.

HMS *Yarmouth*
Built London and Glasgow Co., laid down January 1910, completed April 1912. 1914 China Station. 1914 involved in hunt for *Emden*. October 1914 captured two German colliers. December 1914 2nd Light Cruiser Squadron Grand Fleet. February 1915 3rd Light Cruiser Squadron Grand Fleet. Present at the Battle of Jutland 1916. 1926 sold for scrap.

Bristol Class Second Class Protected Cruisers
Length 430 feet waterline 453 feet overall, beam 47 feet, draught 15 feet 6 inches, displacement 4,800 tons normal, 5,300 tons load. 4 shaft Parsons turbines, 22,000 shp, 25 knots or Bristol 2 shaft

Brown-Curtis turbines. 2 to 0.5in decks. 2 x 6in 50cal Mk XI (2 x 1), 10 x 4in 50cal Mk VIII (10 x 1), 4 x 3 pounder (4 x 1), 2 x 18in TT.

HMS *Bristol*
Built John Brown, laid down March 1909, completed December 1910. 4th Cruiser Squadron West Indies. 6 August 1914 fought with the *Karlsruhe*. Hunted for Admiral Graf von Spee and fought at the Battle of the Falkland Islands. 1915 Mediterranean. 1916 Adriatic. 1918 South America. 1921 sold for scrap.

HMS *Glasgow*
Built Fairfield, laid down March 1909, completed September 1910. 16 August 1914 captured German merchant ship SS *Catherina*. 1 November 1914 fought in the Battle of Coronel. 8 December 1914 Battle of the Falkland Islands. 14 March 1915 along with HMS *Kent* found and sank SMS *Dresden* at Mas a Fuera. 1915 Mediterranean. 1917 8th Light Cruiser Squadron Adriatic. 1927 sold for scrap.

HMS *Gloucester*
Built Beardmore, laid down April 1909, completed October 1910. 2nd Light Cruiser Squadron Mediterranean. August 1914 involved in hunt for SMS *Goeben* and *Breslau*. 1914 hunt for German raiders off west coast of Africa. February 1915 3rd Light Cruiser Squadron Grand Fleet. April 1916 shelled Galway during Easter Uprising. Present at the Battle of Jutland 1916. 1916 2nd Light Cruiser Squadron Grand Fleet. December 1916 8th Light Cruiser Squadron Adriatic. 1921 sold for scrap.

HMS *Liverpool*
Built Vickers, laid down February 1909, completed October 1910. 1st Light Cruiser Squadron Grand Fleet. Fought at the Battle of Heligoland Bight. January 1915 2nd Light Cruiser Squadron Grand Fleet. February 1915 3rd Light Cruiser Squadron Grand Fleet. November 1915 Mediterranean. January 1918 8th Light Cruiser Squadron Adriatic. 1921 sold for scrap.

HMS *Newcastle*
Built Elswick, laid down April 1909, completed September 1910. 1914 China and Pacific. 1917 East Indies. 1918 South America. 1921 sold for scrap.

German Ships by Type

König Class Dreadnought Battleship
Length 575 feet 6 inches overall, 96 feet 9 inches beam, draught 30 feet 6 inches deep load, displacement 25,390 tons normal, 29,200 tons deep load. 3 shaft Parsons/AEG-Vulcan/Bergmann turbines, 31,000 shp at 21 knots. 14 to 3in belt, 12in barbettes, 12in turrets, 2.5in decks. 10 x 12in SKL/50 (5 x 2), 14 x 5.9in (14 x 1), 10 x 3.45in (10 x 1), 5 x 19.7in TT.

SMS *König*
Built Wilhelmshaven Navy Yard, laid down October 1911, completed August 1914, cost 45,000,000 Marks. Trial speed 21 knots. III Battle Squadron. 7 December 1914 collided with SMS *Grosser Kurfürst* near Wilhelmshaven. Present at the Battle of Jutland 1916. Fired 167 x 12in rounds and was hit by 4 x 15in, 9 x 13.5in and 4 x 6in rounds with 45 killed and 27 wounded. Repaired at Kiel. October 1917 operations in the Baltic Islands. 17 October 1917 engaged Russian battleships, sinking the *Slava*. Interned and scuttled at Scapa Flow at the end of the First World War.

SMS *Grosser Kurfürst*
Built Vulcan, Hamburg, laid down October 1911, completed July 1914. Trial speed 21.2 knots. III Battle Squadron. 7 December 1914 collided with SMS *König* near Wilhelmshaven. Present at the Battle of Jutland 1916. Fired 135 x 12in rounds. Hit by 4 x 15in and 3 x 13.5in rounds with 15 dead and 10 wounded. Repaired at Hamburg. 5 November 1916 torpedoed by British submarine J1 off the Danish coast. February 1917 returned from repairs. 9 February 1917 ran aground. 5 March 1917 collided with SMS *Kronprinz Wilhelm*. April 1917 repairs. October 1917 part of operations near the Baltic Islands. 12 October 1917 struck a mine. December 1917 returned from repairs in Wilhelmshaven. 25 April 1918 damaged

entering Wilhelmshaven harbour. May 1918 returned from repairs in Wilhelmshaven. 30 May 1918 ran aground near Heligoland. August 1918 returned from repairs in Wilhelmshaven. Interned and scuttled at Scapa Flow at the end of the First World War.

SMS *Markgraf*

Built Weser, Bremen, laid down November 1911, completed October 1914. Trial speed 21 knots. III Battle Squadron. Present at the Battle of Jutland 1916. Fired 254 x 12in rounds. Hit by 3 x 15in and 2 x 13.5in rounds with 11 dead and 13 wounded. July 1916 repaired at Hamburg. October1917 operations in the Baltic Islands. Interned and scuttled at Scapa Flow at the end of the First World War.

SMS *Kronprinz* (renamed *Kronprinz Wilhelm* in 1918)

Built Germaniawerft, Kiel, laid down May 1912, completed November 1914. Trial speed 21.3 knots. III Battle Squadron. Present at the Battle of Jutland 1916. Fired 144 x 12in rounds, no damage. 5 November 1916 torpedoed by British submarine J1 off the Danish coast. December 1916 returned from repairs. 5 March 1917 in collision with SMS *Grosser Kurfürst* in Heligoland Bight. May 1917 returned from repairs. October 1917 operations in the Baltic Islands. 12 October 1917 struck a mine. 27 January 1918 renamed *Kronprinz Wilhelm*. Interned and scuttled at Scapa Flow at the end of the First World War.

Kaiser Class Dreadnought Battleship

Length 565 feet 7 inches overall, 95 feet 2 inches beam, draught 30 feet deep load, displacement 24,330 tons normal, 27,400 tons deep load. 3 shaft Parsons/AEG-Curtis/Schichau turbines, 31,000 shp at 21 knots. 14 to 3in belt, 12in barbettes, 12in turrets, 2.5in decks. 10 x 12in SKL/50 (5 x 2), 14 x 5.9in (14 x 1), 12 x 3.45in (12 x 1), 5 x 19.7in TT.

SMS *Kaiser*

Built Kiel Navy Yard, laid down December 1909, completed December 1912, cost 44,997,000 Marks. Trial speed 23.4 knots. III Battle Squadron. Present at the Battle of Jutland 1916. Fired 224 x 12in rounds and received 2 x 12in and 4 x 6in hits with one killed and one injured. October 1917 operations in the Baltic Islands. 17 November 1917 engaged with British cruisers in Second Battle of Heligoland Bight. No damage received. Interned and scuttled at Scapa Flow at the end of the First World War.

SMS *Fredrich der Grosse*
Built Vulcan, Hamburg, laid down January 1910, completed January 1913, cost 45,802,000 Marks. Trial speed 22.1 knots. Fleet flagship and part of III Battle Squadron at the start of the war. Present at the Battle of Jutland 1916 as flagship of Vice Admiral Scheer. Fired 72 rounds and received no damage. October 1917 operations in the Baltic Islands. Interned and scuttled at Scapa Flow at the end of the First World War.

SMS *Kaiserin*
Built Howaldtswerke, Kiel, laid down November 1910, completed December 1913, cost 45,173,000 Marks. Trial speed 22.4 knots. Part of III Battle Squadron at the start of the war. Present at the Battle of Jutland 1916. Fired 160 x 12in rounds receiving no damage. October 1917 operations in the Baltic Islands in the Gulf of Riga. 17 November 1917 engaged with British cruisers in Second Battle of Heligoland Bight. No damage received. Interned and scuttled at Scapa Flow at the end of the First World War.

SMS *König Albert*
Built Schichau, Danzig, laid down July 1910, completed November 1913, cost 45,761,000 Marks. Trial speed 22 knots. III Battle Squadron at the start of the war. Missed Jutland owing to condenser problems. October 1917 operations in the Baltic Islands in the Gulf of Riga. Interned and scuttled at Scapa Flow at the end of the First World War.

SMS *Prinzregent Luitpold*
Built Germaniawerft, Kiel, laid down January 1911, completed December 1913, cost 46,374,000 Marks. Trial speed 21.7 knots. III Battle Squadron at the start of the war. Present at the Battle of Jutland 1916. Fired 169 x 12in rounds receiving no damage. October 1917 operations in the Baltic Islands in the Gulf of Riga. Interned and scuttled at Scapa Flow at the end of the First World War.

Helgoland Class Dreadnought Battleship

Length 548 feet 7 inches overall, 93 feet 6 inches beam, draught 29 feet 6 inches deep load, displacement 22,400 tons normal, 25,200 tons deep load. 3 shaft Vertical Triple Expansion, 28,000ihp, 20 knots. 12 to 3in belts, 12 to 2in barbettes, 12in turret, 2.5in decks. 12 x 12in SKL/50 (6 x 2), 14 x 5.9in (14 x 1), 14 x 3.45in (14 x 1), 6 x 19.7in TT.

SMS *Helgoland*

Built Howaldtswerke, Kiel, laid down December 1908, completed December 1911, cost 46,196,000 Marks. Trial speed 20.8 knots. I Battle Squadron at the outbreak of the war. Present at the Battle of Jutland 1916. Fired 63 x 12in rounds and received 1 x 15in hit. After the war taken over by Britain as a replacement for ships scuttled at Scapa Flow. 1924 scrapped.

SMS *Ostfriesland*

Built Wilhelmshaven Navy Yard, laid down October 1908, completed September 1911, cost 43,579,000 Marks. Trial speed 21.2 knots. I Battle Squadron at start of the war as squadron flagship. Present at the Battle of Jutland 1916. Fired 11 x 12in rounds and received no damage. 1 June 1916 returning from the battle hit a mine, 1 dead 10 injured. 26 July 1916 repaired at Wilhelmshaven. After the war taken over by United States. July 1921 sunk as bombing target.

SMS *Thüringen*

Built Weser, Bremen, laid down November 1908, completed September 1911, cost 46,314,000 Marks. Trial speed 21 knots. I Battle Squadron at the outbreak of the war. Present at the Battle of Jutland 1916. Fired 107 x 12in rounds and received no damage. After the war taken over by France and used as target. 1923 scrapped.

SMS *Oldenburg*

Built Weser, Bremen, laid down March 1909, completed September 1911, cost 45,801,000 Marks. Trial speed 21.3 knots. I Battle Squadron at the outbreak of the war. Present at the Battle of Jutland 1916. Fired 53 x 12in rounds and received 1 secondary armament hit. 8 killed and 14 injured. Taken over by Japan after the war. 1921 scrapped.

Nassau Class Dreadnought Battleship
Length 479 feet 4 inches overall, 88 feet 5 inches beam, draught 29 feet 3 inches deep load, displacement 18,570 tons normal, 21,000 tons deep load. 3 shaft Vertical Triple Expansion, 22,000 ihp, 19 knots. 12 to 3in belts, 11 to 2in barbettes, 11in turret, 2.5in decks. 12 x 11in SKL/45 (6 x 2), 12 x 5.9in (12 x 1), 16 x 3.45in (16 x 1), 6 x 17.7in TT.

SMS *Nassau*
Built Wilhelmshaven Navy Yard, laid down July 1907, completed May 1910, cost 37,399,000 Marks. Trial speed 20 knots. I Battle Squadron. Present at the Battle of Jutland 1916. Fired 106 x 11in rounds. Hit twice by 4in rounds and collided with HMS *Spitfire*. 11 killed 16 injured. July 1916 repairs. Post-war taken over by Japan and scrapped in 1920.

SMS *Posen*
Built Germaniawerft, Kiel, laid down June 1907, completed September 1910, cost 36,920,000 Marks. Trial speed 20 knots. Part of I Battle Squadron. Present at the Battle of Jutland 1916. Fired 106 x 11in rounds. Received no damage. Post-war taken over by Britain and scrapped in 1922.

SMS *Rheinland*
Built Vulcan, Stettin, laid down June 1907, completed September 1910, cost 36,916,000 Marks. Trial speed 20 knots. Part of I Battle Squadron. Present at the Battle of Jutland 1916. Fired 35 x 11in rounds. Hit by 2 x 6in rounds with 10 killed and 20 injured. February 1918, assisting Finnish independence. 11 April 1918 ran aground in the Aaland Sea. 8 July 1918 refloated after 6,400 tons of equipment had been removed. Ship not considered worth repairing and was used as a barrack ship in Kiel. 1920 sold for scrap.

SMS *Westfalen*
Built Weser, Bremen, laid down August 1907, completed May 1910, cost 37,615,000 Marks. Trial speed 20.2 knots. Part of I

71

Battle Squadron. Present at the Battle of Jutland 1916. Led the German van during the night, sinking four destroyers. Fired 51 x 11in rounds. Hit by 2 x 4in rounds with 2 killed and 8 injured. July 1916 repairs. 19 August 1916 torpedoed by British submarine E23. October 1916 returned from repairs. February 1918 onwards operations assisting Finish independence. September 1918 became gunnery training ship. Post-war taken over by Britain and scrapped in 1924.

Deutschland Class Battleship
Length 413 feet waterline 418 feet 8 inches overall, beam 73 feet, draught 27 feet, displacement 13,993 tons deep load. 3 shaft Triple Expansion, 19,000 ihp, 18 knots. 9 to 4in belt, 11in turrets, 3in decks. 4 x 11in 40cal (2 x 2), 14 x 6.7in (14 x 1), 22 x 3.4in (22 x 1), 6 x 17.7in TT.

SMS *Deutschland*
Built Germania, Kiel, laid down July 1903, completed October 1906, cost 24,481,000 Marks. Trial speed 18.6 knots. II Squadron High Seas Fleet. Present at the Battle of Jutland 1916. August 1917 became a barrack ship. 1922 scrapped.

SMS *Pommern*
Built A G Vulcan, Stettin, laid down March 1904, completed August 1907, cost 24,624,000 Marks. Trial speed 18.7 knots. II Squadron High Seas Fleet. Sunk at the Battle of Jutland 1916.

SMS *Hannover*
Built Wilhelmshaven Navy Dockyard, laid down November 1904, completed October 1907, cost 24,253,000 Marks. Trial speed 18.5 knots. II Squadron High Seas Fleet. Present at the Battle of Jutland 1916. 1917 guard ship for the Danish Belt. 1944 scrapped.

SMS *Schlesien*
Built Schichau, Danzig, laid down November 1904, completed May 1908, cost 24,920,000 Marks. Trial speed 18.5 knots. II Squadron High Seas Fleet. Present at the Battle of Jutland 1916. 1917 became a training ship. 4 May 1945 scuttled.

SMS *Schleswig-Holstein*
Built Germania, Kiel, laid down June 1904, completed July 1908, cost 24,972,000 Marks. Trial speed 19.1 knots. II Squadron High Seas Fleet. Present at the Battle of Jutland 1916. 1917 accommodation ship. 18 December 1944 sunk by British aircraft.

Braunschweig Class Battleship
Length 413 feet 3 inches waterline 419 feet overall, beam 73 feet, draught 26 feet 7 inches, displacement 14,167 tons deep load. 3 shaft Triple Expansion, 17,000 ihp, 18 knots. 9 to 4in belt, 10in turrets, 3in decks. 4 x 11in 40cal (2 x 2), 14 x 6.7in (14 x 1), 14 x 3.4in (14 x 1), 6 x 17.7in TT.

SMS *Hessen*
Built Germania, Kiel, laid down April 1902, completed September 1905, cost 23,867,000 Marks. Trial speed 18.2 knots. IV Battle Squadron. 1916 II Battle Squadron. Present at the Battle of Jutland 1916. 1917 became a depot ship. About 1960 scrapped.

Königsberg Class Light Cruiser
Length 114.8 m waterline 115.3 overall, beam 13.2 m, draught 5.24 m, displacement 5,440 tonnes load, 7,125 tons full load.
2 shaft triple expansion engines, 13,200 ihp, 23 knots or Stettin 4 shaft Parsons turbines, 13,500 shp, 24 knots. 1.5 to 0.5in decks, 2in gun shields. 10 x 105mm (4.1in) SKL/40cal (10 x 1), 8 x 52mm (2in) (8 x 1), 2 x 450mm (17.7in) TT.

SMS *Königsberg*
Built Kiel Navy Yard, laid down January 1905, completed April 1907, cost 5,407,000 Marks. Trial speed 24.1 knots. Assigned to East Africa. 11 July 1915 sunk.

SMS *Nürnberg*
Built Kiel Navy Yard, laid down January 1906, completed April 1908, cost 5,560,000 Marks. Trial speed 23.4 knots. August 1914 with Admiral Graf von Spee. Present at the Battle of Coronel and sunk at the Battle of the Falkland Islands.

SMS *Stuttgart*
Built Danzig Navy Yard, laid down November 1905, completed February 1908, cost 5,488,000 Marks. Trial speed 23.9 knots. IV Scouting Group. Present at the Battle of Jutland 1916. December 1916 decommissioned. January–May 1918 converted to seaplane carrier. Flagship North Sea Aerial Forces. 1920 ceded to Britain and scrapped.

SMS *Stettin*
Built Vulcan, Stettin, laid down March 1905, completed October 1907, cost 6,398,000 Marks. Trial speed 25.2 knots. Present at the Battle of Heligoland Bight. IV Scouting Group. Present at the Battle of Jutland 1916. 1917 flagship for torpedo boats. 1918 attached to U-Boat training. 1920 ceded to Britain and scrapped in 1921.

Bremen Class Light Cruisers
Length 110.6 m waterline 111.1 m overall, beam 13.3m, draught 5.53 m, displacement 3,278 tonnes load, 3,797 tonnes full load. 2 shaft triple expansion engines, 10,000 ihp, 22 knots or Lübeck 2 shaft Parson turbines, 10,500 ihp, 22.5 knots. 3 to 1in decks, 2in gun shields. 10 x 105mm (4.1in) SKL/40cal (10 x 1), 3 x 17.7in TT.

SMS *Bremen*
Built Weser, Bremen, laid down August 1902, completed May 1904, cost 4,746,000 Marks. Trial speed 23.3 knots. May 1915 refit with four 4.1in guns replaced by 2 x 5.9in. 1915 operated in Baltic. 17 December 1915 sunk by mines.

SMS *Hamburg*
Built Vulcan, Stettin, laid down August 1902, completed March 1904, cost 4,706,000 Marks. Trial speed 23.3 knots. August 1914 command and accommodation ship for German submarines. 21 May 1915 accidentally rammed and sank the torpedo boat S-21. Present at the Battle of Jutland 1916 as part of IV Scouting Group. March 1917 used as stationary command ship. 1944 sunk during British air attack on Hamburg.

SMS *Berlin*
Built Danzig Navy Yard, laid down 1902, completed April 1905, cost 4,545,000 Marks. Trial speed 23.3 knots. 1914 part of coastal defences of the German Bight. 1915–1916 used as a minelayer carrying 80 mines. 1917 decommissioned. 1947 scuttled.

SMS *Lübeck*
Built Vulcan, Stettin, laid down May 1903, completed April 1905, cost 5,436,000 Marks. Trial speed 23.1 knots. 1914 coastal defence ship. 1917 training ship. Post-war ceded to Britain and broken up from 1922 onwards.

SMS *München*
Built Weser, Bremen, laid down August 1903, completed January 1905, cost 5,054,000 Marks. Trial speed 23.3 knots. IV Scouting Group. Present at the Battle of Jutland 1916. 1918 barrack ship. Post-war ceded to Britain and broken up early 1920s.

SMS *Leipzig*
Built Weser, Bremen, laid down July 1904, completed April 1906, cost 5,043,000 Marks. Trial speed 22.1 knots. August 1914 off Mexican west coast, joined up with Admiral Graf von Spee, fought at the Battle of Coronel and sunk at the Battle of the Falkland Islands.

SMS *Danzig*
Built Danzig Navy Yard, laid down July 1904, completed February 1907, cost 4,828,000 Marks. Trial speed 22.9 knots. 1914 coastal defence. Present at the Battle of Heligoland Bight. 18 May 1915 damaged by a mine. December 1916 II Scouting Group. June 1917 training ship. March 1918 decommissioned. Post-war ceded to Britain and broken up early 1923.

Gazelle Class Light Cruisers
Length 104.4 m waterline 105 m overall, beam 12.2 m, draught 5.19 m, displacement 2,643 tonnes load, 2,963 tonnes full load. Gazelle 2 shaft triple expansion engines, 6,000 ihp, 19.5 knots. 1in decks, 2in gun shields. 10 x 105mm (4.1in) SKL/40cal (10 x 1), 3/2 x 450mm (17.7in) TT.

SMS *Frauenlob*
Built Weser, Bremen, laid down 1901, completed February 1903, cost 4,596,000 Marks. Trial speed 21.5 knots. IV Scouting Group. Sunk at the Battle of Jutland 1916.

Karlsruhe Class Light Cruisers
Length 139 m waterline 142.2 m overall, beam 13.7 m, draught 5.79 m, displacement 4,900 tonnes load, 6,191 tonnes full load. 2 shaft Navy turbines, 26,000 shp, 27.8 knots. 2.5 to 0.5in belt, 2.5 to 1in decks. 12 x 105mm (4.1in) SKL/45cal (12 x 1), 2 x 500mm (19.7in) TT, 120 mines.

SMS *Karlsruhe*
Built Germaniawerft, Kiel, laid down September 1911, completed January 1914, cost 8,126,000 Marks. Trial speed 28.5 knots. 1914 operating in the Caribbean. 4 November 1914 destroyed by accidental explosion.

SMS *Rostock*
Built Howaldtswerke, Kiel, laid down 1911, completed February 1914, cost 8,124,000 Marks. Trial speed 29.3 knots. Command ship for torpedo boats. Present at the Battle of the Dogger Bank and sunk at the Battle of Jutland.

Derfflinger Class Battlecruiser
Length 690 feet 3 inches overall, beam 95 feet 2 inches, draught 27 feet 3 inches, displacement 26,180 tons normal, 30,700 tons deep load. 4 shaft Parsons turbines, 63,000 shp, 27 knots. 12 to 4in belt, 10in barbettes, 11in turrets, 3 to 1in decks. 8 x 12in SKL/50 (4 x 2), 12 x 5.9in (12 x 1), 4 x 3.45in (4 x 1), 4 x 19.7in TT.

SMS *Derfflinger*
Built Blohm and Voss, Hamburg, laid down January 1912, completed October 1914, cost 56,000,000 Marks. Trial speed 28 knots. Part of I Scouting Group. 16 December 1914 bombarded Hartlepool. Present at the Battle of the Dogger Bank. February 1915 repairs. 28 June 1915 turbine breakdown. 24 April 1916 took part in bombardment of Great Yarmouth and Lowestoft. Present at the Battle of Jutland 1916. Hit by 10 x 15in, 1 x 13.5in, 10 x 12in, 2 x

6in and 7 x 4in rounds with 157 killed and 26 injured. Took part in sinking of HMS *Invincible* and HMS *Queen Mary* firing 385 x 12in rounds. October 1916 repaired at Kiel. Interned and scuttled at Scapa Flow.

SMS *Lützow*
Built Schichau, Danzig, laid down May 1912, completed August 1915, cost 58,000,000 Marks. Trial speed 28.3 knots. I Scouting Group. 24 April 1916 bombardment of Great Yarmouth and Lowestoft. Took part in sinking of HMS *Invincible* and sunk at the Battle of Jutland.

Seydlitz Class Battlecruiser
Length 657 feet 11 inches overall, beam 93 feet 6 inches, draught 26 feet 11 inches, displacement 24,594 normal, 28,100 tons deep. 4 shaft Parsons turbines, 63,000 shp, 26.5 knots. 12 to 4in belt, 9in barbettes, 10in turrets, 3 to 1in decks. 10 x 11in SKL/50 (5 x 2), 12 x 5.9in (12 x 1), 12 x 3.45in (12 x 1), 4 x 19.7in TT.

SMS *Seydlitz*
Built Blohm and Voss, Hamburg, laid down February 1911, completed August 1913, cost 44,685,000 Marks. Trial speed 28.1 knots. Part of I Scouting Group. 3 November 1914 took part in the bombardment of Great Yarmouth. 16 December 1914 involved in the bombardment of Hartlepool. Damaged at the Battle of the Dogger Bank. 25 April 1916 hit a mine on the way to bombard Great Yarmouth and Lowestoft. 29 May 1916 returned from repair. Present at the Battle of Jutland 1916. Fired 376 x 11in rounds. Hit by 8 x 15in, 6 x 13.5in, 8 x 12in, 1 x 5.5in, 1 x 4in rounds and a torpedo with 98 killed and 55 injured. September 1916 repaired at Wilhelmshaven. Interned and scuttled at Scapa Flow.

Moltke Class Battlecruiser
Length 522 feet waterline 526 feet overall, beam 82 feet 6 inches, draught 31 feet 5 inches, displacement 18,596 load, 22,540 tons deep. 4 shaft Parsons turbines, 52,000 shp, 25.5 knots. 11 to 3in belt, 9in barbettes, 9in turrets, 3 to 1in decks. 10 x 11in SKL/50 (5 x 2), 12 x 5.9in (12 x 1), 12 x 3.45in (12 x 1), 4 x 19.7in TT.

SMS *Moltke*
Built Blohm and Voss, Hamburg, laid down December 1908, completed March 1912, cost 42,603,000 Marks. Trial speed 28.4 knots. I Scouting Group Group. 3 November 1914 took part in the bombardment of Great Yarmouth. 16 December 1914 involved in the bombardment of Hartlepool. Present at the Battle of the Dogger Bank. 19 August 1915 whilst operating near Riga was hit by a torpedo from the British submarine E1. 20 September returned from repairs. 24 April 1916 took part in bombardment of Great Yarmouth and Lowestoft. Present at the Battle of Jutland 1916. Fired 359 x 11in rounds and was hit by 4 x 15in and 1 x 13.5in rounds suffering 17 killed and 23 injured. July 1916 under repairs at Hamburg. 23 April 1918 whilst trying to raid a convoy to Norway was heavily damaged when one of her screws fell off and suffered engine damage resulting in about 2,000 tons of flooding. 25 April 1918 whilst under tow by SMS *Oldenburg* was hit by a torpedo fired by the British submarine E42. Under repair until the end of August 1918. Interned and scuttled at Scapa Flow.

Von der Tann Class Battlecruiser
Length 563 feet 4 inch overall, beam 87 feet 3 inches, draught 26 feet 7 inches, displacement 19,064 tons normal, 21,700 tons deep. 4 shaft Parsons turbines, 43,600 shp, 25 knots. 10 to 3in belt, 9in barbettes, 9in turrets, 2 to 1in decks. 8 x 11in SKL/45 (4 x 2), 10 x 5.9in (10 x 1), 16 x 3.45in (16 x 1), 4 x 17.7in TT.

SMS *Von der Tann*
Built Blohm and Voss, Hamburg, laid down March 1908, completed February 1911, cost 36,523,000 Marks. Trial speed 27.4 knots. I Scouting Group. 3 November 1914 bombarded Great Yarmouth. 16 December 1914 took part in bombardment of Scarborough. 24 April 1916 took part in bombardment of Great Yarmouth and Lowestoft. Present at the Battle of Jutland 1916. Fired 170 x 11in rounds sinking HMS *Indomitable*. Hit by 2 x 15in and 2 x 13.5in rounds with 11 killed and 35 wounded. July 1916 repaired at Wilhelmshaven. November–December 1916 under repair for turbine damage. May–June 1917 under repair. Interned and scuttled at Scapa Flow.

Wiesbaden Class Light Cruisers
Length 141.7 m waterline 145.3 m overall, beam 13.9 m, draught 5.8 m, displacement 5,180 tonnes load, 6,601 tonnes full load. 2 shaft Navy turbines, 31,000 shp, 27.5 knots. 2.5 to 0.5in belt, 2.5 to 1in decks. 8 x 150mm (5.9in) SKL/45cal (4 x 2), 2 x 88mm (2 x 1), 4 x 500mm (19.7in) TT, 120 mines.

SMS *Wiesbaden*
Built Vulcan, Stettin, laid down 1913, completed August 1915. 1915 II Scouting Group. 24 April 1916 took part in bombardment of Lowestoft. Present at the Battle of Jutland 1916.

SMS *Frankfurt*
Built Kiel Navy Dockyard, laid down January 1913, completed August 1915. 1915 II Scouting Group. 24 April 1916 took part in the bombardment of Lowestoft. Prsent at the Battle of Jutland 1916. October 1917 operations in the Baltic Islands in the Gulf of Riga. 17 November 1917 engaged with British cruisers in Second Battle of Heligoland Bight. Interned at Scapa Flow. Attempt to scuttle failed and ceded to USA. 1921 sunk as target.

Pillau Class Light Cruisers
Length 134.3 m waterline 135.3 m overall, beam 13.6 m, draught 5.64 m, displacement 4,390 tonnes load, 5,252 tonnes full load. 2 shaft Navy turbines, 30,000 shp, 27.5 knots. 3 to 0.5in decks. 8 x 150mm (5.9in) SKL/45cal (8 x 1), 2 x 88mm (2 x 1), 2 x 500mm (19.7in) TT, 120 mines.

SMS *Pillau*
Built Schichau, Danzig, laid down 1913, completed December 1914. 1915 II Scouting Group. August 1915 North Sea. Present at the Battle of Jutland 1916. 17 November 1917 took part in the Second Battle of Heligoland Bight. Ceded to Italy after the war and sunk in 1943.

SMS *Elbing*
Built Schichau, Danzig, laid down September 1913, completed September 1915. 1915 Baltic. 1916 II Scouting Group. April 1916 took part in bombardment of Great Yarmouth. Sunk at the Battle of Jutland 1916.

Graudenz Class Light Cruisers
Length 139 m waterline 142.2 m overall, beam 13.7 m, draught 5.79 m, displacement 4,900 tonnes load, 6,191 tonnes full load. 2 shaft Navy turbines, 26,000 shp, 27.5 knots. 2.5 to 0.5in belt, 2.5 to 1in decks. 12 x 105mm (4.1in) SKL/45cal (12 x 1), 2 x 500 (19.7in) TT.

SMS *Graudenz*
Built Kiel Navy Yard, laid down 1912, completed August 1914, cost 8,800,000 Marks. IV Scouting Group and torpedo boat leader.
II Scouting Group. Present at the Battle of the Dogger Bank. April 1916 damaged by mine. Ceded to Italy after the war and scrapped in 1938.

SMS *Regensburg*
Built Weser, Bremen, laid down November 1912, completed January 1915, cost 8,800,000 Marks. Command ship for torpedo boats. II Scouting Group. Present at the Battle of Jutland 1916. Ceded to France after the war and scuttled in 1944.

Chapter Three

Contact

As May dawned both Scheer and Jellicoe were preparing for major offensives. Jellicoe was planning an operation that would be launched on 2 June, when he would use two light cruiser squadrons as bait, in the hope that Scheer would be tempted out to attack them with the German High Seas Fleet. The light cruisers would cross between Denmark and Sweden, lurking behind them would be Beatty's battlecruisers and behind them the Grand Fleet. Jellicoe hoped that his seaplanes could drive off the zeppelins so that Scheer would not be aware of the trap. He needed to draw the Germans out into the North Sea, and trap them. To support this he would lay new mines and position submarines, covering the area between Heligoland Bight and Horns Reef.

At the same time, Scheer had put forward plans for a major operation against Sunderland. He had come to the conclusion that by bombarding Great Yarmouth or Lowestoft he was hitting the British too far south. Beatty, based at Rosyth, would never be able to intercept a German attack and would not, therefore, be drawn into a trap that could be sprung by the High Seas Fleet. Scheer therefore proposed to use Hipper's battlecruisers as bait, knowing that both Beatty and Jellicoe would try to intercept. Lying in wait would be a string of German submarines, covering the exits from Scapa Flow and Rosyth. They would cause damage and confusion to the British fleets, giving Hipper the chance to sail closer to Beatty and draw him south so that Scheer and the main fleet could hit him hard and unsupported near the Dogger Bank.

Scheer initially pencilled in the operation for 17 May 1916, but there were problems. For one thing, there were high winds, preventing the zeppelins from taking off, and Scheer needed them to be his eyes and ears to prevent himself from falling into the same kind of trap he was preparing for Beatty. Initially the operation was postponed until 23 May, even though the submarines had already taken up their positions around Scapa Flow and Rosyth. Scheer then discovered that the *Seydlitz* had not yet been repaired after suffering damage on a raid against Folkestone.

There were other delays, including boiler room problems in some of his battleships, so reluctantly Scheer once again postponed the operation, now intending to launch it on 29 May, in the hope that the weather would be clear enough for his zeppelins. By now his U-boats had been out at sea for nearly two weeks. One had been sunk; another had run into problems and had had to return to base. The bad weather had scattered them, they were running low on fuel and only four of the eighteen U-boats were still in position.

But Scheer was desperate to trap Beatty and therefore decided that the High Seas Fleet would sail north some time around midnight on 30 May.

The British intercepted a signal at 1200 hours on 30 May which was immediately passed on to Jellicoe and Beatty. At this stage the British had no idea what the intended target was and hesitated for a while, finally ordering both men to send their fleets out at 1740.

The German plan was to hug the Danish coast and arrive close to the Skagerrak on the afternoon of 31 May. The intention was to draw Beatty out by launching Hipper against British merchant ships and cruisers. Hipper would then stay close to the Norwegian coast with Scheer in support around 50 miles distant. The Norwegians would tell the British that they had seen Hipper's force and as soon as the Royal Navy was aware that Hipper had ventured as far north as he had, they would not be able to resist the temptation to send Beatty across the North Sea to cut him off and destroy him. Scheer assumed that once Beatty had arrived he could trap him between Hipper's battlecruisers and his own High Seas Fleet.

Unfortunately for the Germans the British had been preparing for their own operation. They already knew that a number of German U-boats had left their bases on 17 May. They also knew that there had been no increase in attacks against merchant ships in the

Atlantic, which could only mean that the Germans were hiding in wait for something in the North Sea. The final clincher was the information that U-boat commanders had been told that German warships would be operating in the North Sea between 30 and 31 May, and had been warned of their presence to avoid accidental torpedoing of German ships.

Initially, as far as the British were concerned, it was clear that the Germans intended to launch an operation somewhere in the North Sea, but it was not obvious what their intentions were or where they would be operating.

As the British ships left their bases only one of the German U-boats, the U-32, managed to launch torpedoes at them, five being fired at HMS *Galatea*, all of which missed. The U-32 compounded its poor performance with an erroneous intelligence support:

> At 5.30, U-32 reported at about 70 miles east of the Firth of Forth, two battleships, two cruisers, and several torpedo boats taking a south-easterly course. At 6.30 a second wireless was received stating that she had intercepted English wireless messages to the effect that two large battleships and a group of destroyers had run out from Scapa Flow. At 6.48 am a third message came from U-66 at about 60 nautical miles east of Kinnairel, eight enemy battleships, light cruisers and torpedo boats had been sighted on a north-easterly course. These reports gave no enlightenment as to the enemy's purpose. But the varied forces of the separate divisions of the fleet, and their diverging courses did not seem to suggest either combined action or an advance on the German bight or any connection with our enterprise, but showed a possibility that our hope of meeting with separate enemy divisions was likely to be fulfilled. We were, therefore, all the more determined to keep to our plan.

Jellicoe had ordered Beatty to rendezvous with him some 90 miles off the entrance to the Skagerrack, at 1400 on 31 May. Meanwhile Jellicoe would make for a position some 70 miles from Beatty's. Beatty was told to search another 20 miles east and turn north. They would then join together and sweep the Horns Reef to the north of Heligoland Bight with the intention of cutting the Germans off from their base.

The bulk of the Grand Fleet began leaving Scapa Flow at 2230 on 30 May. HMS *Iron Duke,* Jellicoe's flagship, led the way, followed by the Fourth then the First Battle Squadrons. At the same time Rear Admiral Horace Hood, in his flagship HMS *Invincible,* steamed out with the Third Battle Cruiser Squadron, supported by the Second Cruiser Squadron. Around them were eleven light cruisers and forty-two destroyers. Around an hour later the Second Battle Squadron of the Grand Fleet set sail from Cromarty Firth. Vice Admiral Jerram on board his flagship, *King George V,* had with him eight Dreadnoughts and eleven destroyers of the First Cruiser Squadron, which were to take almost parallel and then converging courses. Jellicoe and Jerram were due to meet up with one another at around 1200 hours on 31 May.

Almost at the same time as Jerram set sail, Beatty left the Firth of Forth on board HMS *Lion* at the head of the First and Second Battle Cruiser Squadrons. Evan-Thomas, on board HMS *Barham,* followed with the super-Dreadnoughts of the Fifth Battle Squadron. A pair of destroyer flotillas, three light cruiser squadrons and HMS *Engadine,* the seaplane carrier, protected Beatty's force. They would head broadly east-north-east, so that they would be 70 miles to the south of Jellicoe and Jerram at the appointed time.

The British vessels set sail around two hours before the German High Seas Fleet left the Jade Estuary. In addition to the failure of the German submarines, none of Scheer's mines worked either. It would actually take another week for one of these mines, laid by U-75, to claim its first victim, HMS *Hampshire,* off the Orkneys. A significant casualty when the *Hampshire* went down was Field Marshal Lord Kitchener, who was en route to Russia to try and persuade the Russians to continue their war against Germany.

The German High Seas Fleet set sail at 0100 on 31 May with Hipper's flagship, the *Lutzow,* in the lead, one of five battlecruisers belonging to the First Scouting Group. Following Hipper was the Second Scouting Group, comprised of light cruisers and thirty torpedo boats. Almost an hour later Scheer's flagship, the *Friedrich der Grosse,* set off. Accompanying him and leading the way was the Third Battle Squadron, comprised of eight Dreadnoughts, under the command of Rear Admiral Paul Behncke. Following Behncke was Vice Admiral Erhard Schmidt with a further eight vessels. Bringing up the rear was Rear Admiral Franz Mauve's

Second Battle Squadron of six pre-Dreadnoughts, which were the most vulnerable. Mauve had begged Scheer to allow him to come on the sortie, despite the fact that his ships were nicknamed the 'five-minute ships', as this was the amount of time they were expected to survive in a stand-up fight against modern battleships. In all Scheer had 22 battleships, protected by 6 light cruisers and 31 torpedo boats.

Meanwhile, as Beatty neared the rendezvous point at 1358 on 31 May, he signalled for his ships to make a move to the north-east at 1415, in order to bring his battlecruisers close to the position of the Grand Fleet. By this stage, Hipper was around 50 miles to the east of Beatty. In fact, the light cruiser screens were only 16 miles apart.

By pure ill fortune, a vessel belonging to another nation happened to be in the North Sea in precisely the wrong place, at the wrong time. At around 1400 the German light cruiser *Elbing* spotted the Danish tramp steamer, *N J Fjord*; a pair of destroyers was sent to investigate. At 1410 Commodore Edwyn Alexander-Sinclair, on board HMS *Galatea,* the most easterly ship of Beatty's light cruiser screen, also saw the Danish vessel and steamed to investigate, joined by HMS *Phaeton*. As the *N J Fjord* came into closer view they could see a pair of German destroyers alongside, with boats lowered and boarding parties heading to check the Danish ship's documents.

Alexander-Sinclair wrongly identified the two German destroyers as being light cruisers and at 1418 he signalled a report: 'Urgent. Two cruisers probably hostile in sight bearing east-south-east course unknown.'

HMS *Galatea* opened fire on the German vessels at 1428. The two German destroyers fled for protection and the *Elbing* signalled: 'Enemy armoured cruiser in sight bearing west by north.'

The Germans were to score the first hit of the battle:

> At 1432 the first shells were fired at the enemy, and the big battle had started. The distance was 13 to 14 kilometres despite the high speed. We managed to direct the first hit of the battle at the Galatea. The shell hit the bridge through two or three decks. Both English cruisers returned fire but did not hit us.

Both Jellicoe and Beatty received messages from the *Galatea* at around 1420. Jellicoe was still labouring under the misapprehension that the German High Seas Fleet was still in their harbour, but he ordered the Grand Fleet to proceed at full speed. Beatty, meanwhile, ordered his destroyers to form a submarine screen. He then ordered his battlecruisers south-south-east. HMS *Galatea* sent another message at 1430, confirming that they had seen a German light cruiser. Beatty immediately ordered a turn to the south-south-east and increased speed to 22 knots. With him was the First and Second Battle Cruiser Squadron, but the Fifth Battle Squadron was not following him.

HMS *Barham*, the flagship of the Fifth Battle Squadron, had not seen the signal, trying as she was to read flag signals at a distance of 5 miles. The squadron therefore assumed that the signal was just an order to continue their zigzagging pattern that they had been following and steamed on towards the north-west.

Rear Admiral Hugh Evan-Thomas commanded the Fifth Battle Squadron. By continuing on the course and not following Beatty he had made a dreadful mistake. Originally he had been 5 miles from Beatty, sufficiently close to lend almost immediate support. But by now he was 10 miles away and heading in the opposite direction. HMS *Galatea* made another report at 1435: 'Urgent. Have sighted large amount of smoke as though from a fleet bearing east-north-east.'

Hipper had responded to the *Elbing's* signal, which he had received at 1427, and assumed from the message that he was facing a large number of battleships. He turned west-south-west but quickly realized that he was not facing such a formidable foe, only a handful of British light cruisers. Consequently, at 1510, he headed north-west in pursuit of them.

Meanwhile the British battlecruisers were steaming towards the Germans, with the Fifth Battle Squadron eager to catch up with them, having now rectified the misunderstanding with regard to signals. At 1445 HMS *Engadine* was ordered by Beatty to launch an aircraft to confirm the reports received from HMS *Galatea*. This was to become the first air reconnaissance carried out at sea during a battle. Flight Lieutenant Frederick Rutland of the Royal Naval Air Service who flew it, wrote:

After about ten minutes sighted the enemy. Clouds were at 1,000 to 1,200ft, with patches at 900ft. This necessitated flying

1. Admiral Sir John Jellicoe OM GCB, Commander-in-Chief of the Grand Fleet.

2. Vice Admiral Sir David Beatty GCB, Commander-in-Chief of the British Battlecruiser Fleet.

3. Rear Admiral The Hon. Horace Hood, who was lost with his flagship, the *Invisible*, at the Battle of Jutland.

4. Admiral Sir Cecil Burney KCB GCMG, Second-in-Command of the British Grand Fleet.

5. Vice Admiral Sir Charles Edward Madden KCB KCMG CVO, Chief of Staff to the Commander-in-Chief of the Grand Fleet.

6. Rear Admiral Sir Robert Arbuthnot KCB was lost with his flagship HMS *Defence*.

7. Rear Admiral Arthur Cavenagh Leveson CB.

8. Rear Admiral William Edmund Goodenough CB MVO.

9. Vice Admiral Sir F.C. Doveton Sturdee KCB KCMG CVO.

10. Vice Admiral Sir T.H. Martyn Jerram KCB KCMG.

11. Rear Admiral Osmond de Beauvoir Brock CB CMG.

12. Rear Admiral Francis William Kennedy CB.

13. Rear Admiral Sir William Pakenham KCB MVO, commander of the Second Battlecruiser Squadron.

14. Rear Admiral Herbert Leopold Heath CB MVO.

15. Rear Admiral Ernest Frederic Augustus Gaunt CB CMG.

16. Rear Admiral Alexander Ludovic Duff CB.

17. The Kaiser at Wilhemshaven on 5 June 1916.

18. Admiral von Scheer, Commander-in-Chief of the German High Seas Fleet.

19. Vice Admiral von Hipper, Commander of the German Scouting Squadron.

20. Winston Churchill, First Lord of the Admiralty, inspecting naval personnel.

21. Chief Stokers on board HMS *Queen Mary*. Second left is Chief Petty Officer Sparrow, who at the time of the battle was six months short of 32 years service. He held long service, good conduct and South African medals.

22. Morning prayers on board HMS *Shark*. The ship, a destroyer, sank two German destroyers and was then sunk herself by torpedoes.

23. Medal winners. *Left to right*: Chief sick-berth steward A.E. Jones CGM; Officers' Cook (First-Class) H.F. Carter DSM; Chief Petty Officer C. Hucklesby, Medaille Militaire; Leading Signalman W.I. Barrow DSM.

24. HMS *Dreadnought* in dry dock.

25. HMS *King George*, flagship of Vice Admiral Sir Thomas Jerram, commander of the Second Battle Squadron.

26. HMS *Iron Duke*, Jellicoe's flagship.

27. HMS *Lion*, Beatty's flagship.

28. HMS *Monarch*.

29. HMS *Emperor of India* and HMS *Agincourt*.

30. HMS *Orion*, flag-ship of Rear Admiral Leveson, second in command of the Second Battle Squadron.

31. HMS *Benbow* and HMS *Marlborough* in the North Sea.

32. HMS *Neptune*, a Dreadnought of the Fifth Division of the First Battlecruiser Squadron.

33. HMS *Defence*, flagship of Rear Admiral Sir Robert Arbuthnot, commander of the First Cruiser Squadron (sunk).

34. HMS *Colossus*.

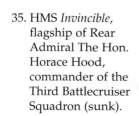

35. HMS *Invincible*, flagship of Rear Admiral The Hon. Horace Hood, commander of the Third Battlecruiser Squadron (sunk).

36. HMS *Birkenhead* of the Third Light Cruiser Squadron.

37. HMS *Indefatigible*, battlecruiser (sunk).

38. HMS *Shannon*, an armoured cruiser of the Second Cruiser Squadron.

39. HMS *Princess Royal*, flagship of Rear Admiral Brock, second in command of the First Battlecruiser Squadron.

40. HMS *Birmingham*, a light cruiser of the Second Light Cruiser Squadron.

41. HMS *Shark*, a destroyer of the Fourth Flotilla (sunk).

42. HMS *New Zealand*, flagship of Rear Admiral Pakenham, commander of the Second Battlecruiser Squadron.

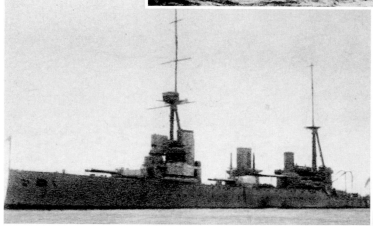

43. HMS *Southampton*.

44. A German torpedo boat at the Battle of Jutland, as depicted in a German newspaper.

45. German U-boat, believed to be the U-35, in Cartegena, June 1916.

46. HMS *Warspite* engaging several German ships at Jutland. She sank or disabled a number of them and despite damage to her steering gear, returned safely home.

47. Scene depicting Beatty's battlecruisers in action at 1548 on 31 May 1916. The battlecruisers are engaging Hipper's squadron.

48. A German Dreadnought cornered by British destroyers. This Dreadnought was sunk with torpedoes.

49. The *Warrior* under heavy fire from the German fleet. She was heavily damaged and attempts to tow her back to port failed

50. Boy, (First-Class) John Travers Cornwell VC, on board HMS *Chester*.

51. A scene on the night of 31 May/1 June. A German light cruiser burns, but she continued to fight until the British fired a torpedo into her.

very low. On sighting the enemy it was very hard to tell what they were, and so I had to close within a mile and a half at a height of 1,000ft. They then opened fire on me with anti-aircraft and other guns, my height enabling them to use their anti-torpedo armament. When sighted they were steering a northerly course. I flew through several of the columns of smoke caused through bursting shrapnel.

Suddenly the Germans changed course, as Rutland later reported:

When the observer had counted and got the disposition of the enemy and was making his w/t report, I steered to about three miles, keeping the enemy well in sight. While the observer was sending one message, the enemy turned 16 points. I drew his attention to this and he forthwith transmitted it. The enemy then ceased firing at me. I kept on a bearing on the boughs, about three miles distant from the enemy, and as the weather cleared a little I observed the disposition of our fleet, and judged by the course of our battlecruisers that our w/t had got through.

Hipper, on board the *Lutzow,* spotted the advancing British battle-cruisers before they spotted him. He continued north but slowed down to 23 knots. At 1525 HMS *New Zealand* and HMS *Princess Royal* reported that they had spotted German battlecruisers. HMS *Lion* saw them five minutes later.

Hipper had already recalled his light cruisers which were pursuing HMS *Galatea.* At 1533 Hipper ordered that his ships turn 16 points to starboard, effectively reversing his course, the original plan that would draw Beatty's six battlecruisers into the arms of Scheer. It now seemed inevitable, with Beatty steaming at full speed toward Hipper, who was fleeing to the south-east, that the long-awaited opportunity to inflict serious damage on the British fleet was possible.

If Jellicoe could fulfil his ambition of ensnaring the Germans in a fruitless pursuit of Beatty, he could bring his Grand Fleet to bear and deal with the German surface fleet once and for all. If the two fleets were taken together it was clear that Scheer was outnumbered. Jellicoe had 24 battleships and Scheer 22, of which only 16 were Dreadnoughts. Jellicoe's strength in battleships outnumbered him nine to five. Jellicoe had eight armoured cruisers and twenty-six light cruisers, even though his armoured cruisers were obsolete and slow. But Scheer could only muster eleven. The Germans had sixty-one torpedo boats, smaller and more lightly armed than the Grand Fleet's seventy-three destroyers.

In total Jellicoe could muster 151 warships compared to Scheer's 99. There has been much talk about the comparative strength in terms of armament on board the vessels. A cursory glance at the larger guns on board these ships shows that the British had 264 and the Germans had 200, however there was a huge difference in terms of destructive power between the 15in and 13.5in guns carried by the British battleships and the 12in or 11in guns carried by the German equivalents. In terms of delivering a broadside, the British had a theoretical total of 286,000lb against the German's total of 144,000lb.

The comparison between Beatty and Hipper is even more marked. Hipper had five battlecruisers, with forty-four large guns, capable of delivering a broadside of 33,000lb. Beatty had six battlecruisers plus four battleships, with eighty large guns and a combined broadside of 118,000lb. So whilst Jellicoe had a theoretical advantage of two to one in terms of broadside ability, Beatty had an even greater advantage of four to one.

Chapter Four

Running South Then North

At 1530 on 31 May Beatty headed at full speed on an easterly course, making straight for Hipper. Hipper meanwhile was heading south-east, but the distance between the two fleets was shortening and in less than fifteen minutes both fleets were within range of one another.

The Germans had a slight advantage inasmuch as they were firing to the west and the light breeze was blowing funnel smoke and gun smoke in front of Beatty's ships.

Beatty was making his own changes to counter this, ordering Rear Admiral William Pakenham, heading the Second Battle Cruiser Squadron in his flagship, HMS *New Zealand,* to take up position in line behind his own First Battle Cruiser Squadron. He also ordered Rear Admiral Evan-Thomas to head east and increase the speed of the Fifth Battle Squadron to 25 knots. There was still a gap between Evan-Thomas's battleships and Beatty's battlecruisers. The Ninth Flotilla took up positions ahead of HMS *Lion* and the Thirteenth Flotilla was arrayed to starboard. Beatty also made sure that Jellicoe was made aware of the situation.

Hipper's greatest fear in facing the British battlecruisers was the fact that his guns were outranged by the British and they could stand off at about 24,000 yards, out of Hipper's range, and blow him to pieces. Inexplicably, however, Beatty did not take advantage of his range advantage and came to within 17,000 yards. The reason for him doing so and not opening fire at 24,000 yards was that his rangefinders were seriously overestimating the range. Beatty's ships were moving at full speed, causing vibrations, which meant that the men operating the Barr and Stroud rangefinders could not estimate the range properly as they needed a pair of images to coincide to make the estimate.

The German rangefinders, on the other hand, were quicker to operate and at around 1548 Hipper gave the order to open fire. The range by now had dropped to 16,400 yards. According to Commander Georg von Hase, on board SMS *Derfflinger*:

> Then began an ear-splitting, stupefying din. Including the secondary armament we were firing on average one mighty salvo every seven seconds. Dense masses of smoke accumulated around the muzzles of the guns, growing into clouds as high as houses, which stood for seconds like an impenetrable wall and were then driven by the wind over the ship. We often could see nothing of the enemy for seconds at a time.

Hipper ordered the *Lützow* to open fire on HMS *Lion*, while *Derfflinger* concentrated on HMS *Princess Royal*, the *Seydlitz* focussed on HMS *Queen Mary*, the *Moltke* fired at HMS *Tiger* and the *Von der Tann* opened up on HMS *Indefatigable*. HMS *New Zealand* was left without an opponent. In return, HMS *Lion* and HMS *Princess Royal* fired at the *Lützow*, HMS *Queen Mary* at the *Derfflinger*, HMS *Tiger* at the *Seydlitz*, HMS *New Zealand* at the *Moltke* and HMS *Indefatigable* at the *Von der Tann*.

It was a confusing engagement: shots were firing left and right, with different-sized splashes landing either beyond or in front of the enemy ships. Both Beatty and Hipper quickly realized that they had got too close to one another. Beatty swung his ships to starboard and Hipper to port, still maintaining virtually parallel courses, the distance opening up to around 1,500 yards.

Jellicoe meanwhile had been informed about the contact. He was 53 miles away and eager to get involved so had increased speed to 20 knots. Scheer, on the other hand, was 46 miles away and making for the area of the engagement at a speed of 16 knots. The two main fleets were still two hours away from one another, with neither of them knowing for sure that the other fleet was even in the North Sea.

Theoretically Beatty, with an extra battleship, had the advantage, but there was confusion with the signals. HMS *Queen Mary* did not fire at the *Derfflinger* as she was ordered to do, but had opened fire on the *Seydlitz*; nearly half an hour passed before HMS *Queen Mary* realized her mistake and started firing at the *Derfflinger*. At the same time HMS *Tiger* was actually firing at the *Moltke* instead of the *Seydlitz*, which meant that both she and HMS *New Zealand* were firing at the *Moltke*.

The German firing turned out to be more effective. In the first five minutes the *Moltke* hit HMS *Tiger* twice, while with her fifth salvo the *Lützow* hit HMS *Lion* twice. In all, in the first twelve minutes of the engagement, every single on of Beatty's ships was hit, with the exception of HMS *New Zealand*. The Germans had scored fifteen hits against the British, who had only scored four. HMS *Lion* had hit the *Lützow* twice and HMS *Queen Mary* had hit the *Seydlitz* twice.

At around 1600 a 12in shell from the *Lützow* hit HMS *Lion*'s Q turret, tearing off the roof and the front of the turret, and killing or maiming most of the gun crew:

> The enemy's shooting at the Lion became extremely accurate and She sheered a little to starboard, the effect as to fall of shot being very noticeable. Just as she came back again she was very heavily hit and I saw a large plate, which I judged to be the top of a turret, blown into the air. It appeared to rise very slowly, turning round and round, and looking very much like an aeroplane. I should say it rose some 400 or 500 feet and looking at it through glasses I could distinctly see the holes in it for the bolts. My attention was drawn from this by a sheet of flame from her second funnel, which shot up about 60 feet and soon died down, but did not immediately disappear. It seemed to have no affect on the ship, except that her mid-ship turret seemed out of action. One gun was about horizontal and the other at a considerable elevation.

This was the view of the hit on HMS *Lion* as seen by Commander Alan MacKenzie-Grieve on board HMS *Birmingham* of the Second Light Cruiser Squadron.

A mortally wounded Major Francis Harvey of the Royal Marines dragged himself to the voice pipe, despite the fact that he had lost both of his legs. He passed an order to close the doors to the magazines and flood them for fear that the flames would spread. Harvey was later awarded a posthumous Victoria Cross for his action, which almost certainly saved the ship. HMS *Lion* staggered out of the line, badly damaged, but there was worse to come.

Commander Gunther Paschen, on board the *Lützow,* described the moments directly after HMS *Lion* reeled away from the engagement:

> Seventeen minutes after fire was opened Lion turned sharply away, until I could see her from aft and Princess Royal pushed in front. I counted six hits in thirty-one salvos. We had been hit three times; one of these exploded between A and B turrets and cleared out the forward action dressing station. All are dead there. Hit number three seems to have hit the belt somewhere, a heavy shot but nothing put out of action.

Just five minutes later, having nearly dealt a crippling blow to HMS *Lion,* the super-Dreadnoughts of the Fifth Battle Squadron had virtually reached maximum range to engage the German light cruisers. HMS *Warspite* opened fire at long range, about 21,000 yards from their target. The shot fell short just as HMS *Barham* and HMS *Valiant* opened fire, adding to the smoke and the confusion.

Lieutenant Heinrich Bassenge, on board the *Elbing,* described the horror of his small vessel being engaged by the British super-Dreadnought monoliths:

> Out of the blue came a heavy barrage of fire from the south-west. We were suddenly surrounded by high fountains of water. Out of the distance four big ships appeared, which Boedicker [Rear Admiral Friedrich] thought to be of the Second British Battle Squadron but very soon we could see a second mast and it was clear that it belonged to the very modern battleships of the Fifth Battle Squadron of the Queen Elizabeth Class. The distance was 17km. We could just see the enemy on the horizon. With our 15cm guns we could only manage about 13-14km and under these circumstances we could hardly fight back. We were not equipped for anything like this. We turned quickly, glad to get out of it.

The Germans believed that they had put Beatty's flagship, HMS *Lion*, out of action, but she was still steaming at full speed and half a dozen of her heavy guns were still firing. As the German light cruisers and a destroyer began to retreat, the British Fifth Battle Squadron moved in.

HMS *Indefatigable* and the *Von der Tann* were firing salvos at one another. Shortly after 1400 hours one from the *Von der Tann* penetrated the 1in deck armour of the British ship and blew up a magazine. As a second salvo of shots from the German ship smashed into HMS *Indefatigable*, there was a huge explosion. Eyewitnesses saw funnels and turrets flying through the air and flames and smoke up to 1,500ft. The ship keeled over and disappeared underwater. Of the 1,019 men on board just two survived, both of them spotters who had been thrown clear of the stricken ship by blast. The men were later picked up by a German torpedo boat.

The Germans were overjoyed but the British reaction was mixed. Lieutenant Chalmers, on HMS *Lion*'s bridge wrote: 'I gazed at this in amazement, and at the same time tumbled to the fact that there were only five battlecruisers in our line. I glanced quickly towards the enemy. How many of them were still afloat? Still five.'

Flag Captain Alfred Chatfield, also on board HMS *Lion*, wrote:

The Lion was hit early several times, but we seemed also to be hitting the Lutzow and were going along joyfully, when, at 4.00pm, the Yeoman of Signal saw the rear ship, the Indefatigable blow up. A vast column of smoke rose to the sky. This seemed at the moment just a disappointment. The Indefatigable was a smaller and more weakly protected ship than those of the First Division and was not a really serious tactical loss.

Both the Germans and the British now had five ships firing at one another. The Fifth Battle Squadron was still too far away, desperately trying to catch up with Beatty. Despite the fact that they were pitching in with shots at the light cruisers, they were not really adding very much to the main engagement.

By 1608 the Fifth Battle Squadron was in range of the German battlecruisers and Evan-Thomas could order his vessels to open fire on the rear ships in the German battle line. HMS *Barham* and HMS

Valiant concentrated in on the *Moltke*, while seconds later HMS *Warspite* and HMS *Malaya* opened fire on the *Von der Tann*. Barely a minute later the *Von der Tann* was hit in the stern and within a few minutes the *Moltke* was also hit, smashing one of her turrets. The Fifth Battle Squadron was now pitching in and scoring significant hits that Beatty's ships had so far failed to achieve. The *Von der Tann* had taken four hits from 15in shells and upwards of 600 tons of sea water was flooding into her.

The Germans were now seriously outnumbered. As the vessels of the Fifth Battle Squadron closed, the *Seydlitz* came into range and was almost immediately hit just below the waterline, although not seriously damaged.

Beatty realized that he should now concentrate his fire on the forward German ships, leaving the Fifth Battle Squadron to take care of the ones in the rear. Ordering the destroyers of the Thirteenth Flotilla to launch an attack on the German ships, he signalled to his own battlecruisers to make a turn to the east, to close with the German ships. Just eight minutes later, at 1617, Hipper made a turn to the west, which meant that the two lines of ships were on a converging course.

Beatty himself had had to order HMS *Lion* out of the line to deal with the turret fire, which had meant that both the *Seydlitz* and the *Derfflinger* were targeting HMS *Queen Mary*. The *Derfflinger* had not intended to be firing at the *Queen Mary* but poor visibility caused her to switch fire from HMS *Princess Royal*, with a spotter trying to see above the smoke, at around 1617.

So far HMS *Queen Mary* had acquitted herself extremely well. She was firing all eight of her big guns and had so far hit the *Seydlitz* four times, but she was now under fire from two German ships. At around 1621 her Q turret was hit and then she was hit again, causing a massive explosion that effectively broke the ship in half, lifting the bow section clean out of the water. In seconds all that was visible was the stern, with repeated explosions tearing parts of the ship to pieces. Of HMS *Queen Mary*'s crew of 1,286 men, only twenty survived. One of the survivors was Petty Officer Ernest Francis:

> I struck away from the ship as hard as I could and I must have covered nearly fifty yards when there was a big smash. Stopping and looking round the air seemed to be full of

fragments and flying pieces, a large piece seemed to be right above my head and acting on an impulse I dipped under to avoid being struck and stayed under as long as I could and then came to the top again. Coming behind me I heard a rush of water, which looked very much like a surf breaking on a beach and I realised it was the suction or backwash from the ship which had just gone. I hardly had time to fill my lungs with air when it was on me. I felt it was no use struggling against it, so I let myself go for a moment or two, then I struck out, but I felt it was a losing game and remarked to myself mentally 'what's the use of you struggling – you're done!' and actually eased my efforts to reach the top, when a small voice seemed to say 'dig out!' I started afresh and something bumped against me. I grasped it and afterwards found it was a large hammock; it undoubtedly pulled me to the top, more dead than alive. I rested on it, but I felt I was getting very weak and roused myself sufficiently to look around for something more substantial to support me. Floating right in front of me was what I believed to be the centre bulk of our pattern four target. I managed to push myself on the hammock close to the timber and grasped a piece of rope hanging over the side. My next difficulty was to get on top and I was beginning to give up hope when the swell lifted me nearly on top and with a small amount of exertion I kept on. I managed to reeve my arms through a strop and I must have become unconscious.

Destroyers HMS *Petard* and HMS *Laurel* hunted for survivors, managing to pick up the majority of them, but two men were later taken prisoner by a German torpedo boat. In the last dying moments of HMS *Queen Mary*, HMS *Tiger* and HMS *New Zealand* came perilously close to running into her. Both ships passed through dense, black smoke, causing great consternation to the crews who thought their own ships were on fire.

Flag Captain Alfred Chatfield, on board HMS *Lion,* made a comment that has immortalized him in Britain's naval history:

I was standing beside Sir David Beatty and we both turned round in time to see the unpleasant spectacle. The thought of my friends in her flashed through my mind; I thought also how lucky we had evidently been in the Lion. Beatty turned to me and said, 'There seems to be something wrong with our bloody ships today!' A remark which needed neither comment nor answer. There was something wrong.

In the space of just forty-five minutes Beatty's flagship had been severely damaged and two of his vessels had been sunk. At this stage the Battle of Jutland was definitely being won by Hipper.

Hipper now ordered the Ninth Torpedo Flotilla, consisting of nine vessels and led by the *Regensburg,* to launch an assault on the British ships, in order to give himself time to extricate his own from the fight. Suddenly, led by HMS *Champion*, the destroyers cut across HMS *Lion* and beat off the German torpedo boat attack, sinking the V-27 and the V-29.

Now it was the turn of the British to launch an attack on the enemy. The British destroyers, led by HMS *Nestor,* fired a number of torpedoes – up to twenty – but only one, fired by HMS *Petard,* scored a hit, hitting the *Seydlitz* and smashing a huge hole in her side. HMS *Nomad* and HMS *Nestor* now came under fire from the German battlecruiser's secondary armament, firing at them at a range of only 3,000 yards. The two destroyers were crippled and would be finished off later on by Scheer's battlecruisers.

Commander Bingham, on *HMS Nestor,* described the moments when his ship was hit:

Two boilers were put out of action by direct hits. From the bridge I saw at once that something of the kind had happened. A huge cloud of steam was rising from the boiler room, completely enshrouding the whole ship and it was painfully apparent that our speed was dropping every second. Although crippled, we had guns that were still intact, and a hostile destroyer, swooping down on what she thought an easy prey, was greeted with volleys of salvos from our invaluable semi-automatic guns. After such a warm reception, the German destroyer sheered off post haste.

Meanwhile, the Second Light Cruiser Squadron was some 2½ miles ahead of HMS *Lion*. At 1630 Commodore William Goodenough, on board HMS *Southampton,* made a terrifying discovery: 'We saw ahead of us, first smoke, then masts, then ships. "Look sir," said Arthur Peters, "this is the day of a light cruiser's lifetime. The whole of the High Seas Fleet is before you!" It was: 16 battleships with destroyers disposed around them on each bow. That was reported.'

With great courage Goodenough remained on course for a further five minutes to ensure that he could inform Beatty and Jellicoe of the exact numbers of the German fleet. His lookouts reported twenty-two battleships with a destroyer screen, in battle formation. By now it was approaching 1645 and the German High Seas Fleet was just 14,000 yards ahead of him: 'We hung on for a few minutes to make sure before confirming the message. My Commander, efficient and cool, said, "If you're going to make that signal, you'd better make it now, sir. You may never make another." Other remarks, some acid, some ribald, passed.'

In the end Goodenough sent his signal at 1648: 'Urgent. Priority. Course of the enemy's battle fleet North Single Line ahead. Composition of van Kaiser class. Bearing of centre east. Destroyers on both wings and ahead. Enemy's battle cruisers joining battle fleet from northwards.'

Goodenough's vessels were approaching the Germans head on, which is why the German Third Battle Squadron, under Rear Admiral Behncke did not open fire – they were easily in range and could have pummelled the British ships with fifty heavy guns had they been approaching from an oblique angle. Goodenough ordered his ships to turn about. As the four cruisers turned, the leading German ships opened fire. HMS *Southampton,* HMS *Birmingham,* HMS *Nottingham* and HMS *Dublin* zigzagged away at 25 knots. The only hit that the Germans achieved was a glancing shot that struck the stern of HMS *Southampton.* Goodenough, meanwhile, continued to signal reports as he pulled away out of range of the German ships.

Meanwhile, the four super-Dreadnoughts of the Fifth Battle Squadron continued to engage Hipper's battlecruisers until around 1650. By 1648 they had reached the point where they were about to pass Beatty's battlecruisers. Beatty ordered Evan-Thomas to alter his course to starboard but the signal was confusing as it would have been normal practice for the ships to turn together, rather than in succession. As it was, the confusion meant that the Fifth Battle Squadron continued south for up to another five minutes. At 1654 Beatty realized that Evan-Thomas had not understood his signal; it was only then that they began to turn.

Beatty had to beat a hasty retreat now that Scheer's High Seas Fleet had arrived – he needed to get out of range without losing any more vessels and draw the German fleet towards Jellicoe. He had an advantage in terms of speed of up to 10 knots and also knew that Hipper would not risk going too far ahead of Scheer.

As Lieutenant Patrick Brind, on board HMS *Malaya,* recalled:

> I must confess to a feeling of relief when I realised we were to turn round, though not at it being done in succession. When it was the turn of the Malaya to turn, the turning point was a very hot corner, as of course the enemy had concentrated on that point. The shells were pouring at a very rapid rate and it is doubtful if we, the last ship in the line, could get through without at least a very severe hammering. However, the captain decided that point by turning the ship early. When we had turned, or rather as I was turning my turret to the starboard side, I saw our battle cruisers who were proceeding northerly at full speed, were already 8,000 yards ahead of us, engaging the German battle cruisers. Then I realised that the four of us alone – Barham, Warspite, Valiant and Malaya – would have to entertain the High Seas Fleet.

At 1643 Beatty had also ordered his destroyers to fall back. It was a confused situation and HMS *Moorsom*, commanded by Lieutenant Commander John Hodgson, found herself in a position to launch an attack against the oncoming High Seas Fleet. At a range of 6,000 yards, Hodgson turned his ship to port and fired a pair of torpedoes and, in the words of Sub Lieutenant Hilary Owen, 'and then we legged it for the safety of our own line'.

Although hit and having taken casualties, HMS *Moorsom* still managed to make 33 knots. When she tried to fire her two remaining torpedoes, one simply sank due to the damage to one of the torpedo tubes.

HMS *Nestor* and HMS *Nomad* had been left to their own devices having been damaged earlier. Lieutenant Commander Paul Whitfield, on board HMS *Nomad*, recalled:

> The High Seas Fleet spotted us, and started battle practice at us with 6in or bigger guns. Salvo after salvo shook us and wounded a few. The ship sinking fast, I gave the order to abandon her and pull clear. About three minutes after, she went down vertically by the stern. It was grand practice for them, but murder for us, and so exasperating that we could not hit back.

HMS *Nestor* was to be next, as recalled by Commander Barry Bingham:

> Very soon we were enveloped in a deluge of shell fire. Any reply from our own guns was absolutely out of the question at a range beyond the possibilities of our light shells; to have answered any one of our numerous assailants would have been as effective as the use of a peashooter against a wall of steel. Just about this time we fired our last torpedo at the High Seas Fleet and it was seen to run well. It was a matter of two or three minutes only before the Nestor, enwrapped in a cloud of smoke and spray, the centre of a whirlwind of shrieking shells, received not a few heavy and vital hits and the ship began to slowly settle by the stern and then to take up a heavy list to starboard.

HMS *Nestor* finally sank at around 1730. Many of the survivors were in the water for some hours, but German destroyers picked some of them up shortly after dark. Commander Bingham was one of the survivors and was later awarded the Victoria Cross.

There were several other British survivors bobbing around in the water, many of whom would have to wait hours before they were picked up. HMS *Petard*, returning from an attack on the German battlecruisers, spotted oil in the water and pulled one man aboard. He was the captain of the after turret of HMS *Queen Mary*. Other men were picked up, including Petty Officer Ernest Francis. The next thing Francis remembers was waking up on a leather settee on board HMS *Petard*.

Thus ended the first phase of the Battle of Jutland, which was later dubbed 'the run to the south'. Beatty's ships had been outgunned and outmanoeuvred by Hipper's battlecruisers. Had it not been for the timely arrival of the Fifth Battle Squadron, his losses may well have been all the more severe. Beatty had begun with six battlecruisers against Hipper's five, but had ended up with only four.

The next phase of the battle is commonly known as 'the run to the north'. In effect it actually covers only a very short period of time – from the moment that Beatty's battlecruisers made their 180-degree turn and began leading Hipper and Scheer into the clutches of Jellicoe's Grand Fleet.

Scheer desperately wanted to crush what remained of Beatty's battlecruiser fleet – he could see them and he wanted a share of the prize that Hipper already had his hands around. If he could destroy Beatty's ships without suffering significant losses himself, the battle would be won, even before Jellicoe arrived on the scene.

As for Beatty, he was concerned not only with drawing Hipper and Scheer on to Jellicoe, but also to survive the encounter with as many of his ships intact as possible. He knew full well that if any of them were seriously hit the Germans would catch up with them and the vessels would be lost.

There was now a strange procession. Hipper and his battlecruisers were pursuing Beatty's battlecruisers; they were around 19,000 yards apart and on a converging course. Evan-Thomas's ships were about 7,000 yards behind Beatty and approximately level with Hipper's ships which were about 17,500 yards away. He was still 21,000 yards ahead of the *Friedrich der Grosse*, Scheer's flagship. The closest ships of the High Seas Fleet were Behncke's, which were only around 19,000 yards short of HMS *Malaya*.

Beatty began to open fire on Hipper's battlecruisers, but the Germans fired back, the *Seydlitz* hitting HMS *Tiger* and the *Lutzow* hitting HMS *Lion* three times. Beatty increased speed to 26 knots, aiming to get ahead of Hipper and force him to the east. This would also serve the purpose of shielding Jellicoe's Grand Fleet and he hoped that if he delayed the German sighting of Jellicoe, there would be no way that the High Seas Fleet could avoid a full-scale action with the Grand Fleet.

At around 1710 Beatty was out of Hipper's range. Hipper was concerned that he was too far ahead of Scheer and, in any case, some of his ships were having problems maintaining speed which meant that he would have to face Evan-Thomas's battleships alone.

But Evan-Thomas had to face both Hipper and Scheer alone, with both Hipper's battlecruisers and up to eight of Behncke's battleships within range. He therefore ordered HMS *Barham* and HMS *Valiant* to fire at Hipper's ships, whilst HMS *Warspite* and HMS *Malaya* tried to engage Scheer's leading ships. By now Evan-Thomas was between Beatty's battlecruisers and the German High Seas Fleet, which was coming on, at maximum speed, on a course north-north-west, their modern Dreadnoughts outpacing some of the slower vessels.

At 1730 Hipper turned north-north-west and reduced his speed just at the point when Evan-Thomas's ships zeroed in on them. HMS *Barham* and HMS *Valiant,* firing at ranges of between 16,000 and 18,000 yards, hit three of Hipper's ships. The *Lützow* was hit four times, the *Seydlitz* six times and the *Derfflinger* three times. Meanwhile HMS *Warspite* and HMS *Malaya* managed to hit the *König,* the *Grosser Kurfurst* and the *Markgraf.* In return, the leading ships of Scheer's fleet failed to hit either of the British vessels, although their fire was getting closer and the *Seydlitz* managed to hit HMS *Warspite* twice. Suddenly, between 1720 and 1735, HMS *Malaya* was hit around seven times by four different battleships.

Meanwhile, Beatty had succeeded in getting ahead of Hipper. At 1741 he swung to the east and opened up at a range of 16,000 yards. HMS *Princess Royal* nearly crippled the *Lützow* and Hipper was forced to turn east.

Scheer's battleships were falling behind Evan-Thomas's, which allowed Evan-Thomas to concentrate on Hipper, and he hit the *Lützow, Derfflinger* and the *Seydlitz.* The only ship of Hipper's five that now remained in full fighting condition was the *Moltke.* The *Von der Tann* had jammed turrets as HMS *Tiger* had knocked out its large guns earlier, but she continued to fire its secondary armament at the battleships, although to no avail.

Jellicoe was now 23 miles away, his six divisions stretching out over 5 miles, but for Hipper there was to be an even more dangerous and immediate problem. His ships had been in action now for two hours and approaching him from the north-east, at a range of about 21,000 yards, was Admiral Horace Hood's Third Battle Cruiser Squadron. Jellicoe had sent Hood to support Beatty and closing on Hipper were HMS *Invincible,* HMS *Inflexible* and HMS *Indomitable*; they were screened by four destroyers with the light cruiser HMS *Chester* around 9,000 yards to their starboard and HMS *Canterbury* the same distance off their port bow.

When HMS *Canterbury* spotted the muzzle flashes to the south-west, Hood was informed and his Third Battle Cruiser Squadron began to close, with HMS *Chester* racing off to find out more information. Visibility to the west was not good, so HMS *Chester* could only pick out a light cruiser and a destroyer; moments later three more light cruisers could be seen. These could easily have been part of Beatty's screen, but at 1738 it became clear that they were Germans, as four of the light cruisers belonging to Hipper's Second Scouting Group opened up on HMS *Chester,* at a range of 7,000 yards.

In the space of the next fifteen minutes the *Frankfurt, Elbing, Pillau* and *Wiesbaden* hit HMS *Chester* seventeen times. Seventy-eight of the 450 men on board her were either killed or wounded; there were holes in her side and four of her guns had been knocked out. She turned about, pursued by light cruisers and destroyers. Hood headed for the gun flashes, saw HMS *Chester* being closely pursued and swung to the north-west.

At 1755 Hood opened fire on the pursuing Germans at a range of 10,000 yards. Boedicker, commanding the Second Scouting Group, ordered his vessels to turn away, but as he did so HMS *Indomitable* and HMS *Invincible* repeatedly struck the *Wiesbaden* with 12in shells. *Wiesbaden* lay dead in the water, both of her engines wrecked. HMS *Inflexible* hit the *Pillau*, knocking out six of her ten boilers before she struggled away, still maintaining 24 knots. Boedicker's force was in imminent danger of being overwhelmed so he ordered his torpedo boats to attack, with the light cruiser *Regensburg* leading, firing twelve torpedoes. Although the torpedoes failed to hit any of Hood's ships, he was forced to order them to turn away. Under the cover of smoke the *Elbing, Pillau* and *Frankfurt* slipped away.

When Boedicker signalled that several battleships had attacked him, Hipper responded by ordering his ships to turn south and make for Scheer's High Seas Fleet. Several of Scheer's battleships had fallen well to the rear and Hipper now took up a position just in front of the High Seas Fleet.

Hood had scattered the enemy and as he steamed to reinforce Beatty, Boedicker launched a second wave of torpedo boats, which were countered by Hood's own destroyers. Commander Loftus Jones, on board HMS *Shark*, led the counter-attack and despite being outnumbered and outgunned, he forced the Germans away. With several German ships firing on *HMS Shark* her engines were disabled and Loftus Jones was mortally wounded.

HMS *Acasta* came alongside and her captain, Lieutenant Commander Barron, signalled to ask Loftus Jones whether he could be of any assistance, to which Loftus Jones simply replied: 'No. Tell him to look after himself.' HMS *Shark* was torpedoed by the S-54 and Loftus Jones's body was later found on the Swedish coastline. He was buried in a village churchyard and was later awarded a posthumous Victoria Cross.

Another Victoria Cross was posthumously awarded for outstanding bravery during this part of the battle, the recipient being Boy Seaman First Class John Cornwell of HMS *Chester*. He was the only survivor of his gun crew and remained at his post, mortally wounded, despite the fact that he was only sixteen years old.

The battle was now slowly swinging in favour of the British. An early ambush had been sprung, both when the Fifth Battle Squadron had arrived and also when Hood had engaged Hipper's Scouting Force. Evan-Thomas's ships had scored some notable hits and by this stage Hipper's battlecruisers had been hit thirteen times by HMS *Barham* and HMS *Valiant*. HMS *Warspite* and HMS *Malaya* meanwhile had struck the leading battleships of Scheer's High Seas Fleet with eighteen 15in shells. In exchange, Beatty's squadron had received six hits, Evan-Thomas had suffered five, while HMS *Malaya* had been hit seven times by Behncke's Third Battle Squadron.

Comparatively speaking, Hipper's battlecruisers were in a far worse state than the ships that remained under Beatty's command. All five of Hipper's ships had been holed, all of them were taking in water, but they still maintained their speed and continued to be active in the battle. Of Beatty's ships, HMS *New Zealand* was virtually undamaged, while HMS *Lion,* HMS *Princess Royal* and HMS *Tiger* all had turrets out of action.

As this phase of the battle ended at around 1800, neither Jellicoe nor Scheer could yet see one another. Both men were suffering from lack of information from their scouts, or at best were receiving confused information. At one point Jellicoe had said: 'I wish someone would tell me who is firing and what they are firing at.'

Suddenly HMS *Marlborough*, far to the west of Jellicoe's Grand Fleet, saw Beatty's battlecruisers firing at something. Jellicoe signalled Beatty, demanding to know where the enemy battle fleet was. Beatty did not know; he had not seen Scheer's ships for nearly an hour. He knew he was to the south and sent the reply: 'Enemy battle cruisers bearing SE.' Jellicoe desperately needed to know whether Scheer was still approaching him so that he could deploy his ships. His twenty-four battleships were approaching in line abreast and he might have to change the formation to a single line. The last words of this phase of the battle must go to the captain of HMS *Princess Royal*, Walter Cowan: 'With the Grand Fleet in sight and within striking distance, we felt like throwing our caps into the air. It looked a certainty we had them.'

Chapter Five

Fleet Engaged

The battle that Jellicoe had been dreaming about and that Scheer had seen in his worst nightmares was about to begin. Jellicoe and his twenty-four Dreadnoughts were heading in a south-easterly direction, in six lines abreast, in columns of four, at a speed of 18 knots. Scheer's fleet, consisting of sixteen Dreadnoughts and six pre-Dreadnoughts, was maintaining a similar speed and heading north.

Jellicoe's ships occupied an area a mile and a half wide and it would take considerable skill to transform that formation into a 7-mile-long, single line. He needed time and plenty warning in order to carry out the difficult manoeuvre under the eyes of the German fleet. Jellicoe still had no clear indication as to where the Germans were, their speed or direction. If he were caught before his ships could create a single broadside line, Scheer would be able to pummel his leading ships and the vessels following them would not be able to see anything. In the ensuing confusion Scheer would be able to pick off some of Jellicoe's other vessels and withdraw before Jellicoe could bring his superior firepower to bear.

Jellicoe had received the first report of contact with the German vessels from HMS *Galatea* at 1418, whereupon he ordered the fleet to proceed at full speed. At 1540 he received news from Beatty that Hipper's battlecruisers were in sight. Jellicoe's fleet had reached a speed of around 20 knots by 1600, at about the same time as Hood was sent to reinforce Beatty. Initially Jellicoe had believed that he was dealing just with Hipper's battlecruisers and that Beatty's force was more than adequate to deal with them.

Confirmation that the German High Seas Fleet was close at hand was received at 1638, when Goodenough reported sighting them. When Jellicoe received this report from Goodenough, on HMS *Southampton,* he believed that his initial plans were still sound:

> At this time I was confident that, under the determined leadership of Sir David Beatty a force of four of our best and fastest battleships and six battle cruisers, very serious injury would be inflicted on the five battle cruisers of the enemy if they could be kept within range. The report of the presence of the German Battle Fleet, which was communicated to our Battle Fleet, did not cause me any uneasiness in the respect of the safety of our own vessels, since our ships of the Fifth Battle Squadron were credited with a speed of 25knots. I did not, however, expect that they would be able to exceed a speed of 24knots; the information furnished to me at this time gave the designed speed of the fastest German battleships as 20.5knots only. Even after making full allowance for the fact that our ships were probably carrying more fuel and stores proportionately than the Germans, and giving the Germans credit for some excess over the designed speed, no doubt existed in my mind that both our battleships and our battle cruisers with Sir David Beatty could keep well out of range of the enemy's Battle Fleet, if necessary, until I was able to reinforce them.

Jellicoe asked the Admiralty to allow Commodore Tyrwhitt's Harwich force to reinforce him. In anticipation of this, Tyrwhitt left base at 1715, but the Admiralty, concerned that some of the German High Seas Fleet might slip away from the engagement and attack targets in the English Channel, sent a signal to Tyrwhitt, ordering him to return to base and await orders. This signal was timed at 1735. Unsurprisingly Tyrwhitt was livid.

Back with the fleet, Jellicoe had warned his Grand Fleet that 'fleet action is imminent'. This signal was timed at 1651. Jellicoe still desperately needed to know exactly where the German fleet was as he had to make an informed decision and deploy his vessels accordingly:

> The plot made on the reports received between 5pm and 6pm from Commodore Goodenough, of the Second Light Cruiser

Squadron, and the report at 4.45pm from Sir David Beatty in the Lion giving the position of the enemy's Battle Fleet, showed that we, of the Battle Fleet, might meet the High Seas Fleet approximately ahead and that the cruiser line ahead of the Battle Fleet would sight the enemy nearly ahead of the centre. Obviously, however, great reliance could not be placed on the positions given by the ships of the Battle Cruiser Fleet, which had been in action for two hours and frequently altering course. I realised this, but when contact actually took place it was found that the positions given were at least twelve miles in error when compared with the Iron Duke's reckoning. The result was that the enemy's Battle Fleet appeared on the starboard bow instead of ahead, as I had expected, and contact also took place earlier than was anticipated. There can be no doubt as to the accuracy of the reckoning onboard the Iron Duke, as the movements of that ship could be plotted with accuracy after leaving Scapa Flow, there being no disturbing elements to deal with.

In fact the *Iron Duke* was some 4 miles further east than Jellicoe believed and Beatty was 7 miles further west. The exact positions when Beatty's force spotted Jellicoe's fleet at 1733 add to the notion that both men were not wholly aware of their true position. HMS *Falmouth,* a light cruiser screening Beatty, was around 4 miles to the north of HMS *Lion.* The light cruiser spotted HMS *Black Prince*, the cruiser on the extreme starboard of Jellicoe's screen. As Beatty approached Jellicoe he shifted course to north-north-east, assuming Jellicoe's position, which meant that he was also closing with Hipper, sparking off another series of salvos at a range of 14,000 yards at 1740.

Fire was concentrated at Hipper's battlecruisers and the *Lützow* received several hits, at least four of which caused superficial damage to the German vessel. The Third Battle Cruiser Squadron, led by HMS I*ndomitable,* continued south-south-east, with HMS *Lion* at this point to their south-west. Hood had despatched HMS *Canterbury* to a position around five miles ahead and HMS *Chester* was five miles to the west. At 1727 HMS *Chester* had been ordered to investigate firing to the south-west, which was when she came in contact with the four German ships belonging to the Second German Scouting Group.

By 1759, with Hipper under fire from the Fifth Battle Squadron and Beatty's battlecruisers, he began to flee to the south-west, joining up with Scheer and his High Seas Fleet shortly before 1814, whereupon Hipper turned about and the entire battle line headed north-east. This was also around the time that HMS *Acasta* was moving away from HMS *Shark*. HMS *Onslow* spotted the stationary *Wiesbaden* and closed to within 2,000 yards. As she closed to finish off the crippled *Wiesbaden*, Hipper's battlecruisers were sighted at a range of around 8,000 yards, but the captain still gave the order to fire torpedoes at the *Wiesbaden*. Just at that moment the *Wiesbaden* opened fire on *HMS Onslow*. As Lieutenant Commander Jack Tovey recalled:

> Immediately there was a big escape of steam completely enveloping both torpedo tubes. On enquiring I received a report that all torpedoes had been fired and consequently turned away at greatly reduced speed, passing about 3,500 yards from the enemy's light cruiser previously mentioned. I sent Sub-Lieutenant Moore to find out the damage done; while doing this he discovered that only one torpedo had been fired and observing the enemy's light cruiser beam on and apparently temporarily stopped, fired a torpedo at her. Sub-Lieutenant Moore, Leading Signalman Cassin, also several other ratings and myself saw the torpedo hit the light cruiser below the Conning tower and explode.

Tovey still had a pair of torpedoes left and his damaged ship could manage around 10 knots. Incredibly he decided to use them against the German High Seas Fleet and not even attempt to flee. Both torpedoes were fired but they missed and with just five casualties, the *Onslow* limped home. Tovey himself would face a vast German ship once more in his career, the *Bismarck,* twenty-five years later.

Jellicoe, it will be recalled, was still confused about the position of the German High Seas Fleet, having not seen them himself, but relying instead on scattered and conflicting pieces of information. He was still receiving snippets of information but nothing concrete enough. As Beatty's battlecruisers drew across the front of Jellicoe's Grand Fleet, HMS *Marlborough,* HMS *Colossus* and HMS *Benbow* of the Grand Fleet spotted the enemy. Lieutenant Thomas Norman, on board HMS *Benbow*, recalled: 'I must confess it was a magnificent sight seeing the Lion, slightly on fire forward, leading the other ships and firing salvo after salvo, with the enemy's flashes visible in the haze, but not the ships themselves, tremendous volumes of water being thrown up by the enemy shots, none of which hit the cruisers when in my vision.'

When Jellicoe finally received confirmation of the location of the German High Seas Fleet at 1814, he now needed to make an absolute decision, a decision that would mark him either as a great naval commander or as a fool. He said of his decision:

The first definitive information received onboard the Fleet-flagship of the position of the enemy's Battle Fleet did not, therefore, come until 6.14pm, and the position given placed it thirty degrees before the starboard beam of the Iron Duke, or fifty-nine degrees before the starboard beam of the Marlborough, and apparently in close proximity. There was no time to lose, as there was evident danger of the starboard wing column of the Battle Fleet being engaged by the whole German Battle Fleet before deployment could be effected. So at 6.16pm a signal was made to the Battle Fleet to form line of battle on the port wing column, on a course southeast by east, it being assumed that the course of the enemy was approximately the same as that of our battle cruisers. Speed was at the same time reduced to 14knots to admit of our battle cruisers passing ahead of the Battle Fleet, as there was danger of the fire of the Battle Fleet being blanketed by them. During the short interval, crowded with events, that elapsed since the first flashes and sound of gunfire had been noted onboard the Iron Duke, the question of most urgent importance before me had been the direction and manner of deployment. As the evidence accumulated that the enemy's Battle Fleet was on our starboard side, but on a bearing well before the beam of the Iron Duke, the point for decision was whether to form a line of battle on the starboard or on the port wing column. My first and natural impulse was to form on the starboard wing column in order to bring the Fleet into action at the earliest possible moment, but it became increasingly apparent, both from the sound of gunfire and the reports from the Lion and Barham, that the High Seas Fleet was in such close proximity and on such a bearing as to create obvious disadvantages in such a movement. I assumed that the German destroyers would be ahead of their Battle Fleet, and it was clear that owing to the mist, the operations of the destroyers attacking from a commanding position in the van would be much facilitated; it would be suicidal to place the Battle Fleet in a position where it might be open to attack by destroyers during such a deployment. The further points that occurred to me were, that if the German ships were as close as seemed probable, there was considerable danger of the First Battle Squadron, and especially the Marlborough's division, being severely handled by the concentrated fire of the High Seas Fleet before the remaining divisions could get in line to assist. Included in the First Battle Squadron were several of our older ships, with only indifferent protection as compared with the German capital ships, and an interval of at least four minutes would elapse between each division coming into line astern of the Sixth Division and a further interval before the guns could be directed onto the ship selected and their fire become effective. The final disadvantage would be that it appeared, from the supposed position of the High Seas Fleet, that the van of the enemy would have a very considerable overlap if line were formed on the starboard wing division, whereas this would not be the case with deployment on the port wing column. The overlap would necessitate a large turn of the starboard wing division to port to prevent the T being crossed, and each successive division coming into line would have to make this turn, in addition to the eight point turn required to form the line. I therefore decided to deploy on the first, the port wing, division.

After considering the situation for a short while Jellicoe announced: 'Hoist equal-speed pendant south-east by east.'

Whilst Jellicoe was ordering the deployment of the Grand Fleet, HMS *Defence* with Rear Admiral Sir Robert Arbuthnot leading the First Cruiser Squadron had found itself in a difficult situation – slap bang between the oncoming German High Seas Fleet and the

Grand Fleet. Arbuthnot moved toward the *Wiesbaden* with HMS *Warrior* and HMS *Duke of Edinburgh* following, his obsolete armoured cruisers cutting across Jellicoe's Grand Fleet just as it was manoeuvring. For a moment it looked as if Arbuthnot's battle cruisers were going to collide with ships of the Grand Fleet as HMS *Defence* and HMS *Warrior* began firing at the *Wiesbaden*. Arbuthnot clearly thought that if the *Wiesbaden* were still capable she would fire torpedoes at the deploying Grand Fleet.

It was an incredibly dangerous manoeuvre, with German battle-cruisers breathing down his neck. As Commander Georg von Has, on board the *Derfflinger* of the First Scouting Group recalled:

> In the misty grey light the colours of the German and the English ships were difficult to distinguish. The cruiser was not very far away from us. She had four funnels and two masts, like our Rostock. She is certainly English, Lieutenant Commander Hauser shouted, May I fire? Yes fire away! I was now certain she was a big English ship. The secondary armament was trained on the new target. Hauser gave the order, 6,000! Then, just as he was about to give the order, fire, something terrific happened. The English ship, which I had meanwhile identified as an old English armoured cruiser, broke in half with a tremendous explosion. Black smoke and debris shot into the air, a flame enveloped the whole ship, and then she sank before our eyes. There was nothing but a gigantic smoke cloud to mark the place where just before a proud ship had been fighting.

Thus ended the heroic attack by Arbuthnot and HMS *Defence*. Just behind her was HMS *Warrior* which was drawing the fire of the German vessels – in a short period of time she received a total of fifteen hits. Initially the engines continued to run, despite the carnage on deck and below, but huge amounts of water were pouring in and the pumps could not cope. Thick smoke covered the ship and leeched down below decks as the German battlecruisers continued to pour fire at her.

Trailing behind HMS *Warrior* was HMS *Duke of Edinburgh*. As she too began to draw fire her crew saw HMS *Defence* burst into flames just as HMS *Warrior* was smashed by a broadside. Amazingly

HMS *Duke of Edinburgh* managed to escape serious damage.

Meanwhile, Evan-Thomas was trying to make sense of the situation. His Fifth Battle Squadron seemed to be leading the entire battle line and he believed that the Grand Fleet had deployed to his starboard. Consequently he headed east, straight into the fire of the leading German vessels, quickly realized his mistake and ordered a turn to the north-east.

Incredibly, just as this was happening HMS *Warspite* headed straight for the Germans, immediately becoming the focus of attention of the *Friedrich de Grosse, König, Heligoland, Kaiserin, Ostfriesland, Nassau, Oldenburg* and *Thuringen*, drawing fire away from HMS *Warrior*. It is still not clear to this day why HMS *Warspite* made this huge, circling manoeuvre. At any rate, the Germans were clearly drawn to it, as it would be far more decisive to deal with a vessel such as *Warspite* than the relatively humble *Warrior*.

With 13 inches of armour protection extending around her main belt, magazines and turrets, HMS *Warspite* was seemingly shrugging off all of the attentions of the German ships. As a member of her crew recalled:

> For about 20 minutes we received the fire of about 20 German ships, using guns of all calibres at what was virtually point blank range. Only the fact that the ship was continuing to turn circles like a kitten chasing its own tail saved us from being sunk. The noise of the shells hitting or bursting close alongside sounded like the rapid independent fire from a battery of 6-inch guns. The ship was heavily hit.

The *Warspite* had been hit several times so that the superstructure was bent and gnarled. Suddenly the firing seemed to stop and everyone, including the Germans, thought the ship was about to sink. In truth no one could see what was going on because of the smoke and spray from the shots. Incredibly, the *Warspite* was in the firing line for ten minutes before eventually pulling away at 16 knots, separating herself from the Grand Fleet. HMS *Warspite* was ordered to return back to base.

Meanwhile Hood, on board HMS *Invincible*, turned his squadron at 1817 to fall in line with HMS *Lion*, just as the German fleet came fully into view, closing from 18,000 to 6,000 yards. The Third Battle Cruiser Squadron continued to fire at the German battlecruisers, but poor visibility was causing problems. HMS *Invincible,* HMS *Inflexible* and HMS *Indomitable* were still scoring spectacular hits on Hipper's battlecruisers, which were was also under fire from Beatty.

As the minutes passed, ships of the British Grand Fleet began to open up on Hipper who realized that to continue would be courting disaster. As Commander Georg von Has, on board the *Derfflinger* put it: 'A severe, unequal struggle developed. Several heavy shells pierced our ship with terrific force and exploded with a tremendous roar, which shook every seam and rivet. The captain had again frequently to steer the ship out of the line in order to get out of the hail of fire.'

Scheer had finally realized that he was facing not just Beatty's battlecruisers, or even Beatty reinforced by elements of the Grand Fleet. He was desperate to know exactly what was out there:

We, on our flagship, were occupied debating how much longer to continue the pursuit in view of the advanced time. There was no longer any question of a cruiser campaign against merchant men in the Skagerrak, as the meeting with the English fighting forces which was to result from such action had already taken place. But we were bound to take into consideration that the English fleet, if at sea, which was obvious from the ships we had encountered, would offer battle the next day. Some steps would also have to be taken to shake off the English light forces before darkness fell in order to avoid any loss to our main fleet from nocturnal torpedo boat attacks.

The truth, however, was beginning to dawn on Scheer. He now knew that he was not facing a small portion of the Grand Fleet, but the entire might that Jellicoe could muster. What had begun as an operation to draw Beatty to his doom by luring him with Hipper's force had now turned full circle and it was Scheer who was being lured into the jaws of destruction:

It was now quite obvious that we were confronted by a large portion of the English fleet and a few minutes later their

113

presence was notified on the horizon directly ahead of us by rounds of firing from guns of heavy calibre. The entire arc stretching from north to east was a sea of fire. The flash from the muzzles of the guns was distinctly seen through the mist and smoke on the horizon, though the ships themselves were not distinguishable. This was the beginning of the main phase of the battle. There was never any question of our line veering round to avoid an encounter. The resolve to do battle with the enemy stood firm from the first.

As each of the ships of the Grand Fleet took up its position in the line they began to open fire. Unfortunately, there was only a short amount of daylight left, but the Germans were trapped. HMS *King George V* led the British line. The massed, heavy guns of the Royal Navy were about to be finally turned on their arch nemesis, the German High Seas Fleet. Everything hitherto had led up to this point: all of the gunnery practice, the drills and exercises, it all had to count now.

In minutes the turrets were thick with the smell or cordite as the 1,350lb shells were levered into place. Broadside after broadside was hurled at the German ships. The first victim was the *Wiesbaden*; she was still afloat and despite being hit several more times she did not sink. Nobody could really tell what they were firing at, with shell splashes landing everywhere. The crew on board HMS *Benbow* thought they were firing at a Kaiser class enemy ship, but later discovered they were actually firing at the battlecruiser, *Derfflinger*.

The poor visibility abruptly improved at 1830 and the Germans could now see the Third Battle Cruiser Squadron straddled in front of them. Shells began landing near HMS *Invincible*, HMS *Inflexible* and HMS *Indomitable*. Taking the worst of the attention was HMS *Invincible*, which for the first time was facing a pair of well-armed and armoured German battlecruisers. There was little chance that she could survive the encounter.

On board the *Derfflinger*, Georg van Has recalls the moment:

Her [HMS Invincible] guns were trained on us and immediately another salvo crashed out, straddling us completely. Range 9,000! roared Leading Seaman Hamel. 9,000 – salvos

114

fire! I ordered, and with feverish anxiety I waited for our splashes. Over. Two hits! Called out Lieutenant Commander von Stosch. I gave the order 100 down. Good. Rapid! And 30 seconds after the first salvo the second left the guns. I observed two short splashes and two hits. Von Stosch called hits! Every 20 seconds came the roar of another salvo. At 6.31pm the Derfflinger fired her last salvo at this ship.

On board the *Lützow*, they saw their salvo hit HMS *Invincible*. A few seconds later there were red glows all over the British ship and at 1834 *Invincible* blew up. A shell had penetrated her midship turret and the magazines below had blown her to pieces. Bryan Gasson was a Royal Marine, operating as a rangefinder in the midship turret of HMS *Invincible*:

Suddenly our starboard mid-ship turret manned by the Royal Marines was struck between the two 12in guns and appeared to me to lift the top of the turret and another of the same salvo followed. The flashes passed down to both mid-ship magazines containing 50 tons of cordite. The explosion broke the ship in half. I owe my survival, I think, to the fact that I was in a separate compartment at the back of the turret with my head through a hole cut in the top. Some of the initial flash must have got through to my compartment as I was burnt on the hand, arms and head – luckily my eyes escaped, I must have instinctively covered them with my hands. The rangefinder and myself had only a light armour covering, I think this came off and, as the ship sunk, I floated to the surface.

Hipper's ships had scored another notable victory. Georg von Has, onboard the *Derfflinger* was delighted:

I shouted into the telephone, our enemy has blown up! And above the din of the battle a great cheer thundered through the ship and was transmitted to the fore-control by all the gunnery telephones and flashed from one gun position to another. I sent up a short, fervent prayer of thanks to the almighty, shouted, bravo Hanel, jolly well measured! And then my order rang out, change target to the left.

Within fifteen seconds all but six of the 1,032 men on board HMS *Invincible* had slipped beneath the surface of the waves with the twisted, metal hulk of their ship.

Men were dying in the water and Beatty sent HMS *Badger* to pick up survivors, but *Badger*'s crew were not even sure if they were British crewmen in the sea. As Royal Marine Bryan Gasson recalled: 'After about half an hour the destroyer HMS *Badger* approached, lowered boats and picked the survivors up. Luckily for me the destroyer carried a doctor and my burns were carefully treated.'

The bow and the stern of HMS *Invincible* remained visible for some time. HMS *Indomitable* and HMS *Inflexible* passed the point where she had sunk, heading for Hipper's flagship, the *Lützow*. Shells were falling all around the German flagship and it was clear that the British were hitting her repeatedly. She was not the only one of Hipper's battlecruisers to be drawing the unwanted attention of British shells.

The German battlecruisers were beginning to take heavy incoming fire from elements of the British Grand Fleet. HMS *Iron Duke* and HMS *Monarch* opened fire on the *König* as Jellicoe himself recalled:

At this time, owing to smoke and mist, it was most difficult to distinguish friend from foe, and quite impossible to form an opinion onboard the Iron Duke, in her position towards the centre of the line, as to the formation of the enemy's Fleet. The identity of ships in sight on the starboard beam was not even sufficiently clear for me to permit fire being opened; but at 6.30pm it became certain that our own battle cruisers had drawn ahead of the Battle Fleet and that the vessels then before the beam were battleships of the Konig class. The order was, therefore, given to open fire, and the Iron Duke engaged what appeared to be the leading battle-ship at a range of 12,000 yards on a bearing 20 degrees before the starboard beam. The fire from the Iron Duke, which came more directly under my observation, was seen to be immediately effective, the third and fourth salvos fired registering several palpable hits. It appeared as if all the enemy ships at that time in sight from the Iron Duke were receiving heavy punishment.

The *König* had indeed been badly hit. One shell had smashed the forecastle deck, which had caused fires, two more had smacked into the port battery, another shell had holed the lower armour and a near miss had wounded Rear Admiral Behncke in the upper bridge. The *Markgraf* was also hit twice, one of which bent the port propeller shaft causing the port engine to be closed down, seriously reducing its speed.

Although Scheer, on board the *Friedrich de Grosse,* could see very little of the British, he now had to make a decision which if he got wrong would probably mean the destruction of the German High Seas Fleet. After consideration he decided to make a battle turn to starboard. Each German ship was to turn individually, the rear ship turning first, and then each ship in the line following its lead. As Scheer said:

> The swing round was carried out in excellent style. At our peace manoeuvres great importance was always attached to these being carried out on a curved line and every means was employed to ensure the working of the signals. The trouble spent was now well repaid; the cruisers were liberated from their cramped position and enabled to steam away south and appeared, as soon as the two lines were separated, in view of the flagship. The torpedo boats, too, on the leeside of the fire had room to move to the attack and advanced.

The II Battle Squadron of pre-Dreadnoughts at the rear of the German fleet did not make the turn, so the rearmost ship, the *West-falen,* a Dreadnought, made the first turn at 1837. It seemed that some of the German vessels were so badly damaged that they would not be able to get away. The *Lützow* could not make more than 15 knots, could no longer lead the battlecruisers and headed south-west, trying to get away. Four German destroyers, pumping out smoke to hide her, escorted her.

Hipper, meanwhile, boarded the G-39, a destroyer. Effectively, Captain Hartog of the *Derfflinger,* now commanded Hipper's battlecruisers. Commander von Has, on board the *Derfflinger,* noted the desperate condition of the vessel:

The masts and rigging had been badly damaged by countless shells, and wireless aerials hung down in an inextricable tangle so that we could only use our wireless for receiving; we could not transmit messages. A heavy shell had torn away two armoured plates in the bows, leaving a huge gap quite six by five metres, just above the waterline. With the pitching of the ship water streamed continually through this hole.

As the German vessels turned away from Jellicoe's Grand Fleet, they launched a destroyer attack on the British ships. HMS *Shark* having been left behind, crippled, incredibly engaged the German destroyers with her last remaining 4in gun, hitting the V-48 at least once and forcing her to stop. Captain Loftus Jones was hit by a shell that did not explode but smashed his leg off below the knee. HMS *Shark* was so battered that she finally sank at 1900. The survivors, around thirty of them, were not picked up for some time, at which stage Loftus Jones was still alive. Of the thirty men who had escaped only six would survive the battle.

Jellicoe, unable to see a great deal, was desperate to regain contact with the German fleet as he headed south-east-by-east. With the range opening up, he signalled for his fleet to turn by divisions to the south, still acutely aware that even though the Germans were in retreat, they could well be laying another trap for his battleships. He was not to know whether or not the Germans had submarines in the area, or whether they had laid minefields. He also had to consider the prospect of a concerted attack by German destroyers. Jellicoe had good reason to worry – throughout the whole battle there had been fragmented reports of periscopes, but these were probably only flotsam and jetsam.

As the Grand Fleet turned south after its quarry, Beatty, on board HMS *Lion*, was leading the battlecruisers with *HMS Inflexible* and HMS *Indomitable* following him. Around 1854 he was about 8,000 yards from the Grand Fleet, but after some odd turns by him the Grand Fleet was considerably closer by 1905.

Earlier, at 1854, HMS *Marlborough* had suffered a dreadful mishap. The V-48, stranded after the survivors of HMS *Shark* had crippled her, fired a torpedo at the British Dreadnought, whose crew recalled a huge explosion and the vessel began to lurch. She had been badly hit and heeled over to starboard, looking as if she was going to sink.

At 1855 Scheer made an incredible decision. He would make another battle turn, heading east, which would bring him directly towards the centre of the British Grand Fleet. But the manoeuvre was not as crazy as it may have seemed, as Scheer explained:

It was still too early for a nocturnal move. If the enemy followed us our action in retaining the direction taken after turning the line would partake of the nature of a retreat, and in the event of any damage to our ships in the rear, the Fleet would be compelled to sacrifice them or else to decide on a line of action enforced by enemy pressure, and not adopted voluntarily, and would therefore be detrimental to us from the very outset. Still less was it feasible to strive at detaching oneself from the enemy, leaving it to him to decide when he would elect to meet us the next morning. There was but one way of averting this – to force the enemy into a second battle by another determined advance, and forcibly compel his torpedo boats to attack. The success of the turning of the line while fighting encouraged me to make the attempt, and convinced me to make still further use of the facility of movement. The manoeuvre would be bound to surprise the enemy, to upset his plans for the rest of the day, and if the blow fell heavily it would facilitate the breaking loose at night. The fight of the Wiesbaden helped also to strengthen my resolve and to make an effort to render assistance to her and at least save the crew. Accordingly, after we had been on the new course about a quarter of an hour, the line was again swung round to starboard on an easterly course at 6.55pm. The battle cruisers were ordered to operate with full strength on the enemy's leading point, all the torpedo boat flotillas had orders to attack, and the First Leader of the torpedo boats, Commodore Michelsen, was instructed to send his boats to rescue the Wiesbaden's crew.

The *König* was leading the line. The German battlecruisers were to the north, while ahead of the advancing Germans was the Second Light Cruiser Squadron, led by Goodenough, who was hoping to

119

have another go at destroying the *Wiesbaden*. All of a sudden HMS *Southampton* and the rest of Goodenough's ships came under fire. He turned back and headed north, signalling to Jellicoe at 1900: 'Enemy battle fleet steering east-south-east. Enemy bears south-south-west, number unknown.'

At 1910 the German fleet now seemed to be heading directly at the Grand Fleet, which was still jockeying around to take up positions. Some of the British ships were masked by others and could not initially fire.

It soon became clear to Scheer that any attempt to try to save the *Wiesbaden*'s crew would only lead to the loss of more German vessels. The destroyers he had sent had drawn the attention of British Dreadnoughts which understandably believed that this was not a mercy mission but a torpedo attack on them.

HMS *Colossus* thought they had hit one of the attacking destroyers, but in all probability they had scored a hit on the V-48, which had regained some power and was creeping south. The German torpedo boats quickly realized that they would be smashed to pieces and abruptly turned away at around 6,600 yards, firing off several torpedoes as they made their turn. The only British ship in immediate danger was HMS *Neptune,* but after taking evasive action she was now safe.

By now the British Grand Fleet was firing heavily at the oncoming German vessels. Scheer ran up a signal flag at 1913, ordering his battlecruisers to turn towards the British and engage their van at close range. Scheer was effectively risking his battlecruisers to allow his destroyers to make a decisive attack.

The destroyers were unleashed at 1918. One of the first German ships to suffer was the *Grosser Kurfurst*, which was hit at least eight times, including some near the waterline.

Meanwhile, Hartog, who had taken over command of Hipper's four battlecruisers, found that his vessels were under fire from eighteen British Dreadnoughts, while the remaining British vessels fired at the German Dreadnoughts.

Several salvos were fired at the *Derfflinger* which was hit a number of times. At 1913 a shell pierced the armour of one of the turrets and a fire broke out, which spread rapidly. Huge gouts of flame shot up from the turrets, killing all but five of the seventy-eight men inside them; a second shell killed another turret crew

120

of eighty men. Around fifteen shells struck the ship in all. Commander Georg von Has, later wrote:

The enemy had got our range excellently. I felt a clutch at my heart when I thought of what the conditions must be in the interior of the ship. So far we in the armoured tower had come off very well. Salvos were still bursting round us, but we could scarcely see anything of the enemy. All we could see was the great reddish gold flames spurting from the guns. I ordered the two forward turrets to fire salvo after salvo. I could feel that our fire soothed the nerves of the ship's company. If we had ceased fire at this time the whole ship's company would have been overwhelmed by despair. So long as we were firing, things could not be so bad.

The Germans were scoring hits too. The *Seydlitz* hit HMS *Colossus* at least twice, but there was relatively little damage done to the enormous British vessel. The German vessel, *Von der Tann,* was unable to fire as all her guns were out of action, but she sailed on, acting as a mobile target. When she was hit again, the conning tower was smashed and all the occupants were either killed or wounded.

The *Lützow* was limping away to the south-west when suddenly, to the horror of her crew, they saw the British Second Battle Squadron, consisting of HMS *Monarch,* HMS *Orion* and HMS *Centurion.* The *Lützow* was hit several more times, thus reducing her ability to fight back and her speed, but she continued to limp on.

Scheer ordered his destroyers, some of which were already trying to protect the *Lützow,* to launch another attack at 1915, but in the confusion only thirteen of them attacked. Leading the charge was the G-41. To their enormous horror they saw the entire British Grand Fleet arrayed in front of them, so they launched their torpedoes at between 7,500 and 9,000 yards; around eleven were fired. HMS *Benbow* was hit by one of them, but it failed to explode.

One of the German destroyers approached HMS *Malaya,* to within 6,000 yards. After five minutes of heavy fire the destroyer, the S-35, sank with all hands lost, including the crew that she had picked up from the V-29.

The German battlecruisers turned at 1920, headed west-south-west and then followed the retreating German High Seas Fleet that was heading west. At 1922 Jellicoe ordered the Fourth Light Cruiser Squadron to launch a counter-attack, while his Dreadnoughts made two separate turns by division. This meant that the British were now facing south-south-east and sailing away from the German High Seas Fleet.

Jellicoe was still concerned about the effect of torpedoes on his Dreadnoughts, but why did he turn away from the torpedoes, rather than turn towards them? He later wrote:

> The alternatives to a turn away were a turn towards, or holding the course and dodging the torpedoes. A turn towards would have led to great danger if the first attack had been followed up by a second and a third, and no one could say that this would not be the case. To hold on and dodge might meet with success if the tracks could be seen. Information had reached me that the Germans had succeeded in making the tracks of their torpedoes more or less invisible. Therefore there was danger in this alternative.

But Jellicoe was working on erroneous information provided to him by Naval Intelligence. He had been told that the Germans had created a torpedo that did not leave a trail, and the number of torpedoes available to the Germans was also seriously overestimated. In fact only thirty-one were fired at the British Dreadnoughts. Despite this, several of the British battleships claimed to have seen torpedoes and took evasive action.

The German destroyer attacks were ineffective and the problem now facing Jellicoe was that he had failing light and needed to close with the German High Seas Fleet. Again his quality of reports let him down. Eventually, at 1935, he turned the Grand Fleet around to where he believed the German High Seas Fleet to be. Both Beatty and Goodenough had told him that they were heading west, so at 1940, the Grand Fleet was ordered to sail south-westerly. The Germans might have fooled Jellicoe temporarily.

Scheer feared that his fleet would be tracked. They had been sailing west and at 1945 he ordered his ships to sail south. Unbeknown to both him and Jellicoe, the British and German vessels were now on converging courses.

Beatty, some 6 miles ahead of the Grand Fleet, saw the Germans change course and signalled to Jellicoe: 'Submit that the van of the battleships follow me: we can then cut off the whole of the enemy's fleet.'

Beatty was clearly willing to get stuck in once again, but wanted back-up in case he ran into more firepower than he could handle. Jellicoe had already decided to turn to the west and ordered Vice Admiral Jerram's Second Battle Squadron to follow Beatty. Unfortunately Jerram could neither see Beatty nor the High Seas Fleet and continued west. The British Grand Fleet was again in six columns, with Beatty 6 miles ahead; the main British fleet was heading west and Beatty was heading south-west. The Germans meanwhile were heading south; the closest German ships to the British were the four battlecruisers. At this stage Scheer had no idea that he was being followed.

At 2011 the British Eleventh Flotilla, led by Commodore James Hawksley, on board HMS *Castor,* spotted German destroyers to his north-west and turned to attack, supported by the Fourth Light Cruiser Squadron. They had found not destroyers, but in fact the main German battle line. By this stage it was 2026.

The German Dreadnoughts were around 8,000 yards away. HMS *Calliope,* with Commodore Charles le Mesurier, commander of the Fourth Light Cruiser Squadron, came under fire and was hit several times before heading back for the safety of the Grand Fleet.

Slightly to the south, Rear Admiral Napier, commanding the Third Light Cruiser Squadron, having been ordered by Beatty to scout to the west, picked up a German scouting group at 2000. They fired at one another at long range, with Beatty moving in to support the British cruisers.

Suddenly Beatty's battlecruisers spotted German battlecruisers and they opened fire on one another at 2019. The German ships were in a desperate state, with holes below the waterline, guns out of action and fires still blazing. The British ships, all five of them, including HMS *New Zealand* and HMS *Indomitable,* were in a better condition to fight. Almost immediately the *Derfflinger* and the *Seydlitz* were hit, but they kept moving and sought the protection of the bigger German vessels. Beatty pursued them and now opened fire on the *Schleswig-Holstein,* the *Pommern* and the *Schlesien* as the pre-Dreadnoughts tried to cover the withdrawal of the battlecruisers.

At 2028 Jellicoe ordered his ships to form a single line by moving west to south-west. The Germans, meanwhile, were once again heading south, on a collision course with the Grand Fleet. HMS *Caroline* and HMS *Royalist* of the Fourth Light Cruiser Squadron were 2 miles ahead of the Grand Fleet, with HMS *Castor* and eight other destroyers belonging to the Eighth Flotilla following them. At 2045 they saw German Dreadnoughts heading towards them from the north-west.

There was confusion. While Captain Crooke, the captain of HMS *Caroline*, ordered a joint torpedo attack, Jerram, on board HMS *King George V*, was certain that they were Beatty's battle-cruisers. There was a considerable delay while the two men argued the case, but Captain Crooke still launched his attack, certain that they were Germans. Shells fired by the approaching ships confirmed he was right; the torpedoes in any event missed. The Eleventh Flotilla turned away from the German battlecruisers, believing that the Grand Fleet would open up, but as suddenly as they had appeared, the German ships turned away and were soon out of sight.

The day's action was over. What now remained to be seen was whether Scheer could extricate himself from the situation or whether Jellicoe could corner him. What was certain was that the Germans could not afford to give battle again. Several of Scheer's ships had been badly damaged and they were outnumbered to the same extent now as they had been when the battle had begun.

Chapter Six

Night Operations

The light was disappearing by 2100. Both Jellicoe and Scheer were concerned not only about what darkness might bring, but also what might happen to them and their fleets come first light. Scheer could easily find his vessels picked off by the British during the night, or worse, he might find the Grand Fleet waiting for him as he tried to sail for home. Jellicoe, on the other hand, faced the prospect of trying to beat off determined attacks by German destroyers and torpedo boats during the night, and had to balance this against his overwhelming desire to close with the German High Seas Fleet and destroy it in the morning.

Scheer had, perhaps, the most difficult of choices as he now found himself to the west of the Grand Fleet. He could either risk a night engagement or try to slip away. Both men knew that whatever might happen in the darkness, it would be a matter of chance. Ships could easily find themselves close by the enemy, and outgunned and destroyed before help could find them. Fleets of that day and age did not have the technology to enable them to fight night actions successfully. They had searchlights, but these were two-edged swords: they could pick out an enemy ship in the night, but they would also signal the searching ship's own position. Any fight, therefore, would have to take place at close quarters.

Jellicoe was still labouring under the misapprehension that the Germans had a surfeit of torpedoes, which could be delivered by all of their destroyers, and feared that this would give the Germans a massive advantage during a night battle. He was also more concerned with what damage the Germans could do to him, rather than what damage he could do to the Germans. After all, Britain still retained its naval supremacy and Jellicoe was not about to risk this advantage, just on the off chance that he could improve Britain's lead by a ship or two.

Therefore, although both men had decided against night action, Jellicoe still wanted to destroy more German ships in the morning by interdicting them before they slipped home the following day. He decided to shift his direction from a west-south-west one to a southerly course. In truth, all he could do was to guess which way the Germans might run, as Scheer had several options.

Jellicoe knew that Scheer would not risk heading for the Baltic. Several of the German ships had considerable damage to their hulls and this would mean a long journey to the north-east, through the Skagerrak and round Denmark. Jellicoe knew that if he decided to make sure the Germans did not go this way it would mean stripping out much of the offensive arm of the Grand Fleet, which could well be needed elsewhere.

Scheer's most direct route meant a 100-mile trip through seas known to be full of British submarines lying in wait. He would have to go around the Horns Reef then around the minefields covering the Heligoland Bight. The alternative to this would be through the minefields, using the same route that the Germans had used on their way out at the start of the operation. The final choice involved a 180-mile trip to the River Ems, around the Friesian coast. As far as Jellicoe was concerned, this was the most likely option. His last positive sighting of Scheer had been that he was headed west-south-west.

Consequently, Jellicoe ordered the fleet south at 17 knots, hoping that he could intercept Scheer. He also sent his destroyers 5 miles behind the Grand Fleet, to ensure that Scheer did not creep around him and make for the Horns Reef channel. At 2132 Jellicoe ordered HMS *Abdiel* to mine the Horns Reef channel, figuring that if the Germans tried to use this route they would be caught unawares.

Shortly before this, at 2117, the Grand Fleet was ordered to close up. The three Dreadnought squadrons formed columns a mile apart. Beatty had already been informed of Jellicoe's intentions. He was to the west-south-west of the Grand Fleet, approximately 13 miles away. As he later recalled:

I did not consider it desirable or proper to close the enemy battle fleet during the dark hours. I therefore concluded that I should be carrying out the Commander-in-Chief's wishes by turning to the course of the fleet, reporting to the Commander-in-Chief that I had done so. My duty in this situation was to ensure that the enemy fleet could not regain its base by passing round the southern flank of our forces. I therefore turned to the south at 9.24pm at 17knots.

Unbeknown to the Germans, this left them in a perilous position – they were, in fact, boxed in and Beatty was actually just ahead of the German battle line.

Scheer was about to make his decision and this was to head for the Horns Reef. At 2110 he ordered the fleet south-south-east three quarters east and assume a speed of 16 knots. His reasoning behind this was:

It might safely be expected that in the twilight the enemy would endeavour by attacking with strong forces, and during the night with destroyers, to force us over to the west in order to open battle with us when it was light. He was strong enough to do it. If we could succeed in warding off the enemy's encircling movement, and could be first to reach Horns Reef, then the liberty of decision for the next morning was assured to us. In order to make this possible all flotillas were ordered to be ready to attack at night, even though there was a danger when the day broke of their not being able to take part in the new battle that was expected. The main fleet in close formation was to make for Horns Reef by the shortest route, and, defying all enemy attacks, keep on that course.

The German High Seas Fleet began to turn at 2146, with the *Westfalen* leading the way. Cruisers were operating ahead and also on the starboard. Hipper's battlecruisers took up the position to the rear of the High Seas Fleet, Hipper having resumed command by boarding the *Moltke* at 2115. Two of the German battlecruisers were finding it very difficult to keep up: the *Von der Tann* was having problems with her furnaces and the *Derfflinger* could not increase her speed due to the holes in her hull. Even now Scheer could not know that he was steering on a collision course with Jellicoe's Grand Fleet.

Some of the British ships were also experiencing difficulties. HMS *Marlborough* was struggling to keep up, torpedoes having restricted her speed to 16 knots. The rest of the Sixth Division, First Battle Squadron tried to pace their speed with her and eventually the four Dreadnoughts were 4 miles behind. Jellicoe had sent the destroyer flotillas out, the Eleventh Flotilla to the west, followed by the Fourth, the Thirteenth and then the Ninth and Tenth, and the Twelfth Flotilla to the east. Soon the British destroyer flotillas were in position, some 5 miles behind the Grand Fleet. Little did they know that the German High Seas Fleet was moving towards them.

At 2158 the German light cruisers, *Frankfurt* and *Pillau*, spotted the Eleventh Flotilla and fired torpedoes, but they missed so they slipped away into the night. At 2205 other German ships from the Second Scouting Group bumped into more British ships. The Germans knew the British recognition codes and these were flashed to HMS *Castor*. When the Germans opened up at around 1,000 yards, HMS *Castor* fired back. An officer on board HMS *Castor* wrote:

They fired only at us, being apparently unable to see our destroyers, which were painted black. We were hit direct four times: one shell hit the forecastle just under the bridge and, bursting inside, made a hole about 5ft in diameter, and the splinters from it wounded a large number of men in the fore ammunition lobby; one shell went right through the fore mess-deck and burst outside the disengaged side of the ship; one hit the motor-barge, bursting in her and setting her on fire; another shell hit the disengaged side of the forebridge and wiped out everyone in the way of signalmen, messengers, etc. who had gathered there, with the exception of one man. Besides these direct hits, the ship was covered with splinter dents from shells, which burst on hitting the water short and several men at the midship guns were laid out by them. We fired a torpedo at the leading Hun and two after six inch guns, which were not being directly fired at, were making very good practice at the enemy.

This was a confusing engagement with searchlights and torpedoes; at one stage HMS *Castor* was firing at a friendly ship. Commodore James Hawksley, on board HMS *Castor,* could not tell the other destroyers what was happening as his wireless had been disabled, as had his signalling lamps.

Meanwhile, at 2220, Goodenough's Second Light Cruiser Squadron, heading south, just to the east of the Eleventh Flotilla, spotted a line of ships sailing towards them. Incredibly, these turned out to be five light cruisers belonging to the German Fourth Scouting Group, with just behind them the *Rostock* and the *Elbing.* Goodenough ordered his ships to make ready to open fire. Challenges were made at 2235 and, according to a lieutenant on board HMS *Southampton,* Goodenough's own ship:

> We began to challenge; the Germans switched on coloured lights at their fore yardarms. A second later a solitary gun crashed forth from the Dublin, who was next astern of us. Simultaneously I saw the shell hit a ship just above the water-line and about 800 yards away. As I caught a nightmare-like glimpse of her interior, which has remained photographed on my mind to this day, I said to myself, my god, they are along-side us! At that moment the Germans switched on their searchlights, and we switched on ours. Before I was blinded by the lights in my eyes, I caught sight of a line of light grey ships. Then the gun behind which I was standing answered my shout of fire.

With five German ships concentrating their fire on HMS *Southampton*, shots were also raining in on HMS *Dublin.* The British returned fire and HMS *Southampton* fired a torpedo which hit the *Fraulenlob.* As a midshipman aboard the *Fraulenlob* reported, the ship did not stay afloat for very long:

> For the first minute the ship merely seemed to sink slightly, but after that it went down rapidly. On reaching the after bridge, I barely had time to fasten on a lifebelt, and glanced hastily at the havoc in the after part of the ship – a shapeless mass of wreckage, cowls and corpses – before the water reached the deck of the after bridge, and I threw myself onto a raft which

was floating in the angle before the fore and aft bridge and the after bridge. I found two men who with great difficulty helped me to clear the raft from the fore and aft bridge, so as not to be caught in the latter. A few seconds later we saw the ship sink without any internal explosion. Some of our guns continued firing when the gunlayers were already standing in water and the ship was sinking. As the last tremor ran through the vessel, three cheers for His Majesty the Kaiser rang out.

With this the *Frauenlob* sank. Out of her crew of 320, only five survived.

In this short engagement HMS *Southampton* had been hit eighteen times, one shell going straight through the ship's side. HMS *Dublin* was also hit, but not as hard as *Southampton*. The Germans seemed to be firing primarily at the bridge area, to literally cut the head off the ship by killing the senior officers. However, as soon as the *Frauenlob* sank they broke off, leaving the British to lick their wounds.

On board the German light cruiser, *Elbing,* there had also been casualties, with four men killed and fourteen wounded when a 4in shell smashed through her hull. Flames had been the principal cause of the casualties. The ship with the highest number of casualties that was still afloat was HMS *Southampton,* on which twenty-nine had been killed and sixty seriously wounded.

The German ships that had turned away from HMS *Southampton* and the other British vessels were about to blunder into the Fourth Flotilla, commanded by Captain Charles Wintour, on board HMS *Tipperary.* Close to him, following in a line, were HMS *Spitfire,* HMS *Sparrowhawk,* HMS *Garland,* HMS *Contest,* HMS *Broke,* HMS *Achates,* HMS *Ambuscade,* HMS *Ardent,* HMS *Fortune,* HMS *Porpoise* and HMS *Unity.* It was Leading Torpedo Man, Maurice Cox, stationed at the foremost torpedo tube on HMS *Garland,* who spotted the German High Seas Fleet at 2315, when he saw the *Westfalen* with some light cruisers heading straight for his ship. The four closest German vessels were the *Stuttgart, Hamburg, Rostock* and *Elbing.*

Initially, Wintour believed that the vessels were the Eleventh Flotilla and when he challenged them at 2330, they were barely 1,000 yards away from him. British recognition signals were hoisted, to be immediately answered by searchlights and a barrage of shots, the German searchlights and guns focusing in on HMS *Tipperary*. Sub Lieutenant Newton William-Powlett recalled that moment:

> They were so close that I remember the guns seemed to be firing from some appreciable height above us. At almost the same instant the Tipperary shook violently from the impact of being hit by shells. I was told afterwards that the first salvo hit the bridge and it must have killed the captain and nearly everyone there. I opened fire with the after guns as soon as the enemy opened on us. Proper spotting was out of the question, but crouching behind the canvas screen of my control position – I felt much safer with this thin weather screen between me and the enemy guns, though it wouldn't have kept out a spent rifle bullet – I yelled at the guns to fire. I don't think they heard me, but they opened fire alright. During this time both our starboard torpedo tubes were fired, but the enemy was so close that I think the initial dive which torpedoes usually take as they enter the water made them go under the enemy ships. The enemy's second salvo hit and burst one of our main steam pipes, and the after part of the ship was enveloped in a cloud of steam through which I could see nothing.

Although HMS *Spitfire*, HMS *Sparrowhawk*, HMS *Garland*, HMS *Contest* and HMS *Broke* all fired their torpedoes before heading to port, it seems that probably only one of them hit a German target. The *Elbing* was certainly struck but at least four of the British ships claim that one hit. The German cruisers sheered off to starboard to avoid the torpedoes, but this brought them close to the German First Battle Squadron, which had also moved away from the threat of the torpedoes. The *Elbing*, having been hit by a torpedo, was unable to manoeuvre past the German Dreadnought, *Posen*. The *Posen* smashed into the *Elbing* which developed a heavy list to starboard.

As the encounter with the British ships had forced the Germans off their course toward Horns Reef, Scheer issued an order to get back on course.

HMS *Spitfire* had been hit several times and was burning, but she turned to help out the stricken HMS *Tipperary*, most of whose upper superstructure was on fire. Suddenly another German vessel appeared out of the darkness, heading straight towards HMS *Spitfire*. Clarence Trelawyn, commanding the *Spitfire,* ordered his ship to face the German vessel head on, otherwise he would have been cut in two, and warned his crew to prepare for a collision.

In the darkness Trelawyn believed he was facing a German light cruiser, but in fact he was facing a German battleship, the *Nassau*. As an officer on board HMS *Spitfire* later recalled:

> The two ships met end on, port bow to port bow, we steaming at almost 27knots, she steaming at not less than 10knots. You can imagine how the eight inch plates of a destroyer would feel such a blow. I can recollect the fearful crash, then being hurled across the deck, and feeling the Spitfire rolling over to starboard as no sea ever made her roll. As we bumped, the enemy opened fire with their foc'sle guns, though luckily they could not depress them to hit us, but the blast of the guns literally cleared everything before it. Our foremast came tumbling down, our for'ard searchlight found its way from its platform above the fore-bridge down to the deck, and the foremost funnel was blown back until it rested neatly between the two foremost ventilation cowls, like the hinging funnel of a penny river steamboat.

The collision caused severe damage to both vessels. HMS *Spitfire* was on fire, but she did not sink. The *Nassau*'s armour plating had been ripped off her port side and 20ft of the plating was sitting on the forecastle of HMS *Spitfire*.

Commander Walter Allen, on board HMS *Broke,* took command of the Fourth Flotilla. There was confusion, understandably considering the circumstances, but once again, at 2340, more shapes were seen in the darkness to starboard. Approaching HMS *Broke* was the *Westfalen*. She was challenged and the same response was received: searchlights then gunfire. HMS *Broke* fired one torpedo before swinging away to starboard as the *Westfalen* poured volleys into her. She was hit several times, killing or wounding nearly all of the gun crews; fifty were killed and twenty wounded in the space of around two minutes.

The next closest British ship was HMS *Sparrowhawk* and she, too, came under fire from the *Westfalen*. In the confusion she could not avoid colliding with *HMS Broke*. One man, Sub Lieutenant Percy Wood, was thrown off the bridge of HMS *Sparrowhawk* and found himself on the deck of HMS *Broke*. He was not the only one to whom this happened as both ships drifted, severely damaged.

Incredibly, a third ship crashed into the pair of destroyers; it was HMS *Contest* which was heading straight for HMS *Sparrowhawk*. Amazingly she veered off at the last minute, slicing off 6ft of *Sparrowhawk*'s stern. It would take the *Sparrowhawk* thirty or more minutes to free herself from this collision.

The Germans were not finished with HMS *Broke*. At around 0130 a destroyer came up close to her and fired several shots, at least six of which hit her. Even more badly damaged, she was now left to her own devices.

A little later, HMS *Contest* and HMS *Ambuscade*, fired off torpedoes at a shape in the darkness, one of which hit the German light cruiser *Rostock*; she was so badly damaged that her crew had to abandon her four hours later.

The leadership of the Fourth Flotilla now passed to the captain of HMS *Achates,* Commander Reginald Hutchinson. Apart from his own vessel, he could now call on only five other destroyers. They formed a line, headed south and incredibly bumped into the Germans once again. They saw four ships ahead of them and were challenged. Searchlights stabbed through the darkness, picking out *HMS Fortune*, which instantly became a target for the German Dreadnought *Oldenberg*, which pumped shells into her. It was a hopeless mismatch – a German Dreadnought against a tiny British destroyer – and it was over very quickly. Many of the crew were to stay in the water until 0630. HMS *Fortune* had continued to fire right up to the moment when she was sinking.

As HMS *Ardent* and HMS *Ambuscade* managed to launch torpedoes in the general direction of the German vessels, Lieutenant Commander Arthur Marsden, captain of *Ardent,* lost sight of the rest of the flotilla. His ship was hit very badly and she slowed down before stopping entirely; the electrics had failed and he knew that his ship was about to sink. After a brief lull in the firing the German vessels suddenly found HMS *Ardent* once again:

> Then all of a sudden we were again lit up by searchlights, the enemy poured in four or five more salvos at point blank range

133

and then switched her lights off once more. This would be about 10 minutes from the first time we were hit. The Ardent gave a big lurch and I bethought myself of my Gieve waistcoat. I blew and blew without any result whatever and found that it had been shot through. Another lurch, which heeled the ship right over and threw me to the ship's side. I could feel that she was going, so I flopped into the sea, grabbing a lifebuoy that was providentially at hand. The Ardent's stern kept up for a few moments, then she slowly sank from view.

Only Marsden and one other crew member were picked up; the rest of the crew went down with the ship.

The engagement between the Fourth Flotilla and the German vessels was over by 0030, but amazingly none of the destroyers had made a report to Jellicoe.

Jellicoe was exhausted. Meanwhile it was clear that there had been some sort of action behind the Grand Fleet even as early as 2345. Several of the ships of the Grand Fleet reported seeing gun flashes and searchlights until 0200.

Things were not all going exactly to plan as far as Scheer and the German High Seas Fleet were concerned. The *Seydlitz* was badly damaged and the crew were struggling to keep her going; their coal was nearly used up and they had resorted to using oil. The *Moltke* had also slowed down because water was coming over her forecastle as her bows were beginning to sink. It was difficult to steer her, but she pulled ahead of the *Seydlitz*. At 2230 the *Moltke* had spotted four large ships to port. Her recognition lights should have been her undoing for she had blundered into four Dreadnoughts of the Second Division of the Second Battle Squadron. Within sight of her were HMS *Orion*, HMS *Monarch*, HMS *Conqueror* and HMS *Thunderer*. If she had been recognized she would have been blown to pieces.

The rear ship, HMS *Thunderer*, did think something was amiss when she saw the German recognition lights, but the captain, James Fergusson, believed that the *Moltke* was just a destroyer and that if he opened up he would be giving away the position of the British Dreadnoughts. HMS *Boadicea*, a light cruiser attached to HMS *Thunderer*, also spotted the *Moltke*. The gunners waited for the order to open fire, but it never came.

The thirty-second window of opportunity passed and the *Moltke* disappeared, desperately trying to slip through the British line. She tried twice more – once at 2255 and again at 2320 – but she was unable to do so and instead headed south in an attempt to circle round the Grand Fleet and make it home alone.

The *Seydlitz,* at times, was in even more dire straits. At 2345, barely able to maintain a speed of 7 knots, the German ship came perilously close to the Sixth Division of the First Battle Squadron, when the aft lookout spotted several large ships approaching the German battlecruiser from astern. They were definitely British and no more than 2,000 yards away. The *Seydlitz* went hard a starboard and flashed the British recognition signal; incredibly, none of the British ships decided to open up. The *Seydlitz* was also spotted later by HMS *Agincourt* but she, too, did not open fire.

The German High Seas Fleet was now approaching the point when it would cross the wake of the British Grand Fleet, as described by Vice Admiral John Harper:

> They steamed down the sides of a very long, very slender v, and it was one of the most curious circumstances of history that they did not come together at the v's point. A matter of minutes – of a quarter of an hour – of the fact that Scheer had sent his leading ships back to the rear of his line, while Jellicoe had drawn the British rear up to form upon the Grand Fleet leaders; of the fact that the British speed was 17knots, while the German speed was 16. Tiny factors and no human plan, caused Jellicoe to arrive at the bottom of the v and pass through the junction point, short minutes before the German ships arrived. The v became an x – the courses of the fleets crossed.

In fact the Germans had crossed some 3 miles behind the trailing vessels of the Grand Fleet. The Fifth Battle Squadron actually spotted the German Dreadnoughts, illuminated by searchlights and shell flashes. It seems amazing that the British ships of the Fifth Battle Squadron did not open fire and, even more implausible that they did not inform Jellicoe.

On board HMS *Barham* of the Fifth Battle Squadron, Captain Craig Waller, later tried to explain the circumstances:

It is doubtful whether the various observations of enemy ships made by ships of our battle fleet ought to have been reported to the Commander in Chief. I was on the bridge all night with my Admiral, and we came to the conclusion that the situation was known to the C-in-C and that the attacks were according to plan. A stream of wireless reports from ships in company with the C-in-C seemed superfluous and uncalled for. The unnecessary use of wireless was severely discouraged as being likely to disclose our position to the enemy. The same reason probably influenced the Marlborough Division. This may have been an error of judgement but cannot be termed amazing neglect.

Many have blamed Jellicoe for the failure of the British ships, bringing up the rear of the Grand Fleet, for not having signalled a report on what they had seen. However, whilst the Grand Fleet battle orders, written by Jellicoe himself, expressly demanded sighting reports, for the last three years radio silence had been drummed into the crews of all ships in the Grand Fleet.

Such inhibitions did not extend to the Germans. Indeed, the Admiralty were intercepting Scheer's wireless messages and already knew he was heading for Horns Reef. At 2241 they sent Jellicoe a message: 'German battle fleet ordered home at 9.14pm. Battle cruisers in rear. Course south-south-east three quarter east.'

What remains a mystery to this day is the fact that, armed with this knowledge, Jellicoe could have ensured that he was ready and waiting for Scheer, off Horns Reef, at dawn. It would have been an opportunity of a lifetime and, assuming that Scheer had not suddenly changed his mind and course, or that the weather conditions were favourable to him, the German High Seas Fleet could have been decimated.

In Jellicoe's defence, however, the Admiralty had confidently told him that the German High Seas Fleet was still in harbour, and he had been given inaccurate information even more recently. A signal sent by the Admiralty at 2158 had told him that the German fleet was 8 miles to his south-west. Jellicoe had received that message at 2223. In fact, the German fleet at that time was to his north-west. In truth, however, it was not the Admiralty's fault that they had sent this false information. The German ship that had signalled its position had actually miscalculated its exact location. Jellicoe had already received reports that German battlecruisers were to the north-east and heading south. This information had been sent by HMS *Birmingham* but what the vessel had actually seen was the Germans making a turn to starboard when they had encountered the Fourth Flotilla. After this southern turn they would resume their course for Horns Reef.

At 2338 Jellicoe received another signal, this time from Goodenough, who reported that he had engaged enemy cruisers bearing west-south-west. What is most perplexing is why the Admiralty did not pass on all the information they knew to Jellicoe, as it would surely have swayed his mind. They had translated Scheer's orders to his fleet, which he had issued at 2110, four minutes before Scheer sent a signal requesting an aerial reconnaissance first thing in the morning over Horns Reef. Another signal was intercepted, timed at 2232, ordering the German destroyers to assemble near Horns Reef at 0200. What happened was that only the bare bones of the information had been passed on to Jellicoe. But what still remains an absolute mystery is why Jellicoe did not respond to the sounds of battle behind him. In his own words, he later explained:

> The evident signs of destroyer fighting in the rear, at a long distance astern led me to think that our torpedo boat destroyers were in action with enemy torpedo boat destroyers and supporting light cruisers, and I considered that the effect of such fighting would be to turn the enemy to the northward or westward, even if he had originally intended to take passage by the Horns Reef. There was nothing to indicate that our destroyers were still in action with enemy battleships.

The other covering destroyer flotillas steered away from the sounds of battle – had they turned and supported the Fourth Flotilla, it would have been possible to launch devastating torpedo attacks on the German ships. Captain James Farie, on board HMS *Champion*, commanded the Thirteenth Flotilla, which took up position behind the Ninth and Tenth Flotillas. The three British flotillas turned to take up a south-westerly course at 0010 and steered directly in front of a line of ships. Following the commander of the Ninth and Tenth Flotillas, Commander Malcolm Goldsmith, on board HMS *Lydiard,* was a column of ships, including HMS *Unity,* from the Fourth Flotilla. Goldsmith did not recognize the significance of the ships ahead of him and planned to run across the head of the column of ships, taking into consideration only his own five vessels and not the full twelve. HMS *Petard* and HMS *Turbulent* were to pay the price. *Petard* passed the *Westfalen* just 200 yards ahead of the German vessel, but *Turbulent* was even closer and for a moment it appeared that she was going to be rammed. Abruptly she turned to starboard and for a moment or two sailed alongside the German ship – which promptly blew her to pieces. There were no survivors and Goldsmith steamed on, not realizing what had happened until 0600. *HMS Petard* had also been badly hit.

So far the German fleet had managed to slip across the rear of the Grand Fleet without major loss. Admittedly the *Elbing* and the *Rostock* were badly damaged, but five British destroyers had been sunk and another five were in a bad way. It seemed that the *Elbing* was not going to make it and preparations were being made to abandon her, rather than risk her sinking, taking her crew with her. A German torpedo boat came alongside, and the crew of the *Elbing* and many wounded from HMS *Tipperary,* who were also on board, clambered aboard the destroyer S-53. A skeleton crew remained aboard the *Elbing* to try and nurse her home, but eventually they were also forced to abandon ship and board a small vessel. As they passed a group of survivors from HMS *Tipperary,* still in the water, the German crew lit flares to alert British destroyers. The German crew were picked up by a Dutch vessel and were returned home.

The *Lützow* was in no better shape. A huge amount of water had flooded into her compartments since she had first been hit at 1815, and the crew were exhausted, but each hour saw another part of the ship fill with water – it seemed only a matter of time before the ship would be dragged below the surface. By around 2400 the crew of the *Lützow* estimated that around 7,500 tons of water was already on board. Captain Harder believed that she would be lucky to be still afloat at 0600 so he reluctantly decided to abandon ship, making the decision only just in time because the ship finally gave up the fight and sank at 0145.

This was around the same time as the *Wiesbaden* finally sank, with incredibly only one survivor. The vast majority of the crew were already dead, even before she sank. Hugo Zenne, a stoker, clung to a raft for thirty-eight hours before being finally rescued from the sea by a Norwegian ship.

Meanwhile, at 0145, the British Twelfth Flotilla spotted large vessels ahead of them on a south-easterly course. The commander of the Twelfth Flotilla was Captain Anselan Stirling, on board HMS *Faulkner*. From this distance he could not immediately identify them, but something told him that they were not British so he ordered the First Division of the Twelfth Flotilla to launch an attack and straight afterwards signalled Jellicoe: 'Enemy's battle fleet steering south-east, approximate bearing south-west. My position ten miles astern of First Battle Squadron.'

In fact, Stirling was not 10 miles astern, but 26 miles astern and out on the port quarter. Although the signal did not get through to Jellicoe, the First Division of the Twelfth Flotilla, under Commander George Campbell, moved in to attack in thickening mist. Campbell was on board HMS *Obedient* and was accompanied by HMS *Mindful*, HMS *Marvel* and HMS *Onslaught*.

Campbell was leading and assumed that in the misty conditions the Germans had turned away from him, so he headed south-east. Suddenly, looming in front of him, were a host of light cruisers and the German battlecruisers *Von der Tann* and *Derfflinger*. Campbell launched his attack at 0203. At a range of 2,000 yards, HMS *Onslaught*, HMS *Obedient*, HMS *Marvel* and HMS *Falconer* fired twelve torpedoes at the German ships, which tried desperately to avoid the oncoming missiles. One of the torpedoes went straight under the *Grosser Kurfurst* and another exploded prematurely, but a pair of them struck the *Pommern* at 0210. The effect was devastating – as fire swept into her magazine, she blew up, claiming the lives of 844 crew members.

If the Germans had doubted whether these were British ships, they now knew that the enemy was on to them. As the British destroyers generated smoke, the last one, HMS *Onslaught*, was still visible to the Germans, who poured shells into her; the bridge was on fire, the steering gear smashed. The captain, Lieutenant Commander C.R. Onslow, was taken below, mortally wounded. His last words were

'Is the ship alright?' to which someone replied that it was. He then said, 'I'll have a little sleep now then' and died.

More British destroyers were now moving in to attack the German line. The Second Division of the Twelfth Flotilla, led by Commander John Champion on board HMS *Meanad*, fired torpedoes at the Germans. HMS *Narwhal*, HMS *Nessus* and HMS *Noble* managed to get their torpedoes broadly on target, but HMS *Meanad* missed the turn away and found herself heading directly for the German line, as Commander Champion recalled:

We dashed ahead to get ready to attack them. I got separated from the others and attacked three times about 2.15am. Just before 2.30, one of our torpedoes blew up the fourth ship of the line, 1,000ft high, just like the Defence. There is no doubt about one and everything points to there having been two sunk. Anyhow I claimed one and at the very least the Twelfth Flotilla got one between them. Of course in these attacks we were fired at. Shots just short and just over and certainly between the funnels and the bridge. We bore charmed lives, it is a miracle and nothing less.

The *Pommern* had been hit, but the attack was not yet over. With the Germans firing back at the British destroyers, there was a confused mêlée between the huge, lumbering ships. German light cruisers had also joined in.

Meanwhile, Captain James Farie, on board the light cruiser HMS *Champion*, was heading south-easterly with HMS *Obdurate* and HMS *Moresby* towards the sound of the attack being pressed home by the Twelfth Flotilla. Quickly they turned west and picked up HMS *Marksman* and HMS *Meanad*, which had become separated from the Twelfth Flotilla. At 0234, they spotted four German battleships ahead of them, 4,000 yards away. They were Deutschland pre-Dreadnoughts.

Captain Farie turned away to the east, but HMS *Moresby* fired a torpedo at 0237 which hit the German destroyer, V-4. The unlucky destroyer had its bow blown off and sank almost immediately.

Dawn was at 0300. Jellicoe still hoped that he could close with Scheer, but in fact Scheer had already escaped the noose that had threatened to strangle him all night. The High Seas Fleet, or at least the main body of it, was already at the Horns Reef entrance to the Heligoland minefield. Jellicoe still believed that the Germans were to the west of him.

Instead of seeing the German fleet, all the British spotted was a zeppelin which was fired at by HMS *Revenge*. The zeppelin was following Scheer's orders to reconnoitre the Horns Reef area. Several other ships opened up, including HMS *Conqueror*, HMS *Benbow* and HMS *Royal Oak*. On board the Zeppelin, the L-11, was Commander Victor Schulze:

> The enemy opened fire on the airship from all vessels with anti-aircraft guns and guns of every calibre. The great turrets fired broadsides; the rounds followed each other rapidly. The flash from the muzzles of the guns could be seen although the ships were hidden by the smoke. All the ships that came in view took up the firing with the greatest energy, so that L-11 was some-times exposed to fire from 21 large and numbers of small ships. Although the firing did not take effect, that and the shrapnel bursting all around so shook the ship's frame that it seemed advisable to take steps to increase the range.

There was to be one last flurry of action. The destroyers following Captain Farie aboard HMS *Champion* spotted four German destroyers. Both sides opened up on one another and torpedoes were fired, before the four German destroyers peeled away. No serious damage was done and the four destroyers disappeared into the distance carrying 1,000 extra men on board: the crew of the *Lützow*.

Scheer and the High Seas Fleet finally reached Horns Reef. Although, in his own words, it seems that he was willing to resume the battle, he was not in fact going to consider this even for one moment:

> From the main fleet itself no signs of the enemy were visible at daybreak. The weather was so thick that the full length of a squadron could not be made out. In our opinion the ships in a southwesterly direction as reported by L11 could only just have come from the Channel to try, on hearing the news of the battle, to join up with their main fleet and advance against us.

There was no occasion for us to shun an encounter with this group, but owing to the slight chance of meeting on account of visibility conditions, it would have been a mistake to have followed them. Added to this the reports received from the battle cruisers showed that Scouting Division I would not be capable of sustaining a serious fight, besides which the leading ships of Squadron III could not have fought for any length of time, owing to the reduction in their supply of munitions by the long spell of firing. The Frankfurt, Pillau and Regensburg were the only fast light cruisers now available, and in such misty weather there was no depending on aerial reconnaissance. There was, therefore, no certain prospect of defeating the enemy reported in the south. An encounter and the consequences thereof had to be left to chance. I therefore abandoned the idea of further operations and ordered the return to port.

The British had one last chance to do serious injury to the German High Seas Fleet. Three British submarines – the E55, the E26 and the D1 – had left Harwich on 30 May. Unfortunately they had been told to stay below the surface until 2 June, so they were unable to receive any signals.

Meanwhile, HMS *Abdiel* had reached the Horns Reef at 0124 and managed to lay eighty mines in thirty minutes. As the German Dreadnought, *Ostfriesland,* passed the Horns Reef at 0520 she hit one of the mines. Although she took on a huge amount of water, she was still able to creep back home under her own steam. Strangely enough, the mine which had struck the German ship was not one that had just been laid, but one that had been put there by HMS *Abdiel* on 4 May.

The German High Seas Fleet arrived home between 1300 and 1444. Even the *Seydlitz* made it back as she had linked up with the rest of the fleet at 0600. She had been hit by a torpedo, twenty-one shells, had four main guns and two secondary guns knocked out, and had lost ninety-eight men dead and fifty-five injured – but she would be ready to fight again just four months later.

The Battle of Jutland was now over and all that would be left would be the recriminations.

Chapter Seven

Notable Accounts

In this chapter we briefly look at five notable accounts of the battle, which have no doubt added considerably to the mystique of the Battle of Jutland. Selected parts of these accounts are drawn from Kipling, Grant, von Edidy, Foerster and von Hase.

Rudyard Kipling described the Battle of Jutland in his series of reports in the London *Daily Telegraph*; for security reasons he used fictitious names for the destroyers. He describes the action between the screening British destroyers and the German fleet during the night:

> Towards midnight our destroyers were overtaken by several three- and four-funnel German ships (cruisers, they thought) hurrying home. At this stage of the game anybody might have been anybody – pursuer or pursued. The Germans took no chances, but switched on their searchlights and opened fire on *Gehenna*. Her Acting Sub Lieutenant reports: "A salvo hit us forward. I opened fire with the after guns. A shell then struck us in a steampipe, and I could see nothing but steam. But both starboard torpedoes were fired."
>
> *Eblis*, *Gehenna*'s next astern, at once fired a torpedo at the second ship in the German line, a four-funnelled cruiser and hit her between the second funnel and the mainmast, when "she appeared to catch fire fore and aft simultaneously, heeled right over to starboard, and undoubtedly sank." *Eblis* loosed off a second torpedo and turned aside to reload, firing at the same time to distract the enemy's attention from *Gehenna*,

who was now ablaze fore and aft. *Gehenna*'s Acting Sub Lieutenant (the only executive officer who survived) says that by the time the steam from the broken pipe cleared he found *Gehenna* stopped, nearly everybody amidships killed or wounded, the cartridge boxes round the guns exploding one after the other as the fires took hold, and the enemy not to be seen. Three minutes or less did all that damage.

Eblis had nearly finished reloading when a shot struck the davit that was swinging her last torpedo into the tube and wounded all hands concerned. Thereupon she dropped torpedo work, fired at an enemy searchlight which winked and went out, and was closing in to help *Gehenna*, when she found herself under the noses of a couple of enemy Cruisers . . . the enemy did her best. She completely demolished the *Eblis*'s bridge and searchlight platform, brought down the mast and the forefunnel, ruined the whaler and the dinghy, split the foc's'le open above water from the stern to the galley which is abaft the bridge, and below water had opened it up from the stern to the second bulkhead. She further ripped off *Eblis*'s skin plating for an amazing number of yards on one side of her, and fired a couple of large-calibre shells into *Eblis* at point-blank range narrowly missing her vitals. Even so, *Eblis* is as impartial as a prize court . . .

After all that *Eblis* picked herself up, and discovered that she was still alive, with a dog's chance of getting to port. But she did not bank on it. That grand slam had wrecked the bridge, pinning the commander under the wreckage. By the time he had extricated himself he "considered it advisable to throw overboard the steel chest and dispatch box of confidential and secret books." [These] are never allowed to fall into strange hands, and their proper disposal is the last step but one in the ritual of the burial service of His Majesty's ships at sea. *Gehenna*, afire and sinking, out somewhere in the dark, was going through it on her own account. This is her Acting Sub Lieutenant's report: "The confidential books were got up. The First Lieutenant gave the order: 'Every man aft,' and the confidential books were thrown overboard. The ship soon afterwards heeled over to starboard and the bows went under. The First Lieutenant gave the order: 'Everybody for themselves.' The ship sank in about a minute, the stern going straight up into the air."

But it was not written in the Book of Fate that stripped and battered *Eblis* should die that night as *Gehenna* died. After the burial of the books it was found that the several fires on her were manageable, that she "was not making water aft of the damage," which meant two thirds of her were, more or less, in commission, and, best of all, that three boilers were usable in spite of the cruiser's shells. So she "shaped course and speed to make the least water and the most progress towards land".

On the way back the wind shifted eight points without warning – and, what with one thing and another, *Eblis* was unable to make any port till the scandalously late hour of noon June 2, "the mutual ramming having occurred about 11:40 P.M. on May 31." She says, this time without any legal reservation whatever, "I cannot speak too highly of the courage, discipline, and devotion of the officers and ship's company."

In that flotilla alone there was every variety of fight, from the ordered attacks of squadrons under control, to single ship affairs, every turn of which depended on the second's decision of the men concerned; endurance to the hopeless end; bluff and cunning; reckless advance and redhot flight; clear vision and as much of blank bewilderment as the Senior Service permits its children to indulge in. That is not much. When a destroyer who has been dodging enemy torpedoes and gunfire in the dark realizes about midnight that she is "following a strange British flotilla, having lost sight of my own," she "decides to remain with them," and shares their fortunes and whatever language is going.

If lost hounds could speak when they cast up next day, after an unchecked night among the wild life of the dark, they would talk much as our destroyers do.

'Through the Hawse Pipe' were the unpublished memoirs of Captain Alexander Grant CBE DSC. During the Battle of Jutland, Grant was a gunner on board HMS *Lion*. The memoirs are held by the Imperial War Museum.

I had no particular special duty in action. To use a naval phrase I had a roving commission, to be here, there and everywhere.

My first concern however was the supply of ammunition to the turret guns, as the new supply method was being used and therefore I wanted to see it applied in its entirety. There were four turrets named A, B, Q and X. Each one had four separate magazines. As soon as fire had opened I made for A and B magazines. They were in the fore part of the ship and in close proximity to each other. I found everything quite satisfactory, no delay, only one door opened, and not more than one full charge in the handing room. The supply was meeting the demand. I left orders that if there was a lull in the firing the party must not forget to close the door of the magazine in use. "Aye, aye, sir," was the reply. The men were in real good fettle. I then made for Q which was in the centre of the ship. To reach it entailed a climb up a Jacob's Ladder on to the mess deck and a walk aft. En route I had to pass several parties at their allotted stations. "How is it going Sir" they asked, "alright" I would reply. "The Admiral is on the Bridge." "That's good" they would say. To get to Q one had to descend into a small flat where a first aid and electric light party was stationed, and then down into the handing room. Here everyone was standing about in silence. When I asked what was the matter, the Sergeant in charge said that something had gone wrong in the turret and that the Major in charge of the turret had ordered the magazines to be flooded. I inquired how long the valves for flooding had been opened, and when I learned that they had been opened some time I was convinced that the magazine was now completely flooded. It was also reported that the supply cages were full. It would therefore appear that there was outside the magazine at least two full charges in the supply cages and there may have been two more in the loading cages in the working chamber which was immediately under the guns. While I was making these inquiries, men from the working chamber were coming down the trunk into the handing room. I asked them what had happened and they informed me that a shell had pierced the turret, exploding inside, killing the gun's crew, and that the turret was completely out of action. Q turret was manned by the Royal Marines, with Major Harvey in charge. Major Harvey, although lying mortally wounded, to his everlasting glory thought of the safety of the ship and ordered the magazines to be flooded. For this gallant deed in safeguarding the ship he was posthumously awarded the Victoria Cross.

I thought at first of going up the trunk to see at first hand what had happened. The turret was out of action however, and as I had not yet been to X magazine I decided to go there, first ordering the men who came from the working chamber to go up into the flat above as the handing room was overcrowded. I have ever regretted not going up into the disabled turret as a subsequent disaster might, or might not have been averted. In X magazine everything appeared to have been in order. There was a lull in the firing at the time so the door was closed with no charges in the handing room. I did not stay very long, feeling rather uneasy about the flooded magazine of Q, and made to the place again. I had reached the hatchway leading to the flat above the magazine and by the Providence of God had only one foot on the step of the Jacob's Ladder, when suddenly there was a terrific roar, followed by flame and dense smoke. Had I been a few seconds earlier and thus farther down the Ladder, I would have met the same fate as all those fine men below who were burned to death. I instantly ran into the next compartment thinking the end had come. I regained my breath and self-possession and immediately went back to the hatchway and down to the bottom of the ladder. I could not get any further for smoke and fumes of cordite and scorched paint. Gas masks of those days were rather primitive and it was found that they were no use in this atmosphere. Numbers of my shipmates were either in their last agonies or already dead. I could see there was no fire and as soon as we got below endeavoured with the help of other men to rescue any who might be alive. We hauled up a few through the small hatchway but by this time all hope of saving life was gone.

I consider that the cause of this tragedy was that early in the action, an enemy shell, by a thousand chances to one, struck the armoured turret where the two guns protrude, exploding and so lifted one of the armoured plates clean off the turret. At the same time the force of explosion apparently killed or mortally wounded all those in the gun position and played havoc with the hydraulic machinery, thus putting the turret out

147

of action. It was when this happened that Major Harvey gave the order to flood magazines. Sometime had therefore elapsed between the time the turret was placed out of action and the explosion. There are two theories as to the cause of this explosion. The first is that a second enemy shell entered and exploded in the turret, thus causing a fire. With part of the roof open, the draught caused by the speed of the ship would be forced down through the turret, resulting in the flame igniting the cordite which would be in the gun-loading cages. This in turn must have ignited the cordite in the supply trunk which contained two full charges, and being in a confined space, the gases concentrated there exploded. According to the second theory, a fire may have been caused by the first shell that put the turret out of action. If so, then the strong draught of air being forced down ignited the cordite in the gun-loading cages and supply trunk. It is this second theory that has always made me regret not going into the turret to see that no fire was about. It was by the providence of God that the hatchway leading from the flat to the magazine handing room was open. This opening formed a vent though which the gases set up by the ignition of the cordite could escape. As it was, the bulkheads of the magazines were found to be saucer-shaped on examination from the force of explosion. It is difficult to say what might have happened had the hatchway been closed, or charges of cordite been left in the handing room at the time of flooding. As it was the grim fact remains that over sixty of my shipmates lost their lives in tragic circumstance without an opportunity of escape.

When I was satisfied there was no danger of fire in the vicinity of Q Magazine, I reported to the Bridge through the transmission station, for the information of the Captain. During the action the ship received several hits. Some of these passed through the ship in a most erratic way, others exploded causing casualties and fire which were promptly dealt with. One large shell landed on the upper deck, close to our foremost funnel, failed to explode, and was subsequently rolled overboard as it was considered dangerous should the ship again be engaged. As I performed this operation I thought wistfully, what a trophy it would have made for "EXCELLENT".

I do consider that for men in big ships a sea engagement is a particularly trying experience. There they are cramped and confined down below in so many small compartments, with no certain knowledge of events. If they have work to occupy their minds they are fortunate, but in such a well organised community many have not much to do during the actual battle. They listen to the thud of an enemy shell and the explosion of another. This unavoidable lack of occupation, together with the rumours that get about (and they certainly do get about), to effect that some ship has been blown to pieces, is more than enough to arouse uneasiness in their minds. It is the bounded duty of all those in authority to dispel these rumours, even if they know them to be true, and so keep up the men's spirit to the job in hand, the annihilation of the enemy.

In due course, owing to the manoeuvring of the enemy, our Squadron's firing ceased. It again opened up round about nine o'clock for a short period. Visibility then became very poor and firing ceased altogether. Orders were given that everyone had to remain at his station during the night, as it was expected that a night action might take place, and that at any rate we must be prepared to meet the enemy at dawn. Meals had to be taken in relays. During the night we pumped the water out of Q Magazine and attended to many things in readiness to meet the enemy again and, as I fervently hoped, add another glorious First of June to the annals of our Service. This action as everyone knows did not materialise. The enemy escaped to his Base, and we had no choice but to make reluctantly for the Forth. During the forenoon I had to supervise the removal of the dead from Q turret handing room and the flat above. They were all carried reverently to the Quarter Deck, and in the afternoon, our Admiral, officers and men assembled to pay homage to their shipmates who had made the supreme sacrifice. The Captain read the service (our Chaplain being amongst the dead), after which their bodies were committed to the deep. On the following forenoon we anchored in the Forth. The wounded were landed. Colliers and ammunition lighters came alongside and in less than twenty-four hours the Squadron was ready to put to sea.

The captain of SMS *Seydlitz* was Kaptain zur See von Egidy and this is his account of the battle:

When at 1400 hours the message "Enemy in sight" came in, bugles and drums sounded the General March to call all hands to battle-stations. Within minutes, every station reported to the bridge that it was ready for action.

Soon the British light cruisers came in view, and behind them dense clouds of smoke. Then tripod masts and huge hulls loomed over the horizon. There they were again, our friends from Dogger Bank. At 1545 hours we opened fire. After a short time, HMS *Indefatigable* blew up, followed 20 minutes later by HMS *Queen Mary*, our target as Tactical Number Three. The spectacle was overwhelming, there was a moment of complete silence, then the calm voice of a gunnery observer announced "Queen Mary blowing up", at once followed by the order "Shift target to the right" given by the gunnery officer in the same matter-of-fact tone as at normal gunnery practice.

Now four fast British battleships came up and directed heavy fire against our rear ships. But our main fleet came up, too; the British battle-cruisers turned away to the north, and we took up station ahead of our own battleships. We had not gone unscathed. The first hit we received was a 12-inch shell that struck Number Six 6-inch casemate on the starboard side, killing everybody except the Padre who, on his way to his battle-station down below, had wanted to take a look at the men and at the British, too. By an odd coincidence we had, at our first battle practice in 1913, assumed the same kind of hit and by the same adversary, the *Queen Mary*. Splinters perforated air leads in the bunker below and gas consequently entered the starboard main turbine compartment.

Somewhat later the gunnery central station deep down reported: "No answer from 'C' turret. Smoke and gas pouring out of the voice pipes from 'C' turret." That sounded like the time of Dogger Bank. Then it had been "C" and "D" turrets. A shell had burst outside, making only a small hole, but a red-hot piece of steel had ignited a cartridge, the flash setting fire to 13,000 pounds of cordite. 190 men had been killed, and the two turrets had been put out of action. Afterwards, a thorough examination showed that everything had been done in accordance with regulations. I told the gunnery officer: "If we lose 190 men and almost the whole ship in accordance with regulations then they are somehow wrong." Therefore we made technical improvements and changed our methods of training as well as the regulations. This time only one cartridge caught fire, the flash did not reach the magazines, and so we lost only 20 dead or severely burned, and only one turret was put out of action. When Beatty turned to the north, we had a wonderful view of the British destroyer flotillas going full speed into the attack. They were intercepted by two of our flotillas, but we did not have much time to watch the furious engagement between the lines. Our foretop reported first one, then more torpedo tracks. We tried to avoid them by sharp turns, but finally one got us a bit forward of the bridge. The blow was much softer than gunnery hits or near misses, no loud report, but only a rattling noise in the rigging. It was almost the same spot near the forward torpedo flat where we had struck a mine five weeks before. For the damage control party it was a repeat performance, and although they grinned it was otherwise not much of a joke. The torpedo bulkhead held, but it was seriously strained, as were parts of the armoured deck. Where the rivets had gone completely, the holes could be stopped with wooden pegs. Where they only leaked, which they did in great numbers – more than enough for our needs – they became a distinct menace because there was no way to plug them effectively.

Both forward generators were casualties; one stopped entirely, while the other ran but failed to generate any current. Soon all this part of Compartment XIII was flooded, and with one third of our electric supply gone, all circuits had to be switched to the generators aft. There the air leads had been damaged by splinters, and in the dynamo room the temperature rose to 72 C (164 F). The men had to don gas masks but some fainted and had to be carried out. Eventually, the room had to be evacuated, although a stoker returned from time to time to lubricate the bearings. The lights failed, but the petty officer at the electrical switchboard succeeded in re-switching all the circuits from memory. In view of the intricate battle arrangements this was quite a feat. He could do it only because he simply lived for his work and among his work. Besides this, the turbo-fans, the strong lungs of the ship, repeatedly failed because their leads were damaged, casings bent and vents perforated. However, the repair parties took special note of them and got them working again every time.

In the conning tower we were kept busy, too. "Steering failure" reported the helmsman and automatically shouted down from the armoured shaft to the control room: "Steer from control room." The order: "Steer from tiller flat" was the last resort. We felt considerable relief when the red helm indicator followed orders. The ship handling officer drew a deep breath: "Exactly as at the admiral's inspection." "No," I said, "then we used to get steering failure at the end whereas now the fun as only just started." Fortunately, we soon found some springs holding down levers in the steering heads had not been strong enough for the concussions caused by the hits. Quite simple, but try finding that under heavy fire.

The helmsman was a splendid seaman but every six months or so he could not help hitting the bottle. Then he felt the urge to stand on his head in the market square of Wilhemshaven. Each time this meant the loss of his Able Seaman's stripe. At Jutland he stood at the helm for 24 hours on end. He got the stripe back and was the only AB in the fleet to receive the Iron Cross 1st Class. The first casualty in the conning tower was a signal yeoman, who collapsed silently after a splinter had pierced his neck. A signalman took over his headphone in addition to his own. In our battle training we had overlooked this possibility.

Meanwhile, visibility decreased and there seemed to be an endless line of ships ahead. But we saw only incessant flashes, mostly four discharges in the peculiar British "rippling" salvoes. Our ship received hit after hit but our guns remained silent because we could not make out any targets. This put us under a heavy strain which was relieved, to some extent, by ship handling, changes of formation and zigzagging towards and away from previous salvoes. The port casemates suffered heavy damage, and chains had to be formed to get ammunition from the lee battery. In B turret, there was a tremendous crash, smoke, dust, and general confusion. At the order "Clear the Turret" the turret crew rushed out, using even the traps for the empty cartridges. Then they fell in behind the turret. Then compressed air from Number 3 boiler room cleared away the smoke and gas, and the turret commander went in again, followed by his men. A shell had hit the front plate and a splinter of armour had killed the right gunlayer. The turret missed no more than two or three salvoes.

In the port low-pressure turbine, steam leaked out and the men had to put on gas masks. The leak was repaired by a man creeping on his belly in the bilge directly under the turbine casing. Electric light and boiler room telegraphs also ceased under the frequent concussions. Fortunately we had practised working in the dark. Our men called these exercises "blind-man's-bluff" because they were blindfolded to learn handling valves etc by touch. The stokers and coal trimmers deserved the highest praise, for they had to wield their shovels mostly in the dark, often up to their knees in water without knowing where it came from and how much it would rise. Unfortunately, we had very bad coal, which formed so much slag that fires had to be cleaned after half the usual time, and grates burnt through and fell into the ash-pits. The spare ones had to be altered in the thick of the battle because even the beams supporting the grates were bent by the heat.

Our repair parties were very efficient, the efforts of the electricians eclipsing all the others. They found solutions for the trickiest problems, invented new connections, created electric bypasses, kept all necessary circuits going and crowned their achievements by repairing the electric baking-oven so that on the morning we got pure wheat bread, a rare treat for us

Our aerials were soon in pieces, rendering our ship deaf and dumb until a sub-lieutenant and some radio operators rigged new ones. The anti-torpedo net was torn and threatened to foul the propellers, but the boatswain and his party went over the side to lash it. They did it so well that later, in dock, it proved difficult to untie it again. According to regulations our paymasters were expected in a battle to take down and certify last wills, but we preferred them to prepare cold food forward and aft, and send their stewards round to battle-stations with masses of sandwiches.

Around 2000 hours we came under especially heavy fire, and then there followed a distinct lull, during which turrets could

153

be opened and fresh air blown through the whole ship. When we left the conning tower we stood before a frightful scene. One of the last shells had passed through the admiral's charthouse and burst in the lee of the conning tower, killing or mutilating my aide and his party of messengers and signal ratings there.

Korvettenkapitan Richard Foerster was the I Artillerie Offizier of the *Seydlitz*; he describes the terrifying night on board with the ship in dire straits and how the vessel limped home:

The condition of our ship became ever graver. Hour by hour more water penetrated into the foreship, so that the stem almost lay in the water. The danger always increased that the forward bulkheads would break. Our men of the Leak Security Service, under the direction of *Korkpt.* von Alvensleben and *Marineingenieurs* d Res. Lucke, worked like slaves during the night! The untiring, energetic work of each man had a single aim, that we still believed in, to bring the ship safely to harbour. Special thanks should go to our commander, who through his quiet, definite orders inspired all on the ship during the battle, and forgot his understandable tiredness and always spurred us to new performances. We all wanted to save our heavily damaged ship, cost what it may, and there were still many difficulties to overcome.

During the battle almost all our navigation aids were destroyed, and we had been out of FT contact for some considerable time, the antenna was shot away. Our ships position was not known accurately after the innumerable twists and turns during the battle and frequent changes in speed. Where would we find ourselves at dawn? Would we be in sight of the Horns Reef light vessel? And weren't the English standing between us and our fleet, and we almost defenceless?

It was dawn, a beautiful clear June morning. There was nothing to be seen around us, neither light vessel, nor our own nor enemy ships. We ran with as much speed as our frail ship could tolerate.

During the morning hours the FT Officer successfully made the reserve FT arrangements serviceable and we were again connected to the outside world. We learned only little; the fleet was ahead of us and retiring, and an airship reported enemy battleships north of Helgoland. However, we could report our situation and especially request support. As the enemy was not in sight *Pillau* and some *torpedobootes* would be sufficient, and they would skilfully find us and pilot us.

Always we went slower and in the Amrum Bank passage we finally ran aground in a water depth of 15 metres. What now? Remain sitting here? Certainly not, we wanted to survive. Astern into deep water and on to Heligoland. With our low speed and unmanoeuvrability on the return journey we would be an easy target for English submarines: we didn't want to bother them. Therefore we tried with all means to come free. *Pillau* came close to us and lowered a boat that brought a thick steel line over to us, so as to take us in tow. The line was made fast and *Pillau* began the tow; the arm thick line stretched tight, dead straight and – bing! – it rent like an insipid thread and finished up in the water with a clap. A second attempt finished with the same outcome and the tow attempt was given up. Could we attempt to go astern? The engines and rudder were totally undamaged and behind the ship lay considerably deeper water. Therefore we turned and went astern; and see there, slowly, however steadily we went over the sandy bottom of Amrum Bank and again were on our way. Thereon *torpedobootes* came from seawards behind us, and we recognized them as our own. As they approached we could see hundreds of men on their decks; and these gave three hurras for S.M.S. *Seydlitz*. Through blinker signal we learned that the boats had picked up the crew of S.M.S. *Lützow*. In the latter part of the battle *Lützow* had fared just like us; heavy hits, especially in the fore ship had brought flooding and finally the water came over the forecastle. It was no longer possible to hold the position. There were two *torpedobootes* in the immediate vicinity and they came alongside and took *Lützow's* survivors aboard. Shortly afterwards the proud *battlekreuzer* sank beneath the waves, as the only German fleet dreadnought loss; we had sunk three English battlecruisers.

Would we share the same fate? With each hour our situation became graver, we already had enormous amounts of water in the ship, and the strenuous work was not possible to stop new water masses penetrating the ship. Two pump steamers came out from Wilhelmshaven and they put themselves alongside us and pumped water out of the ship. However, as quickly as they pumped the water out more water poured in through the innumerable holes, that could only poorly be closed. We expected a catastrophe to overtake our ship at any moment. Everything now depended on the transverse bulkhead of the forward boiler room; if it held then it was quite possible that we could remain capable of buoyancy, if it failed then it meant the end. I knew that the *I Offizier, Korvkpt.* von Alvensleben and his bulkhead men had been in the questionable boiler room and strengthened the bulkhead with available means. With innumerable wooded supports they had propped the bulkhead but water seeped through in many places, and death lurked nearby. Undeterred they did their duty in this horrible room and it was only thanks to them that the ship was saved.

Slowly we proceeded, and slowly we neared our goal. Shortly before we reached the Jade mouth we had one more desperate battle with the elements, on Friday morning. During the night a storm came up from the NW and heavy seas threatened to destroy the fatally wounded ship, just short of the safety of harbour. We had 4000 tonnes of water in the ship and within a few hours a further 1000 tonnes entered. However we survived this trial and on a sunny evening toward 6hrs we arrived on Wilhelmshaven Roads to the cheers of the ships lying there.

Commander Georg von Hase, a First Gunnery Officer of the *Derfflinger*, describes the action shortly after 0900 when the German battlecruisers came under intense fire:

Followed by the Seydlitz, Moltke, and Von der Tann, we altered course south at 9.13 p.m. and headed straight for the enemy's van. The Derfflinger, as leading ship, now came under a particularly deadly fire. Several ships were engaging us at the same time. I selected a target and fired as rapidly as possible. At first the ranges recorded by my faithful log- keeper in the transmitting station were 12,000, from which they sank to

8000. And all the time we were steaming at full speed into this inferno, offering a splendid target to the enemy while they were still hard to make out. Commander Scheibe, in his description of the battle, describes this attack as follows: "The battle-cruisers, temporarily under the command of the Captain of the Derfflinger, while Admiral Hipper was changing ship, now hurled themselves recklessly against the enemy line, followed by the destroyers. A dense hail of fire swept them all the way.

Salvo after salvo fell round us, hit after hit struck our ship. They were stirring minutes. My communication with Lieutenant-Commander von Stosch was now cut off, the telephones and speaking-tubes running to the fore-top having been shot away. I was now left to rely entirely on my own observation of the splashes to control the gun-fire. Hitherto I had continued to fire with all four heavy turrets, but at 9.13 P.M. a serious catastrophe occurred. A 38-cm. shell pierced the armour of the "Caesar" turret and exploded inside. The brave turret commander, Lieutenant-Commander von Boltenstern had both his legs torn off and with him nearly the whole gun crew was killed. The shell set on fire two shell-cases in the turret. The flames from the burning cases spread to the transfer chamber, where it set fire to four more cases, and from there to the case-chamber, where four more were ignited. The burning cartridge-cases emitted great tongues of flame which shot up out of the turrets as high as a house; but they only blazed, they did not explode as had been the case with the enemy. This saved the ship, but the result of the fire was catastrophic. The huge tapering flames killed everyone within their reach. Of the seventy-eight men inside the turret only five managed to save themselves through the hole provided for throwing out empty shell-cases, and of these several were severely injured. The other seventy-three men died together like heroes in the fierce fever of battle, loyally obeying the orders of their turret officer.

Chapter Eight

Official Reports and Despatches

It is not possible to reproduce all the despatches of Jellicoe, Beatty and Scheer, but there follow fragments of those despatches prepared by the three men after the action. They are informative inasmuch as they provide different views of the sequence of the battle and the outcome.

We have used Scheer's account of the battle as the spine of this comparison. His account was given by the German Admiralty to the Associated Press and is dated 20 June 1916. In all cases Scheer's account is in normal typeface, Jellicoe's in italics and Beatty's in bold:

The High seas fleet consisting of three battleship squadrons, five battle cruisers, a large number of small cruisers, several Destroyer flotillas, cruising in Skaggerack on 31st May, purpose as on earlier occasions offering battle British fleet. The vanguard of small cruisers at 4.30 in the afternoon suddenly encountered ninety miles west of Hanstholm a group of eight newest cruisers of the Calliope class, fifteen to twenty of the most modern Destroyers.

While German light forces and first cruiser squadron under Hipper were following the Britons retiring north-westward, the German battlecruisers sighted to westward Beatty's battle cruiser squadron of six ships, including four Lions and two Indefatigables, which developed battle line south-easterly course.

At 2.20 p.m. reports were received from Galatea (Commodore Edwyn S. Alexander-Sinclair, M.V.O., A.D.C., indicating the

*presence of enemy vessels. The direction of advance was im-
mediately altered to S.S.E., the course for Horn Reef, so as to
place my force between the enemy and his base. At 2.35 p.m.
a considerable amount of smoke was sighted to the eastward.
This made it clear that the enemy was to the northward and
eastward, and that it would be impossible for him to round the
Horn Reef without being brought to action. Course was
accordingly altered to the eastward and subsequently to north-
eastward, the enemy being sighted at 3.31 p.m. Their force
consisted of five battle cruisers.*

Hipper formed line ahead same general course approached for
running fight, and opened fire at 5.40 in the afternoon with
heavy artillery at a range of 13,000 metres against superior
enemy. The weather was clear, light sea, light north-west wind.
After about a quarter of an hour a violent explosion occurred,
last cruiser Indefatigable caused heavy shell destroyed
Indefatigable. About 6.20 afternoon five Queen Elizabeths
coming west joined the British battle cruiser line, powerfully
reinforcing with fifteen inch guns remaining after 6.20 five
British battle cruisers. To equalise this superiority Hipper
ordered Destroyers to attack enemy British Destroyers small
cruisers interposed; bitter close range engagement ensued
wherein light cruiser participated. Germans lost two torpedo
boats whose crews were rescued by sister ships under heavy fire.
Two British Destroyers sunk by artillery; two other Nestor and
Nomad remained crippled scene, later destroyed by main fleet
after German torpedo boats rescued all survivors. While this
engagement was in progress a mighty explosion caused by big
shells broke Queen Mary third ship in the line asunder at 6.30
when smoke cloud disappears. Soon thereafter German main
battleship fleet sighted southwards, steering north. Hostile fast
squadrons there-upon turned northward closing first section of
the fight lasting about an hour. British retired high speed before
sharply following German fleet, German battle cruisers
continued artillery combat, increasing intensity, particularly
with division Queen Elizabeths, wherein leading German
battleship division intermittently participated hostile ships
showed desire to run in flat curve ahead point our line cross it.

159

Seven forty five in the evening British small cruisers and destroyers launched an attack against our battle cruisers which avoided torpedoes by manoeuvring while British battle cruisers retired from the engagement wherein later they did not participate as far as can be established. Shortly thereafter a German re-connoitering group, parrying Destroyer attack, received heavy fire from the northeast whereby the cruiser Wiesbaden was soon put out of action, parts German torpedo flotillas which immediately attacked heavy ships appearing shadow-like from bank of haze north east, made out long line at least twenty five battleships which first on northwest to westerly course sought junction British battle cruisers and Queen Elizabeths, then turned to easterly to south-easterly course. With the advent of the British main fleet, whose centre consisted of three squadrons eight battleships with fast divisions of three Invincibles on northern wing and three newest Royal Sovereigns armed with fifteen inch guns at southern end began about eight in the evening third section of the engagement embracing combat main fleets Vice Admiral Scheer determined to attack British main fleet which as now recognised was completely assembled and about doubly superior.

The action between the battle fleets lasted intermittently from 6.17 p.m. to 8.20 p.m. at ranges between 9,000 and 12,000 yards, during which time the British Fleet made alterations of course from S.E. by E. to W. in the endeavour to close. The enemy constantly turned away and opened the range under cover of destroyer attacks and smoke screens as the effect of the British fire was felt, and the alterations of course had the effect of bringing the British Fleet which commenced the action in a position of advantage on the bow of the enemy) to a quarterly bearing from the enemy battle line, but at the same time place us between the enemy and his bases.

At 6.55 p.m. Iron Duke passed the wreck of Invicible (Captain Arthur L. Cay), with Badger (Commander C.A. Fremantle) standing by.

German battleship squadrons headed by battle cruisers steered first toward extensive haze bank in north east wherefrom

160

crippled Wiesbaden was still receiving heavy fire. Around the Wiesbaden stubborn individual fights in quickly changing conditions now occurred; enemy light forces supported by armoured cruiser squadron of five ships of Minotaur, Achilles, Duke of Edinburgh classes coming from north-east; apparently surprised by decreasing visibility of our battle cruisers and leading battleship divisions they thereby came under violent heavy fire, whereby smaller cruiser and Defence and Black Prince were sunk, Warrior regained its own line as a wreck and sank later, small cruiser was severely damaged. Two destroyers had already fallen victims to the attack by German torpedo-boats against leading British battleships, small cruiser and two destroyers were damaged. German battle cruisers and leading battleship divisions had in these engagements and under effect of increased fire of enemy battleship squadron which shortly after eight could be made out in haze turned to north-easterly finally easterly course. Germans observed amidst artillery combat shelling of great intensity signs of effect of good shooting particularly eight-twenty thirty [2020 + thirty seconds]. Several officers of German ships observed that battle-ship Queen Elizabeth class blowing up under conditions similar to Queen Mary. Invincible sank after being severely hit. Ship of Iron Duke class had earlier received a torpedo hit; one Queen Elizabeth class running around in circle apparently hit in steering arrangements. Luetzow was hit at least by fifteen heavy shells and was unable to maintain place in the line: Vice Admiral Hipper therefore transhipped by torpedo-boat under heavy fire to Moltke. Derfflinger in the meantime temporarily took the lead. German torpedo flotillas attacked enemy main fleet, heard detonations. Germans therein lost torpedo-boat by heavy hit. Enemy destroyer seen hit by torpedo and in sinking condition. After this first violent onslaught into mass of supe-rior enemy opponents lost sight of each other in smoke power cloud. After short cessation of artillery combat, Scheer ordered new attack with all available forces. German battle cruisers which with several light cruisers and torpedo-boats again headed the line encountered soon after nine renewed heavy fire from mist which was answered by them and then by leading division main fleet. Armoured cruisers now flung themselves

161

in reckless onset at extreme speed against enemy line in order to cover the attack; torpedo-boats approached it though covered with shot to 6,000 metres. Several German torpedo flotillas dashed forward to attack, delivered torpedoes and returned, losing only one boat, despite most severe counter-fire. Bitter artillery fight again interrupted after this second violent onslaught, in smoke from guns and funnels several torpedo flotillas which were ordered to attack somewhat later found after penetrating smoke cloud enemy fleet no longer before them. Nor when fleet commander again brought German squadrons upon southerly and south-westerly course where enemy last seen could opponents be found. Only once more shortly before 10.30 did the battle flare up for a short time; in late twilight German battle cruisers sighted towards four enemy capital ships and opened fire immediately. As two German battleship squadrons attacked enemy turned and vanished in the darkness; older German light cruisers of fourth reconnaissance group were also engaged with older enemy armoured cruisers in a short fight. This ended day battle.

I continued on a south-westerly course with my light cruisers spread until 9.24 p.m. Nothing further being sighted, I assumed that the enemy were to the north- westward, and that we had established ourselves between him and his base. Minotaur (Captain Arthur C.S.H. D'Aeth) was at this time bearing north 5 miles, and I asked her the position of the leading battle squadron of the Battle Fleet. Her reply was that it was not in sight, but was last seen bearing N.N.E. I kept you informed of my position, course, and speed, also of the bearing of the enemy.

In view of the gathering darkness, and the fact that our strategic position was such as to make it appear certain that we should locate the enemy at daylight under most favourable circumstances, I did not consider it desirable or proper to close the enemy Battle Fleet during the dark hours. I therefore concluded that I should be carrying out your wishes by turning to the course of the Fleet, reporting to you that I had done so.

German divisions which after losing sight of enemy took up night mark in southerly direction were attacked until dawn by enemy light forces in rapid succession. The attacks were favoured by general strategic situation and particularly dark night. Cruiser Frauelob was severally damaged during engagement of fourth reconnaissance group with superior cruiser force and was lost from sight missing then on. Armoured cruiser Cressy class suddenly appeared close to German battleship, was shot into fire after four seconds and sank four minutes. Florent Destroyer 60 (names hard to decipher in darkness, therefore uncertainly established) and four destroyers three, seventy-eight, nought-six, twenty-seven destroyed by four fire partly in course seconds. One destroyer was cut in two by ram of German battleship seven destroyers thirty hit and severely damaged, these including Tipperary, Turbulent which after saving survivors were left behind in sinking condition and drifted past our lines some burning bow to stern. Tracks of countless torpedoes were sighted by German ships but only the Pommern fell immediate victim to torpedo. Cruiser Rostock was hit but remained afloat. Elbing was damaged by German battleship in unavoidable manoeuvre. After vain endeavour to keep the ship afloat the Elbing was blown up after crew embarked on torpedo boats. German post torpedo boat struck mine laid by enemy.

The 13th Flotilla, under the command of Captain James U. Farie, in Champion, took station astern of the Battle Fleet for the night. At 0.30 a.m. on Thursday, 1st June, a large vessel crossed the rear of the flotilla at high speed. She passed close to Petard and Turbulent, switched on searchlights, and opened a heavy fire, which disabled Turbulent. At 3.30 a.m. Champion was engaged for a few minutes with four enemy destroyers. Moresby reports four ships of "Deutschland" class sighted at 2.35 a.m., at whom she fired one torpedo. Two minutes later an explosion was felt by Moresby and Obdurate.

Fearless and the 1st Flotilla were very usefully employed as a submarine screen during the earlier part of the 31st May. At 6.10 p.m., when joining the Battle Fleet, Fearless was unable to follow the battle cruisers without fouling the battleships, and therefore took station at the rear of the line. She sighted during the night a battleship of the "Kaiser" class steaming fast

163

and entirely alone. She was not able to engage her, but believes she was attacked by destroyers further astern. A heavy explosion was observed astern not long after.

The 1st and 3rd Light Cruiser Squadrons were almost continuously in touch with the battle cruisers, one or both squadrons being usually ahead. In this position they were of great value. They very effectively protected the head of our line from torpedo attack by light cruisers or destroyers, and were prompt in helping to regain touch when the enemy's line was temporarily lost sight of. The 2nd Light Cruiser Squadron was at the rear of our battle line during the night, and at 9 p.m. assisted to repel a destroyer attack on the 5th Battle Squadron. They were also heavily engaged at 10.20 p.m. with five enemy cruisers or light cruisers, Southampton and Dublin (Captain Albert C. Scott) suffering severe casualties during an action lasting about 15 minutes. Birmingham (Captain Arthur A.M. Duff), at 11.30 p.m., sighted two or more heavy ships steering South. A report of this was received by me at 11.40 p.m. as steering W.S.W. They were thought at the time to be battle cruisers, but it is since considered that they were probably battleships.

At daylight, 1st June, the battle fleet, being then to the southward and westward of the Horn Reef, turned to the northward in search of enemy vessels and for the purpose of collecting our own cruisers and torpedo- boat destroyers. At 2.30 a.m. Vice-Admiral Sir Cecil Burney transferred his flag from Marlborough to Revenge, as the former ship had some difficulty in keeping up the speed of the squadron. Marlborough was detached by my direction to a base, successfully driving off an enemy submarine attack en route. The visibility early on 1st June (three to four miles) was less than on 31st May, and the torpedo-boat destroyers, being out of visual touch, did not rejoin until 9 a.m. The British Fleet remained in the proximity of the battlefield and near the line of approach to German ports until 11 a.m. on 1st June, in spite of the disadvantage of long distances from fleet bases and the danger incurred in waters adjacent to enemy coasts from submarines and torpedo craft. The enemy, however, made no sign, and I was reluctantly

164

compelled to the conclusion that the High Sea fleet had returned into port. Subsequent events proved this assumption to have been correct. Our position must have been known to the enemy, as at 4 a.m. the fleet engaged a Zeppelin for about five minutes, during which time she had ample opportunity to note and subsequently report the position and course of the British Fleet.

The waters from the latitude of the Horn Reef to the scene of the action were thoroughly searched, and some survivors from the destroyers Ardent (Lieutenant-Commander Arthur Marsden), Fortune (Lieutenant-Commander Frank G. Terry), and Tipperary (Captain (D) Charles J. Wintour), were picked up, and the Sparrowhawk (Lieutenant-Commander Sydney Hopkins), which had been in a collision and was no longer seaworthy, was sunk after her crew has been taken off. A large amount of wreckage was seen, but no enemy ships, and at 1.15 p.m., it being evident that the German Fleet has succeeded in returning to port, course was shaped for our bases, which were reached without further incident on Friday, 2nd June. A cruiser squadron was detached to search for Warrior, which vessel had been abandoned whilst in tow of Engadine on her way to the base owing to bad weather setting in and the vessel becoming unseaworthy, but no trace of her was discovered, and a further subsequent search by a light cruiser squadron having failed to locate her, it is evident that she foundered.

The Fleet fuelled and replenished with ammunition, and at 9.30 p.m. on 2nd June was reported ready for further action.

I deeply regret to report the loss of H.M. ships Queen Mary, Indefatigable, Invincible, Defence, Black Prince, Warrior, and of H.M. T.B.D.'s Tipperary, Ardent, Fortune, Shark, Sparrowhawk, Nestor, Nomad, and Turbulent, and still more do I regret the resultant heavy loss of life. The death of such gallant and distinguished officers as Rear-Admiral Sir Robert Arbuthnot, Bart., Rear-Admiral The Hon. Horace Hood, Captain Charles F. Sowerby, Captain Cecil I. Prowse, Captain Arthur L. Cay, Captain Thomas P. Bonham, Captain Charles J. Wintour, and Captain Stanley V. Ellis, and those who perished with them, is a serious loss to the Navy and to the country. They led officers and men who were equally gallant, and whose death is mourned by their comrades in the Grand Fleet. They fell doing their duty nobly, a death which they would have been the first to desire.

The enemy fought with the gallantry that was expected of him. We particularly admired the conduct of those on board a disabled German light cruiser which passed down the British line shortly after deployment, under a heavy fire, which was returned by the only gun left in action.

Chapter Nine

Who Won Jutland?

At dawn on 1 June 1916, Jellicoe confidently expected to find the enemy fleet somewhere off to the west. Visibility was extremely poor, but he needed to close on Scheer before the German vessels could slip away to safety.

Scheer meanwhile had hoped that zeppelins would be launched to carry out a reconnaissance for him, but the zeppelin base had not received the signal. Nonetheless, there were zeppelins in the sky that morning but only one, the L11, spotted a dozen or so enemy ships, which promptly fired at her to drive her away. The position of the British vessels was immediately passed on to the German navy.

Despite the fact that only the L11 confirmed sightings of the British ships, several other zeppelins came close to discovering the enemy. Between 0315 and 0345 on 1 June, nine or more British ships reported hearing zeppelins overhead.

Jellicoe now decided that if British ships had heard the zeppelins, then the zeppelins must have seen his fleet, which meant that Scheer had the upper hand and Jellicoe was unlikely to be able to bring him to battle. The Admiralty sent a coded message, timed at 0329, giving him the precise location and speed of the German main fleet. By the time it was fully decoded it was 0410. Scheer, by this stage, was less than 40 miles from the entrance to the German defence minefield and had passed the Horns Reef. Jellicoe concluded: 'This signal made it evident that by no possibility could I catch the enemy before he reached port, even if I disregarded the danger of following him through the minefields.'

One British officer summed up the British mood when he wrote:

'[There] came a gradual realisation, the mounting disappointment, that we should not see the High Seas Fleet that day; there was to be no completion of yesterday's work.'

All Jellicoe could now hope to achieve would be to mop up any German stragglers, yet he did not contact Beatty. At 0404 Beatty signalled Jellicoe: 'When last seen Enemy was to the W, steering SW and proceeding slowly. Zeppelin has passed astern of me steering west. Submit I may sweep SW to locate Enemy.'

At 0430, Beatty signalled his battlecruisers: 'Damage yesterday was heavy on both sides, we hope today to cut off and annihilate the whole German Fleet. Every man must do his utmost. Lutzow is sinking and another German battlecruiser expected to have sunk.'

However, at 0440, Beatty received a reply from Jellicoe, responding to his signal of 0404: 'Enemy has returned to harbour. Try to locate Lutzow.'

Beatty was crushed by this news and reluctantly abandoned his search for the enemy fleet. Jellicoe too gave up the pursuit at 0716. By 1100, the Grand Fleet was gone, heading back to their bases. After sixteen hours it was over, a battle that had been sparked by the *N J Fjord* and ended in disappointment for both admirals. Quite simply, it had begun too late in the day and in poor weather conditions, which had affected visibility. Scheer's plan to inflict sufficient casualties to gain parity at sea had failed and Jellicoe's attempt to crush the German High Seas Fleet had ended in frustration. Jellicoe's Grand Fleet now had to endure a 400-mile journey, with the possibility of enemy torpedo boats, mines and submarines all the way home. Beatty's force was some 300 miles from Rosyth.

At 0600 on the morning of 2 June, Beatty's ships arrived in the Firth of Forth; Jellicoe's vessels made it to Scapa Flow at around midday; some of the smaller, damaged ships did not make it home until 4 June.

At 2145 on 2 June, Jellicoe signalled the Admiralty that his force would be ready to leave at four hours' notice. He could muster some 25 Dreadnought battleships, 6 battlecruisers, 25 cruisers and 60 destroyers. All Scheer would be able to scrape together, had the need arisen, was a dozen battleships, a pair of battlecruisers, three cruisers and a handful of torpedo boats.

The German fleet steamed unmolested in the mouth of the Jade, even passing over three British submarines, which had explicit instructions not to surface until 2 June.

There was panic at 0520 for the Germans when the *Ostfriesland* hit a mine, and when the ships reached Amrum Bank, the crippled *Seydlitz* ran aground. Rather than risk the same fate, the captain of the *König* waited for three hours before he attempted to cross the sandbank. The *Seydlitz* was eventually floated off at high tide, but she was so badly damaged she had to be towed in and nearly sank twice more, but finally made it home. By the look of the German High Seas Fleet that morning, they would not be capable of putting up a fight for some time.

The German press picked up on the inaccurate claims that Scheer had reported, believing that they had scored a significant victory against the Royal Navy. They had a full day's lead in making the most of the propaganda as the British fleet was still at sea.

Confidently, a Frankfurt paper stated: 'Great sea battle in the North Sea. Many British battleships destroyed and damaged.'

So far, apart from the Admiralty and certain others in the establishment, no one else actually knew that the Battle of Jutland had even happened. The First Lord of the Admiralty, Arthur Balfour, released a communiqué on the morning of 3 June which did not allay any fears, nor did it necessarily contradict the claims being made by the Germans.

On 3 June, the British papers were full of the news that the British had lost the Battle of Jutland, although some were more cautious. No one suspected the truth, that after a poor start in the battle, the Royal Navy had given the German High Seas Fleet a pasting. Added to that, the German ships had had to break off the engagement and make for safety. Admittedly, more British ships may have been sunk, but comparatively speaking, the Germans were now considerably weaker than they had been before the first shots had been fired in the battle.

The Germans, however, were convinced that victory had been achieved. Henceforth, they would refer to the battle as *Skagerrakschlact*, although the battle had not taken place near the Skagerrak, which was some 100 miles distant. Laterally the battle would earn its name from Jellicoe's description – the Battle of Jutland Bank.

The Kaiser, Wilhelm II, was desperate to see the victorious fleet. After dishing out countless Iron Crosses and Ordres pour le Mérite, he told the assembled ranks of naval men:

The journey I have made today means very much to me. I would like to thank you all. Whilst our army has been fighting our enemies, bringing home many victories, our fleet had to wait until they eventually came. A brave leader led our fleet and commanded the courageous sailors. The superior English armada eventually appeared and our fleet was ready for battle. What happened? The English were beaten. You have started a new chapter in world history. I stand before you as your Highest Commander to thank you with all my heart.

Meanwhile, the British had released another communiqué, written by Churchill. It had Churchill's touch and helped to restore confidence in the situation and in the Royal Navy.

The Admiralty sent a copy of Jellicoe's despatch to King George V. As an ex-Navy man himself, he replied:

I am deeply touched by the message which you have sent me on behalf of the Grand Fleet. It reached me on the morrow of a great battle, which has once more displayed the splendid gallantry of the officers and men under your command. I mourn the loss of brave men, many of them personal friends of my own, who have fallen in their country's cause. Yet even more do I regret that the German High Seas Fleet, in spite of its heavy losses, was enabled by the misty weather to evade the full consequences of an encounter they have always professed to desire, but for which when the opportunity arrived they showed no inclination.

The Admiralty issued a final statement on the evening of 4 June, leading to statements, closer to the truth, in the newspapers the following morning, such as: '[Jellicoe] having driven the enemy into port, returned to the main scene and scoured the sea in search of disabled vessels.'

Any lingering doubts were dispelled on 4 June when the Germans admitted the full extent of their losses at the Battle of Jutland. The naval correspondent of the *Daily Express* remarked: 'If there is anyone left in this country who still has doubts about the character of the British victory, he is a fit subject for a mental specialist.'

A New York journalist was all the more cutting: 'The German Fleet has assaulted its jailer, but it is still in jail.'

So who really won the battle of Jutland? If the measure of victory is purely in terms of ships sunk then there can be little doubt that the Germans won the battle. Total British losses amounted to a displacement of 113,000 tons or fourteen vessels; total German losses were 61,000 tons or eleven vessels.

Losses at the Battle of Jutland

Type	British	German
Battlecruisers	*Indefatigable* *Queen Mary* *Invincible*	*Lützow*
Pre-Dreadnoughts		*Pommern*
Armoured cruisers	*Black Prince* *Defence* *Warrior*	
Light cruisers		*Elbing* *Frauenlob* *Rostock* *Wiesbaden*
Destroyers	*Ardent* *Fortune* *Nestor* *Nomad* *Shark*	S35 V4 V27 V29 V48
	Sparrowhawk *Tipperary* *Turbulent*	
Crew killed	6,097	2,551

This table really only shows part of the story, as do the bald comparisons between fourteen lost vessels against eleven. Both HMS *Queen Mary* and the *Lützow* were ultra-modern vessels. The *Invincible* and the *Indefatigable* were effectively obsolete, still first-line, but not as powerful as Beatty's battlecruisers. HMS *Black Prince*, HMS *Defence* and HMS *Warrior* were over ten years old and obsolete, as was the German pre-Dreadnought, the *Pommern*. With the exception of the obsolete *Frauenlob,* the other three German light cruisers were brand new. As for the destroyers or torpedo boats, they were all new and none more than five years old. Some of the damaged ships would soon be back in operation, although many of these dates are disrupted:

Capital Ship Dry Dock Repair Completion Dates

Tiger	1/7/1916	*Helgoland*	16/6/1916
		Grosser	
Barham	4/7/1916	*Kurfurst*	16/7/1916
Malaya	10/7/1916	*Markgraf*	20/7/1916
Warspite	20/7/1916	*König*	21/7/1916
Princess Royal	21/7/1916	*Ostfriesland*	26/7/1916
Marlborough	2/8/1916	*Moltke*	30/7/1916
Lion	13/9/1916	*Von der Tann*	2/8/1916
		Seydlitz	16/9/1916
		Derfflinger	15/10/1916
		Rheinland	2/1/1917
		Westfalen	17/6/1916

It does seem that the German High Seas Fleet had suffered more long-term damage than the British. It would take some time for many of the German ships to be capable of operations once again. Unfortunately, the damage reports for four of the German vessels have not survived – the *Kaiser, Oldenburg, Schlesien* and the *Schleswig-Holstein.*

Even by the late summer of 1916 the Germans would be lacking their two most powerful battlecruisers. Jellicoe, on the other hand, was actually able to set sail the day after the Battle of Jutland with an impressive Grand Fleet.

The vast majority of the British casualties relate to the five large ships that exploded during the battle. In actual fact, three of the battlecruisers that the British had lost blew up after particularly lucky, or unlucky, shots, depending on your point of view. The pair of armoured cruisers that had blown up were simply too old and too weakly armoured; this had also been the fate of the Germans' *Pommern*. If the large ships had not blown up, causing such horrific loss of life, then the casualties by gunfire alone would have been fairly even.

Much has also been made of the comparative accuracy of the British and the Germans. The Germans fired 2,424 x 12in shells and a further 1,173 x 11in shells. With these they had scored just 120 hits – in other words just over 3 per cent were on target. The British figures, however, are slightly worse and their hit rate was only just over 2 per cent. However, these figures must be taken with a pinch of salt – some of the German hits include only those that were made at point-blank range when it would obviously be far easier to hit an enemy target than at extreme range. Equally the Germans did not provide accurate figures as to the type of shells that hit their vessels. Many of the large-calibre British shells are actually described by the Germans as clusters of smaller calibre shells.

More recent investigations into the hit rate suggest that the British capital ships fired 4,480 rounds of heavy shells. Of these 123 were on target, giving a hit rate of 2.75 per cent. In comparison the German High Seas Fleet expended 3,597 heavy shells and scored 122 hits. Their hit rate was therefore 3.39 per cent. Again, these figures, compiled from data over the past decade, fail to recognize the fact that of the 122 German hits, 49 of them were at point-blank range, the majority of which were fired into the defenceless HMS *Warspite*. By means of comparison, nineteen of the hits scored by the British were made at ranges of between 8,000 and 18,000 yards.

If we compare the shots to hit ratios of the capital ships themselves when they were firing at one another, we can see that even if we include the fact that the *Warspite* was hit fifteen times at close range, the Germans scored 85 hits against 104 by the British.

Around half of all the hits scored by the Royal Navy during the Battle of Jutland were made at targets travelling at a speed of at least 8 knots at distances of around 8,000 yards. On average, therefore, both the Germans and the British were scoring hits at a rate of around 3 per cent. Before the First World War, studies had been carried out that suggested that at ranges between 10,000 yards and 20,000 yards, the hit rate would be 5 per cent.

Which of the ships performed most creditably in terms of gunnery during the Battle of Jutland? For the Germans, the First Scouting Group of Hipper's force were scoring a hit for every twenty-six shells fired, which works out at nearly 4 per cent. The British comparison was Hood's Third Battle Cruiser Squadron which was scoring a hit with every twenty-three shells, equating to a 4.3 per cent success rate.

The worst performers as far as the British were concerned were the First and Second Battle Cruiser Squadrons. Collectively they fired 1,469 rounds of heavy shells and only scored twenty-one hits, which meant that these battlecruisers, all six of them, were taking seventy rounds to score a single hit. In other words, they scored a pitiful 1.4 per cent success rate. However, these were not the worst performers on the battlefield that day. HMS *Tiger* and HMS *New Zealand* fired off 723 rounds and scored just six hits.

For the British, the most effective ships were HMS *Invincible*, HMS *Inflexible*, HMS *Barham*, HMS *Valiant* and HMS *Iron Duke*. As far as the Germans were concerned, the *Derfflinger*, *Moltke* and the *Lützow* achieved the best results.

It was clear that the British, using a bracketing system, were probably more effective than the Germans. Typically a British ship would fire off a salvo at an enemy vessel, wait for the shells to fall and then, using the splashes in the water, adjust the range accordingly. Once they were on target, straddling or bracketing the enemy ship, they were more able to stick to the target than their German adversaries. The Germans relied on stereoscopic range-finders, but the noise of battle obviously had a detrimental effect on their ability to maintain accurate assessments of range.

It was, perhaps, the fact that Beatty's battlecruiser squadrons had less opportunity to practise their gunnery than Jellicoe's Grand Fleet that caused their poor gunnery performance during the Battle of Jutland. The two notable exceptions were Hood's Third Battle Cruiser Squadron and Evan-Thomas's Fifth Battle Squadron, which had the opportunity for gunnery practice at Scapa Flow. Hood's squadron only fired 25 per cent of the number of shells fired by

Beatty's ships. Beatty's six ships scored twenty-one hits yet Hood's squadron scored sixteen. At the same time Evan-Thomas's ships, whilst firing three quarters of the number of shells that Beatty's had fired, scored twenty-nine hits.

Much has been made of the fact that fewer German capital ships were destroyed than British capital ships – the simple answer is that the German capital ships were far more robust and able to take punishment. It took twenty-four hits to destroy the *Lützow*, but the *Derfflinger* and the *Seydlitz* were hit almost as many times without sinking.

Another key determining factor was the British shells' tendency to explode before they penetrated the German armour. They were far too sensitive. It is also believed that, despite testing, between 30 and 70 per cent of the British shells were duds.

As for the final analysis of who won the Battle of Jutland, it is important to appreciate that the battle was won and lost at various stages. Initially, Hipper performed well and probably won the battle against Beatty. However, Beatty had fulfilled his role and had drawn the German fleet into a trap to be sprung by the Grand Fleet. On two occasions Jellicoe had effectively forced Scheer to retreat. To begin with it was a disorganized withdrawal but, once again, the Germans turned the tables and were able to extract the bulk of their fleet from the clutches of Jellicoe's pursuing vessels.

Although this was not a clear-cut victory, Jellicoe had succeeded inasmuch as he had control of the battlefield with his enemy in retreat. However, Jellicoe failed in his primary objective which was the annihilation of the German High Seas Fleet. Admittedly Scheer was forced to withdraw, but he saved the bulk of his fleet perhaps to fight another day. Jellicoe, understandably, was as concerned with making sure that his Grand Fleet was not defeated as he was with ensuring that the German fleet was destroyed. The best we can conclude about Jutland is that it was indecisive.

It had convinced Scheer, however, of the notion that he would lose a head-to-head fight against the Royal Navy. German losses were severe and considering the disparity of forces before the battle, they were even more marked after it. Scheer, however, was confident in a report he wrote to the Kaiser on 4 July 1916, in which he told the Kaiser that the German High Seas Fleet would be prepared to resume offensive operations by the middle of August 1916. He concluded, however:

> Nevertheless there can be no doubt that even the most successful outcome of a Fleet action in this war will not force England to make peace. A victorious end to the war within a reasonable time can only be achieved through the defeat of British economic life – that is, by using the u-boats against British trade.

As it was, however, the unrestricted use of U-boats did not begin again until February 1917. From the Battle of Jutland onwards the German High Seas Fleet would only be used in a supporting role. Scheer said: 'The High Seas Fleet was reduced to the hilt of the weapon whose sharp blade was the u-boat.'

Meanwhile, the Royal Navy's blockade of Germany continued. The only place it was not in effect was in the Baltic Sea. Shortages became acute and there were even food riots. The best the Germans could achieve was a form of counter-blockade using their submarines.

Chapter Ten

Surrender and Controversy

It is certain that the individual crew members on every single ship, whether British or German, during the Battle of Jutland could not have made any greater efforts. It is harder to appraise the three key commanders during the battle.

As far as Jellicoe is concerned, he was undoubtedly a good professional Royal Navy officer. He had spent two years with his fleet at Scapa Flow, attempting to bring it to a peak of perfection in terms of gunnery and manoeuvres. What is less clear is whether he had the tactical ability to use it. He had certainly not been trained as a tactician and so he was somewhat inflexible. His seventy-page Grand Fleet Battle Orders were quite limiting and probably prevented many individual captains from showing any independence, ingenuity or flair.

Jellicoe favoured long, single lines of ships, firing at the enemy in parallel lines from a distance – he considered most other tactics to be far too dangerous – and was obsessed with the need to dominate the battlefield with superior firepower. Jellicoe was not keen on delegating, a fact that is amply borne out by his attitude towards reinforcing Beatty, thus allowing him to take a wider range of independent actions, without the involvement of the Grand Fleet. He knew the weaknesses of his own force as well as their strengths; he also knew that he could not underestimate the Germans.

In terms of tactical brilliance on the battlefield, Jellicoe undoubtedly pulled off an extremely impressive and complex manoeuvre when he crossed Scheer's T, which he achieved by deploying to port. Jellicoe had often been criticized for not following up failed German attacks with strong and determined counter-attacks of his own, and had always been afraid of counter-attack by torpedo boats, the German's use of the submarines and their deployment of mines. When Scheer retired for the second time, covered by torpedo boats, it has been argued that Jellicoe should have pressed home his advantage and not turned away. Many believe that the small number of German torpedo boats would not have presented a major risk to the British fleet.

More perplexing is why Jellicoe did not use his scouts to find Scheer after the latter had withdrawn for the second time. At this stage Jellicoe still had two hours of daylight, so he could easily have fallen on the German rearguard and scored some spectacular hits on the retreating German force.

By the time night fell, Jellicoe, for many of the same reasons for which he was reluctant to risk his Grand Fleet against underwater or smaller enemy vessels, did not press home any advantage – neither he nor Scheer were willing to risk their fleets against one another at night. Consequently Jellicoe had to wait until daylight. Above all, he had to place the Grand Fleet between the Germans and their safe home bases.

Scheer had tried to escape to the east on two occasions, so Jellicoe sent the bulk of his scouting force to the west and south. As it was, Scheer managed to pass through Jellicoe's rearguard and escape.

In the introduction and at the beginning of this book, Jutland was compared to the Battle of Trafalgar. It is certainly the case that Jellicoe and Nelson were very different men, yet Nelson had a considerable psychological advantage – he knew that if he had been defeated at the Battle of Trafalgar, there was an equally large fleet waiting to protect the British Isles. Jellicoe did not have this safety blanket to allow him to make more aggressive and risky decisions. If the British fleet had been badly mauled or even destroyed at Jutland then the German High Seas Fleet would rule the North Sea, if not all the waters around the British Isles.

Beatty was a very different man. Many believed that he had worked with precision to draw the German High Seas Fleet on to Jellicoe's Grand Fleet; many others have equally accused him of being impetuous. Beatty was dying to get into action. Just two months before the Battle of Jutland he wrote to his wife: 'If I meet Hipper and his battle cruisers, I can deal with them.'

Beatty was certainly inspirational and his subordinates trusted him implicitly. He did not have a great relationship, however, with Evan-Thomas and Moore, although he was happy for his subordinates to make independent decisions and often allowed them to do so.

Despite all this Beatty did lack experience and he never seemed to learn from his past mistakes. Prior to his appointment to the Battle Cruiser Squadrons he had not been given command of an important squadron. During the battle he made some basic errors, as Churchill later pointed out: 'Beatty's six battle cruisers were in themselves superior in numbers, speed and gun power to the whole of the German battle cruisers. Why should he wait to become stronger when by every test of paper and every memory of battle he was already strong enough?' Put simply, Beatty did not deploy all of the assets he had when the opportunity arose.

In support of Beatty, however, he could not have known whether Hipper was on his own or whether other vessels were available in support. When he came to engage Hipper, Beatty should have ordered his ships to open fire at longer ranges in order to take advantage over the range superiority between his own vessels and those of Hipper. By the time Beatty had closed in to open fire he was already under fire from Hipper's ships.

Another mistake occurred when Scheer's fleet arrived. Beatty delayed the order to turn north, putting Evan-Thomas's squadron in great danger. Beatty was overwhelmingly outmanoeuvred by Hipper as the Germans fled to the south.

In the next major phase of the battle, however, Beatty acquitted himself well. He drew away from the pursuing German vessels, even cutting across their line of advance, causing Hipper to move to the east. He then held course until Jellicoe could fall on the unsuspecting Germans.

Beatty has also been criticized for the poor signalling performance which led to confusion amongst his battlecruiser squadrons. What can never be forgotten, however, is that even after using up a huge amount of ammunition, Beatty still failed to score impressive hits on the German fleet. In fact, although not a completely fair comparison, during one afternoon of the Battle of the Falklands, Sturdee sank more ships than Beatty managed to sink in the three battles in which he was involved. In a letter to the King's private secretary, Sir Hedworth Meux said:

> Jellicoe's despatch stating that his battle fleet was engaged for two hours is most disingenuous and has naturally created a false impression in the country. Practically the whole of the fighting was done by our battle cruisers, and our battle fleet only fired a very few rounds – hardly any of them were touched and probably did a similar amount of damage to the enemy.

This sums up perfectly the age-old argument that the Battle of Jutland was, essentially, a battle between Beatty's battlecruisers, Hipper's force and Scheer's German High Seas Fleet. It is not strictly true, but there was enormous resentment between Beatty's crews and the battleships of the Grand Fleet. The truth was that Jellicoe's battleships fired far more shells than Beatty's vessels had done. In fact, in their two encounters lasting a total of no more than an hour, they had still managed to fire more shells than Beatty's ships had managed in three and a half hours of continued fighting. In the end, however, Beatty was lauded for his boldness and considered to be most like Nelson.

The British media portrayed Beatty as a dashing admiral, definitely in the Nelson mould. It was strongly believed that had Beatty commanded the Grand Fleet and not Jellicoe, he would have annihilated the German High Seas Fleet – he would have taken advantage of all of the tactical opportunities and crushed them without mercy. As a result, Jellicoe, the quiet and unassuming man, did not match the press or the public's view of a Nelson figure, but Beatty, rightly or wrongly, did.

Ranged against Jellicoe and Beatty were, of course, Scheer and Hipper. Scheer, the senior man, had an offensive approach to his tactics. He had been aggressive in the past and would openly embrace new tactics and ideas. Scheer preferred to give his ships' commanders far more freedom in decision-making. In fact, throughout the first period of contact on 31 May until nightfall, Scheer issued just fifty-six signals to his captains. The British, on the other hand, sent out 732.

Scheer's overriding concern was that the German High Seas Fleet should try to take on only part of the British Grand Fleet at any one time. In effect, his tactics could be boiled down to the simple approach of delivering temporarily overwhelming firepower against a portion of the British fleet and then withdrawing once the British started to reinforce their vessels. The standard procedure, once the withdrawal was under way, was to cover the retreat with smoke and torpedo boats.

What is not clear about Scheer's tactics during the Battle of Jutland is why he so easily fell for Beatty's ruse in retreating after he had engaged Hipper's fleet. If Beatty had truly been beaten and was retreating for his life then he would not have been proceeding in a northerly direction, but would have been heading north-west for a safe port. Beatty must have been up to something and Scheer must have known that lying somewhere out there to the north was Jellicoe's Grand Fleet. Nonetheless Scheer took the bait and pursued Beatty.

When Scheer made his 180-degree turn for the first time he caught Jellicoe on the hop, but why, later, did he make another 180-degree turn to now face Jellicoe once again? He had turned away and then turned back towards Jellicoe in the space of thirty minutes, but now his leading ships were his slowest and most heavily damaged. Scheer then had to make another turn to prevent his entire fleet from being cut off, surrounded and destroyed. There was panic as the German vessels were under fire from Jellicoe's fleet. In fact, had some of the German ships not begun the turn too early, a lot of Scheer's fleet would have found itself in a very difficult predicament. Once he had broken clear of Jellicoe, he headed for home, although he confusingly wrote later that he had wished to renew the battle at daylight the following day.

Scheer did manage to save the German High Seas Fleet. He had allowed himself to be crossed twice, but had extricated the fleet each time it got in danger. In effect, Scheer had not won a battle; he had just prevented his fleet from being destroyed.

The final significant commander during the Battle of Jutland was Franz von Hipper. He was considered to be somewhat impulsive and he had a good reputation in Germany because of his aggressive actions against British coastal towns. At least Hipper's fleet was actually inflicting damage on the enemy and not sitting and waiting for the ideal opportunity in a German port.

During the battle Hipper led his ships against almost overwhelming odds, managing to survive duels against battleships. To use his own words: 'It was nothing but the poor quality of their bursting charges that saved us from disaster.'

Hipper adroitly led Beatty into a trap and throughout his flight south, drawing Beatty on to Scheer, he kept the more senior man fully appraised of the situation. Although Hipper did fall into the British trap, he had been given direct orders by Scheer to head north and therefore had no option but to obey.

Throughout the battle, despite some tactical lapses, Hipper kept his nerve. His squadron had borne the brunt of the British attack and in truth, only Hipper out of the four men came out of the Battle of Jutland with an enhanced reputation.

Worthy of mention is the fact that both Jellicoe and Scheer had access to other weapons that they did not actually use. The British had a pair of seaplane tenders, *Engadine* and *Campania* – in effect prototype aircraft carriers – that would have been ideal to find out where the German forces were. But the *Engadine* was only used as a tugboat and the *Campania* had engine problems, causing Jellicoe to order her to return to port.

The Germans had zeppelins. They could not be used on the day of the battle because of high winds, and when they did take off the cloud cover prevented them from seeing anything. They were only any use after the battle had been fought, when they carried out a reconnaissance of the Horns Reef area.

The submarine could have been a decisive weapon during the Battle of Jutland. The problem was that they could not communicate if they were underwater. If they were above water they could be spotted and sunk, but below the waves, although they could move without being spotted, they could not be told where the battle was actually being fought. The Germans were terrified in any case of involving submarines in a pitched surface battle as a stray torpedo might well hit a German ship.

There had been an opportunity to inflict considerable damage on the Grand Fleet after the battle. U-boats could have been used to ambush the Grand Fleet as it steamed towards Scotland, but someone had neglected to tell them to remain at sea.

British submarines had no better luck. Although some had been stationed close to the Vyl Lightship, they could not be contacted owing to communication difficulties.

During the Battle of Jutland around 200 torpedoes were fired. Two Dreadnoughts were hit, one British and one German, but in all only six of the 200 torpedoes hit anything at all. The other hazard was mines. Jellicoe was particularly cautious in his pursuit of Scheer on account of the belief that the German admiral would order the sewing of a minefield behind them. Had the British continued in pursuit, there was every possibility that they would run into a German minefield, but because of Scheer's tactics of turning about, he could not risk running into his own mines. In fact, during the whole Jutland operation only one ship was hit by a mine, and that was a German one – HMS *Abdiel* had laid the mine that damaged the German vessel, the *Ostfriesland*.

In the aftermath of the Battle of Jutland the British set about making root-and-branch changes in the Royal Navy. Tactics would be markedly improved, with command being decentralized and more emphasis being placed on the use of the torpedo, a better signal book, clearer scouting instructions and a host of other minor adjustments. On the technical front, additional armour plate was added to the decks of ships, additional armour protection was added to the hulls, anti-flash devices were fitted and, above all, there would be a vast improvement in armour-piercing shells. Within a few months of the battle the British could muster thirty-one battleships. The battlecruisers lost would be replaced and Jellicoe had forty Dreadnoughts.

In comparison the Germans had nineteen battleships and just a single pair of battlecruisers. In terms of Dreadnoughts alone, the British outnumbered the Germans two to one. Jutland had given the Germans their opportunity, they had not taken it and the chance had now passed and gone forever.

It was not only the British who learned lessons from the Battle of Jutland. Whilst Scheer hung on to the notion that the way to defeat the Royal Navy ultimately would be to cut off sections of the fleet and destroy them, the means of doing this had changed. Henceforth he proposed that the flanks of his force would be protected by U-boats, so that if the Germans were sucked into a trap they could not be surprised and surrounded.

It was the Germans who were to make the next aggressive move as they planned to: 'Bombard Sunderland, to force the English fleet to come out and show the world the unbroken strength of the German fleet.'

The attack was planned for 18–19 August 1916 and would be led by Hipper, with his pair of battlecruisers backed up by three of Scheer's battleships. He would attack Sunderland at dawn with Scheer lying in wait, with his sixteen battleships, about 20 miles away. Protecting Scheer's flanks were twenty-four U-boats. This time Scheer was not prepared to be caught unawares – he had sent ten zeppelins ahead of his force on a reconnaissance mission.

The British had intercepted the signals and Jellicoe was sent to deal with the situation with twenty-nine battleships and a dozen battlecruisers under Beatty, the whole force setting off two hours before Scheer and Hipper left the Jade. This time Jellicoe would be just 30 miles from Beatty so that he could be reinforced instantly.

The much anticipated re-engagement between the two fleets was not to happen, however. The day had started with all the ingredients for an ideal set of weather conditions, but Scheer received a signal from Zeppelin L13 which reported that they had seen a force of around thirty ships sitting off the Norfolk coast, confidently adding that among these were battleships. The zeppelin had actually seen the Harwich force, consisting of five cruisers and twenty destroyers.

Scheer took immediate action and swung south-east. This was exactly the kind of situation that he had been looking for: a chance to destroy, in detail, a portion of the Grand Fleet.

Jellicoe headed south as soon as Scheer signalled his intentions, whereupon HMS *Nottingham* was hit by what Jellicoe believed to be the edge of a minefield. In fact, she had not been hit by a mine but by three torpedoes, fired by the German U-52. This diverted Jellicoe from his southbound course and it would take him three hours to work his way around again, until he was heading on the same bearing. It also meant that the two fleets missed one another, although at one stage they were only 40 miles apart. When Scheer received information from U-53 that Jellicoe was steaming south, he cancelled his sortie against Sunderland and headed for home.

Scheer had come within a whisker of encountering the entire Grand Fleet. In the end only three vessels were lost: the light cruisers HMS *Falmouth* and HMS *Nottingham* were lost to German submarines, while one of Jellicoe's own submarines, the E-23, managed to damage the German battleship *Westfalen.*

Despite the German submarines' success, it was decided that they would be withdrawn from operations with the German High Seas Fleet and would be used against merchant ships. As for the German High Seas Fleet, it was now reduced to a supporting role, this being the last time that surface vessels steamed so far into the North Sea.

There would be only two more sorties by the German High Seas Fleet. There was an abortive operation to attack the British east coast in October 1916, but the British intercepted some of the signals and the Grand Fleet was prepared to move to intercept Scheer. As it was the operation was cancelled prematurely when the British submarine, E-38, torpedoed the *München* just off the German coast.

The final operation mounted by Scheer and the German High Seas Fleet was in April 1918, when they attacked a Scandinavian convoy, without managing to achieve very much. In effect, the two fleets had cancelled one another out.

Meanwhile, the U-boat offensive continued apace, with German submarines managing to sink 2 million tons of British shipping throughout the whole of 1916. Something had to be done in order to break the growing hold that German submarines had on British commerce and their ability to wage war.

Jellicoe left the Grand Fleet on 22 November 1916 to take up his post as First Sea Lord. As his successor, Jellicoe recommended Vice Admiral Madden, but the position was offered to Beatty, despite the fact that several other men were senior to him. He accepted on 27 November 1916. Rather than adopting an aggressive stance from the outset, Beatty proved as cautious as Jellicoe had been.

Meanwhile, the German fleet was languishing in port. There were poor rations, poor pay and agitators were at work, breeding discontentment. In the summer of 1917, there was even a mutiny, which Scheer suppressed by shooting the ringleaders.

On 1 February 1917 Germany decided to reimpose unrestricted warfare on merchant vessels once again. The result was the loss of 6.15 million tons of Allied shipping in 1917, but the Germans were playing a dangerous game for they were receiving constant demands from the United States to stop attacking their merchant ships. The Americans were finally pushed once too often and declared war on Germany on 6 April 1917. They immediately sent six battleships to join the British Grand Fleet and by the end of 1917 dozens of destroyers were patrolling the merchant sea lanes and attacking German U-boats.

Huge numbers of mines, some 70,000 in total, were laid through the entrance to the English Channel and in the North Sea, making it incredibly difficult for German submarines to gain access.

The US Navy and the Royal Navy provided a model of co-operation. Despite the continued U-boat success, which saw 2.75 million tons of Allied ships sunk in 1918, the anti-submarine offensive was beginning to work. In fact, by the end of the war the Germans had lost 178 U-boats, while in January 1918 German cities were racked with food riots.

Scheer was appointed as Chief to the German Naval Staff Headquarters on 11 August 1918 and Hipper took over as Commander of the German High Seas Fleet. He found a fleet riddled with dissention, secret sailors' unions had been established on every ship, men refused to obey orders and, once again, the fleet mutinied on 30 October 1918.

Unfortunately for Hipper he had planned a major offensive on 29 October in which he intended to sail for the Thames Estuary and offer the Royal Navy a stand-up fight. He considered that if he could achieve a creditable performance in the battle, when the armistice negotiations came it would strengthen the German cause. When the fleet was ordered to set sail on 29 October, four vessels refused to obey orders. The mutiny was spreading and Hipper had his hands full to try and regain control.

Germany finally surrendered on 11 November 1918, with hostilities formally ceasing at 1100 hours. There was still much to negotiate. The German High Seas Fleet had not formally surrendered and so it was decided that they would be interned at Scapa

Flow. On 21 November 1918, what remained of the German High Seas Fleet, consisting of 9 battleships, 5 battlecruisers, 7 light cruisers and 49 torpedo boats, left their bases for the last time. They were crewed by a minimum number of men, under the command of Rear Admiral Ludwig von Reuter, and were to rendezvous with the British Grand Fleet off the coast of Scotland.

What awaited the Germans was the entire Grand Fleet, a French cruiser and an American battle squadron. As the German ships sailed between lines of Allied ships, the Allies were ready in case there was a last attempt to fight, but they entered temporary anchorage in the Firth of Forth without incident. Beatty signalled to the German ships: 'The German flag will be hauled down at sunset today, Thursday, and will not be hoisted again without permission.'

The German ships were sent to Scapa Flow just two days later, where they would languish at anchor for the next six months. In the meantime, von Reuter decided to scuttle the fleet and on 21 June 1919, at 1030, he sent a signal to each ship ordering them to open their seacocks. All doors, tubes and drains were to be opened and slowly the seventy-four vessels of the German fleet began to sink for ever.

The British were angry and considered this to be a betrayal. There were some attempts to board the German ships and stop them from being scuttled; some Germans were prevented from going ashore. The last casualties of the First World War lost their lives on 21 June 1919, over six months after the end of hostilities. Captain Schumann of the *Markgraf* was killed, as were eight other German sailors, with sixteen others wounded. In six hours most of the German fleet had been sunk. The British managed to salvage three cruisers and eighteen torpedo boats, but half a million tons of war materials were now only worth scrap.

Over the next ten years, whilst the masts and funnels of the *Hindenburg* were visible at Scapa Flow and the *Derfflinger* floated upside down, newspapers and critics savaged Jellicoe. Now that the war was over blame for the lack of a decisive victory at Jutland could be attributed. Jellicoe was variously described as being indecisive, or even a coward.

The major problem with any analytical dispute, with hindsight, on the rights and wrongs, was that no detailed account of the battle actually existed. Questions were raised in the House of Commons about Jellicoe's conduct, but neither Jellicoe nor Beatty would be drawn into the debate. As far as Beatty was concerned, his silence seemed to damn Jellicoe all the more.

Jellicoe was, in fact, preparing his own book, entitled *The Grand Fleet, 1914–1916*, which was published in 1919 and, rather than defending his position, it was simply long and dull. Meanwhile, the Admiralty was urged to produce its own account of the Battle of Jutland and consequently five naval officers were assigned the duty of producing the official account of the battle. They would have access to all reports, logs, charts and records. Facts were checked and rechecked, and what became known as the *Harper Record,* named after the Chairman, Captain John Harper, was finished in October 1919. It was straightforward, but there were personal comments.

The conclusion of the report was that as far as the British were concerned the Battle of Jutland was a partial defeat. It was sent to the Admiralty for approval, but there was a problem: it was about to be approved on 24 October 1919 by Rear Admiral Brock when Harper was told that it must have the approval of Beatty, when he became First Sea Lord.

Beatty assumed his position on 1 November 1919, having managed to surround himself with men who had served with him for several years and were all battlecruiser men. Beatty did not like the sections of the *Harper Record* that covered his own battle-cruisers. Over the next few weeks Captain Harper was brought before Beatty on several occasions and each time was asked to make minor changes. On 11 February 1920 Beatty ordered Harper to amend the sections dealing with the battlecruisers' shooting ability. All this in spite of the fact that when the report had been commissioned it had been agreed that neither Jellicoe nor Beatty would read it before it was published.

In the meantime, on exactly the same day as Beatty ordered Harper to make his amendments, Carlyon Bellairs' book, *The Battle of Jutland: The Sowing and the Reaping*, was published. Bellairs was pro-Beatty and anti-Jellicoe. The book was highly critical of Jellicoe and one heading read: 'I came, I saw, I turned away'.

Even this new book was not sufficient for Beatty, who continued to try to make Harper change the content of his report, even providing Harper with a new diagram, showing that HMS *Lion* had made an S-shaped manoeuvre rather than a 360-degree turn. The provenance of this diagram has always been hotly disputed. The diagram itself was dated 17 July 1916 and was not signed, but this was remedied by Beatty in 1920, making it official.

On 14 May 1920 the report was submitted once again for approval, with a note that said that nothing had been changed in it since the Navy Board had approved it. Beatty once again asked for changes and sent Harper a list of these on 26 May.

As far as Harper was concerned the changes did not match the evidence that he had uncovered. Beatty suggested the following two paragraphs should appear in the Preface:

> The following narrative of events, amplified by detailed proceedings of each Squadron and Flotilla, shows that the enemy's advanced forces were reinforced by the main Fleet some hours before the British main Fleet was able to reach the scene of action. During this period, therefore, the British were in greatly inferior force.
>
> On learning of the approach of the British main Fleet the Germans avoided further action and returned to base.

This was, of course, not the case. Beatty had only been unsupported for around an hour and in any case he had had a superior force at the beginning of the engagement. The two paragraphs also suggest that the Grand Fleet paid no part in the battle whatsoever.

When Jellicoe was sent a copy of the report, he strongly objected to the amendments that Beatty had made, especially the Preface. At this point Jellicoe was on the verge of taking up the post of Governor General of New Zealand, but he put this off until the report reflected the truth in his eyes. Jellicoe's objections were considered on 14 July. Harper stuck to his point of view, as did Beatty. Beatty would not accept references to the Grand Fleet even being within gun range of the Germans, but in the end he gave in, saying, 'Well, I suppose there is no harm in the public knowing that someone in the Battle Fleet got wet, as that is about all they had to do with Jutland.'

Harper wanted to be relieved of the responsibility and the First Lord of the Admiralty, Long, concurred. Long called a meeting on 22 September, suggesting that Harper's work be abandoned.

Everyone, apart from Beatty, agreed – Beatty wanted the amended signals, despatches and charts to be published, but not the text. The result was an impasse and plans to release an official record were put aside indefinitely.

The government had already announced that an official account was being prepared as early as March 1919, and again promised that a narrative would be produced when they confirmed its progress on 29 October of the same year. A year later, on 27 October, the government admitted:

It is not now proposed to publish an Official Account. Any record based on British official evidence only would inevitably present a one-sided version. Moreover, Sir Julian Corbett's *Naval History of the War* includes Jutland [and] is likely to be published within the course of the next year. All materials prepared by the Admiralty will be placed at Sir Julian Corbett's disposal.

On 4 November 1920, the Prime Minister, Lloyd George, said, 'In view of the general wish for the immediate publication of documents relating to the battle of Jutland, a Parliamentary Paper will be issued at an early date containing all these documents whether reports, despatches or signals.'

Finally, in December 1920, the government produced *The Battle of Jutland: Official Despatches with Indices*. There were some 603 pages, incorporating every single signal, despatch and ship's report. There was no analysis, no linking of the documents and none of the charts and tables prepared by Harper were used. It was about as unintelligible as it could possibly have been made.

A private *Naval Staff Appreciation* was prepared by a pair of inexperienced junior officers, known to be admirers of Beatty, and distributed only to the Royal Navy. These two men were brothers, Alfred and Kenneth Dewar, and their work was completed in August 1921. The only person who came out of this appraisal with any degree of acclaim was, of course, Beatty.

It was an odd version of the Battle of Jutland, primarily focusing on the importance of the battlecruiser fleet, downplaying the role of everyone else. In 1930, when Admiral Madden took over as First Sea Lord, he ordered that the *Naval Staff Appreciation* be destroyed and that all copies were to be burned. Madden was Jellicoe's former chief of staff. Luckily some copies survived.

In 1923, Volume III of the British history of the war at sea was released; the series was called *Naval Operations*. Volume III covered the period May 1915 to June 1916 and was written by Sir Julian Corbett. He had seen the *Harper Record* and the *Naval Staff Appreciation*, and had access to all documents, but was refused permission to make any reference to the interception and deciphering of German signals.

Corbett concentrated on the facts and Jellicoe came out well from the accounts. Meanwhile, Corbett unfortunately died suddenly soon after completing the final draft of his account. He had prepared the account under the direction of the Committee of Imperial Defence (CID) and they were to resist attempts by the pro-Beatty Board of Admiralty to make changes to the text. In the end, there was a disclaimer printed on the first page, which read as follows:

NOTE BY THE LORDS COMMISSIONERS OF THE ADMIRALTY

The Lords Commissioners of the Admiralty have given the author access to official documents in the preparation of this work, but they are in no way responsible for its production or for the accuracy of its statements.

Their Lordships find that some of the principles advocated in the book, especially the tendency to minimise the importance of seeking battle and forcing it to a conclusion, are directly in conflict with their views.

Throughout the whole writing procedure, the Board of Admiralty, Beatty and Churchill had harassed Corbett. Churchill actually delayed the publication.

In August 1924 the Admiralty produced its own account of the battle, entitled *Narrative of the Battle of Jutland*. It was probably prepared by the Dewar brothers and was a disjointed account, again pro-Beatty and with an emphasis on his battlecruisers, rather than the Grand Fleet. It also exaggerated the number of hits Beatty's ships had scored on the Germans.

Jellicoe had the opportunity to look at this account and made several objections, some of which were included, although his comments were consigned to Appendix G. Even this had a preface:

This Appendix has been added to by the Admiralty Narrative, to meet the wishes of Admiral of the Fleet, Viscount Jellicoe. Where, however, the Appendix differs from the Admiralty Narrative Their Lordships are satisfied that the Narrative is more in accordance with the evidence available. Notes have been added, where necessary, mainly in amplification or elucidation of the text criticised in the Appendix.

When the *Narrative of the Battle of Jutland* appeared in 1924, another book, written by Admiral Bacon, called *The Jutland Scandal,* was published. His dedication set the tone of the book: 'Those Two Neglected Goddesses, Justice and Truth, Now Worshipped in an Obscure Corner of the British Pantheon.'

Bacon's account defended Jellicoe as he believed that the Admiralty's own account of the battle unnecessarily discredited Jellicoe. Bacon's book was roundly criticized, particularly by a journalist working for the *Sunday Express*. Filson Young had written a book called *With the Battle Cruisers*, which had been published in 1921. At the time Young had been on Beatty's staff and unsurprisingly it not only criticized Jellicoe as a leader, but also embellished Beatty's tactical ability and strategic genius. Bacon, in turn, refuted Young's criticisms of Jellicoe and it looked as if the two would meet one another in court.

The German account of the Battle of Jutland was released in 1926, and was far better than Scheer's original account of the battle. The author, Otto Groos, stood by the point of view that the Battle of Jutland had been a German victory. He admitted that the German High Seas Fleet had been badly mauled but made no criticism of Scheer. Groos was not complimentary about Beatty's force and made comments that seemed to favour Jellicoe's view of the battle.

Churchill added to the controversy when his version of the Battle of Jutland appeared in Volume III of *The World Crisis*. It must be borne in mind that Churchill had chosen Beatty in the first place and to find fault with Beatty could be seen as a criticism of himself, therefore his account criticized Jellicoe. Churchill had based his account on the Dewars' original *Naval Staff Appreciation*.

Lord Sydenham wrote a book entitled *The World Crisis by Winston Churchill: A Criticism*, which included a criticism of Churchill's version of Jutland, written by Bacon. Bacon had pointed out the inaccuracies and the prejudices.

There were two more books on Jutland published soon after this. The first was written by Harper and was called *The Truth About Jutland,* in which he made restrained criticism of Beatty and was complimentary about Jellicoe. Madden authorized the publication of the *Reproduction of the Record of the Battle of Jutland*. This had changes to the text and the maps and diagrams had been removed.

It is understandable that Jellicoe, as the overall commander of the operations, was likely to draw criticism for any mistakes made by any of his subordinates. However, any positive comments made about Beatty's contribution were Beatty's alone. It seemed that the British government had made their own judgement on the situation. Jellicoe had become a viscount, but Beatty had become an earl. As far as many commentators were concerned, the comparisons were clear. Field Marshal Haig, who had led the British Expeditionary Force on the Western Front, had also been made an earl, like Beatty. But Allenby, who had masterminded the campaigns in the Middle East, had only been made a viscount, like Jellicoe. Parliament had also made disproportionate grants to both Jellicoe and Beatty – Jellicoe had been given £50,000 and Beatty twice that amount. Part of this iniquity was dealt with in 1925, when Jellicoe returned from New Zealand and was made an earl.

The debate between those who favoured Jellicoe and those who favoured Beatty continues to rage. New interpretations of the battle and decisions made continue to be included in accounts of British naval operations during the First World War. What can never be properly squared is the debate on the one hand which asserts that the Grand Fleet was hardly engaged during the Battle of Jutland – after all, Jellicoe's ships had suffered virtually no casualties or damage. On the other hand, there is the contention that in Jellicoe's two encounters with the German High Seas Fleet that day, they fired far more heavy shells and scored three times as many hits as Beatty's battlecruisers which were engaged for the most part throughout the whole battle.

Whatever the view taken with regard to the involvement of the Grand Fleet in the Battle of Jutland, what is absolutely clear is that Scheer considered his contact with the Grand Fleet to be sufficiently dangerous that he never risked a confrontation with the British again.

Appendix 1

Battle of Jutland Orders of Battle

British Grand Fleet

The Battle Fleet

2nd Battle Squadron/1st Division
HMS *King George V* – Captain Field, Vice Admiral Jerram
HMS *Ajax* – Captain Baird
HMS *Centurion* – Captain Culme-Seymour
HMS *Erin* – Captain Stanley

2nd Division
HMS *Orion* – Captain Backhouse, Rear Admiral Leveson
HMS *Monarch* – Captain Borrett
HMS *Conqueror* – Captain Tothill
HMS *Thunderer* – Captain Fergusson

4th Battle Squadron/3rd Division
HMS *Iron Duke* – Captain Dreyer, Admiral Jellicoe
HMS *Royal Oak* – Captain MacLachlan
HMS *Superb* – Captain Hyde-Parker, Rear Admiral Duff
HMS *Canada* – Captain Nicholson

4th Division
HMS *Benbow* – Captain Parker, Vice-Admiral Sturdee
HMS *Bellerophon* – Captain Bellerophen

HMS *Temeraire* – Captain Underhill
HMS *Vanguard* – Captain Dick

1st Battle Squadron/6th Division
HMS *Marlborough* – Captain Ross, Vice Admiral Burney
HMS *Revenge* – Captain Kiddle
HMS *Hercules* – Captain Bernard
HMS *Agincourt* – Captain Doughty

5th Division
HMS *Colossus* – Captain Pound, Rear Admiral Gaunt
HMS *Collingwood* – Captain Ley
HMS *Neptune* – Captain Bernard
HMS *St Vincent* – Captain Fisher

3rd Battlecruiser Squadon
HMS *Invincible* – Captain Cay, Rear Admiral Hood
HMS *Inflexible* – Captain Heaton-Ellis
HMS *Indomitable* – Captain Kennedy

1st Cruiser Squadron (Armoured Cruisers)
HMS *Defence* – Captain Ellis, Rear Admiral Arbuthnot
HMS *Warrior* – Captain Molteno
HMS *Duke of Edinburgh* – Captain Blackett
HMS *Black Prince* – Captain Bonham

2nd Cruiser Squadron (Armoured Cruisers)
HMS *Minotaur* – Captain d'Aeth, Rear Admiral Heath
HMS *Hampshire* – Captain Savill
HMS *Cochrane* – Captain Leatham
HMS *Shannon* – Captain Dumaresq

4th Light Cruiser Squadron
HMS *Calliope* – Commodore Le Mesurier
HMS *Constance* – Captain Townsend
HMS *Caroline* – Captain Crooke
HMS *Royalist* – Captain Meade
HMS *Comus* – Captain Hotham

Attached Light Cruisers

HMS *Active* – Captain Withers
HMS *Bellona* – Captain Dutton
HMS *Blanche* – Captain Casement
HMS *Boadicea* – Captain Casement
HMS *Canterbury* – Captain Royds
HMS *Chester* – Captain Lawson

4th Destroyer Flotilla

HMS *Tipperary* – Captain Wintour

HMS *Acasta*
HMS *Ambuscade*
HMS *Broke*
HMS *Contest*
HMS *Garland*
HMS *Midge*
HMS *Owl*
HMS *Shark*
HMS *Spitfire*

HMS *Achates*
HMS *Ardent*
HMS *Christopher*
HMS *Fortune*
HMS *Hardy*
HMS *Ophelia*
HMS *Porpoise*
HMS *Sparrowhawk*
HMS *Unity*

11th Destroyer Flotilla

HMS *Castor* (Light Cruiser) – Commodore Hawksley

HMS *Kempenfelt*
HMS *Mandate*
HMS *Marne*
HMS *Michael*
HMS *Minion*
HMS *Moon*
HMS *Mounsey*
HMS *Ossory*

HMS *Magic*
HMS *Manners*
HMS *Martial*
HMS *Milbrook*
HMS *Mons*
HMS *Morning Star*
HMS *Mystic*

12th Destroyer Flotilla

HMS *Faulknor* – Captain Stirling

HMS *Maenad*
HMS *Marvel*
HMS *Menace*
HMS *Mischief*
HMS *Narwhal*
HMS *Noble*

HMS *Marksman*
HMS *Mary Rose*
HMS *Mindful*
HMS *Munster*
HMS *Nessus*
HMS *Nonsuch*

HMS *Obedient*   HMS *Onslaught*
HMS *Opal*

Others
HMS *Abdiel* (Minelayer)
HMS *Oak* (Destroyer tender)

The Battlecruiser Fleet/1st Battlecruiser Squadron
HMS *Lion* – Captain Chatfield, Vice Admiral Beatty
HMS *Princess Royal* – Captain Cowan, Rear Admiral O de Brock
HMS *Queen Mary* – Captain Prowse
HMS *Tiger* – Captain Pelly

2nd Battlecruiser Squadron
HMS *New Zealand* – Captain Green, Rear Admiral Pakenham
HMS *Indefatigable* – Captain Sowerby

5th Battle Squadron
HMS *Barham* – Captain Craig, Rear Admiral Evan-Thomas
HMS *Valiant* – Captain Woollcombe
HMS *Warspite* – Captain Philpotts
HMS *Malaya* – Captain Boyle

1st Light Cruiser Squadron
HMS *Galatea* – Commodore Alexander-Sinclair
HMS *Phaeton* – Captain Cameron
HMS *Inconstant* – Captain Thesiger
HMS *Cordelia* – Captain Beamish

2nd Light Cruiser Squadron
HMS *Southampton* – Commodore Goodenough
HMS *Birmingham* – Captain Duff
HMS *Nottingham* – Captain Miller
HMS *Dublin* – Captain Scott

3rd Light Cruiser Squadron
HMS *Falmouth* – Captain Edwards, Rear Admiral Napier
HMS *Yarmouth* – Captain Pratt

HMS *Birkenhead* – Captain Reeves
HMS *Gloucester* – Captain Blunt

Seaplane Carrier
HMS *Engadine*

1st Destroyer Flotilla
HMS *Fearless* (Light Cruiser) – Captain Roper

HMS *Acheron*	HMS *Ariel*
HMS *Attack*	HMS *Badger*
HMS *Defender*	HMS *Goshawk*
HMS *Hydra*	HMS *Lapwing*
HMS *Lizard*	

9th and 10th Destroyer Flotillas (combined)
HMS *Lydiard* – Commander Goldsmith

HMS *Landrail*	HMS *Laurel*
HMS *Liberty*	HMS *Moorsom*
HMS *Morris*	HMS *Termagant*
HMS *Turbulent*	

13th Destroyer Flotilla
HMS *Champion* (Light Cruiser) – Captain Farie

HMS *Moresby*	HMS *Narborough*
HMS *Nerissa*	HMS *Nestor*
HMS *Nicator*	HMS *Nomad*
HMS *Obdurate*	HMS *Onslow*
HMS *Pelican*	HMS *Petard*

German High Seas Fleet

The Battle Fleet

III Battle Squadron/5th Division
König – Captain Bruninghaus, Rear Admiral Behncke
Grosser Kurfurst – Captain Goette
Kronprinz – Captain Feldt
Markgraf – Captain Seiferling

6th Division
Kaiser – Captain von Keyserlingk, Rear Admiral Nordmann
Kaiserin – Captain Sievers
Prinzregent Luitpold – Captain Heuser
Fredrich der Grosse – Captain Fuchs, Vice Admiral Scheer

I Battle Squadron/1st Division
Ostfriesland – Captain von Natzmer, Vice Admiral Schmidt
Thuringen – Captain Kusel
Helgoland – Captain von Kameke
Oldenburg – Captain Redlich

2nd Division
Posen – Captain Lange, Rear Admiral Engelhardt
Rheinland – Captain Rohardt
Nassau – Captain Klappenbach
Westfalen – Captain Redlich

II Battle Squadron/3rd Division
Deutschland – Captain Meurer, Rear Admiral Mauve
Hessen – Captain Bartels
Pommern – Captain Bolken

4th Division
Hannover – Captain Heine, Rear Admiral von Dalwigk zu Lichtenfels
Schlesien – Captain Behncke
Schleswig-Holstein – Captain Barrentrapp

IV Scouting Group (Light Cruisers)
Stettin – Captain Rebensburg, Commodore von Reuter
Munchen – Captain Bocker
Hamburg – Captain von Gaudecker
Frauenlob – Captain Hoffmann
Stuttgart – Captain Hagedorn

Light Cruisers & Torpedo Boats
Rostock – Captain Feldmann, Commodore Michelson

Torpedo Boat Flotilla

G39 – Commander Albrecht

G38	G40
S32	

III Torpedo Boat Flotilla

S53 – Commander Hollmann

V71	V73
G42	G88
S54	V48

V Torpedo Boat Flotilla

G11 – Commander Heinecke

V1	V2
V3	V4
V6	G7
G8	G9
G10	V5

VII Torpedo Boat Flotilla

S24 – Commander von Koch

S15	S16
S17	S18
S19	S20
S23	V186
V189	

The Battlecruiser Force

I Scouting Group (Battlecruisers)

Lützow – Captain Harder, Vice Admiral von Hipper
Derfflinger – Captain Hartog
Seydlitz – Captain von Egidy
Moltke – Captain von Karpf
Von der Tann – Captain Zenker

II Scouting Group (Light Cruisers)

Frankfurt – Captain von Trotha, Rear Admiral Bodicker
Wiesbaden – Captain Reiss

Pillau – Captain Mommsen
Elbing – Captain Madlung

Light Cruisers & Torpedo Boats
Regensburg – Captain Heuberer, Commodore Heinrich

II Torpedo Boat Flotilla
B98 – Captain Schuur

B97	B109
B110	B111
B112	G101
G102	G103
G104	

VI Torpedo Boat Flotilla
G41 – Commander Schultz

G37	G86
G87	S50
V44	V45
V46	V69

IX Torpedo Boat Flotilla
V28 – Commander Goehle

V26	V27
V29	V30
S33	S34
S35	S36
S51	S52

Appendix 2

Losses at the Battle of Jutland

31 May 1916
British
Indefatigable, Indefatigable class battlecruiser
Queen Mary, Queen Mary class battlecruiser
Invincible, Invincible class battlecruiser
Fortune, Acasta class destroyer
Shark, Acasta class destroyer
Nestor, M class destroyer
Nomad, M class destroyer
Defence, Minotaur class armoured cruiser

German
V27, V25 class destroyer
V29, V25 class destroyer
V48, V43 class destroyer
S35, S31 class destroyer

1 June 1916
British
Ardent, Acasta class destroyer
Sparrowhawk, Acasta class destroyer
Tipperary, Faulknor class destroyer leader
Turbulent, Talisman class destroyer
Black Prince, Duke of Edinburgh class armoured cruiser
Warrior, Warrior class armoured cruiser

German

V4, German, V1 class destroyer
Frauenlob, German, Gazelle class light cruiser
Rostock, German, Karlsruhe class light cruiser
Elbing, German, Pillau class light cruiser
Wiesbaden, German, Wiesbaden class light cruiser
Pommern, German, Deutschland class pre-Dreadnought battleship
Lützow, German, Derfflinger class battlecruiser

Bibliography

Bacon, Admiral Sir Reginald, *The Jutland Scandal* (London, 1925).

Bennett, Geoffrey M., *The Battle of Jutland* (London, Batsford, 1964).

Bennett, Geoffrey M., *Naval Battles of the First World War* (London, Pan Books, 1974).

Breyer, Siegfied, *Battleships and Battlecruisers* (London, Macdonald and Jane's, 1973).

Burt, R.A., *British Battleships of World War One* (Annapolis, Md., Naval Institute Press, 1986).

Campbell, John, *Jutland: An Analysis of the Fighting* (London, Conway Maritime Press, 1986).

Corbett, Sir Julian, Official History of the War, *Naval Operations*, Volume III (London, Longmans & Co., 1920–31) Reprint 1940.

Costello, John and Terry Hughes, *Jutland 1916* (London, Futura Publications, 1976).

Falls, Cyril Bentham, *The First World War* (London, Longmans, 1960).

Gordon, Andrew, *The Rules of the Game: Jutland and British Naval Command* (London, John Murray, 1996).

London, Charles, *Jutland 1916, Clash of the Dreadnoughts* (Osprey Campaign Series, Osprey Publishing, 2000).

MacIntyre, Captain Donald, *Jutland: The Mightiest Naval Battle of All Time* (London, Pan Books, 1957).

Marder, Arthur J., *From the Dreadnought to Scapa Flow*, Volume II: The War Years to the Eve of Jutland, 1914–1916 (Oxford, Oxford University Press, 1978).

Marder, Arthur J., *From the Dreadnought to Scapa Flow*, Volume III: Jutland and After, May 1916–December 1916 (Oxford, Oxford University Press, 1978).

Massie, Robert K., *Castles of Steel: Britain, Germany, and the Winning of the Great War at Sea* (New York, Random House, 2003).

Steel, Nigel and Hart, Peter, *Jutland 1916: Death in the Grey Wastes* (Cassell, 2003).

Tarrant, V.E., *Jutland: The German Perspective – A New View of the Great Battle* (London, Arms and Armour Press, 1986).

Yates, Keith, *Flawed Victory: Jutland 1916* (London, Chatham Publishing, 2000).

Index

212